# Computer Programming for Beginners
# 3 Books in 1

*Step by Step Beginners' Guide to Learn Programming, Python For Beginners, Python Machine Learning*

By

Kevin Cooper

versions of the work, physical, digital, and audio unless express consent of the Publisher is provided beforehand. Any additional rights reserved.

Furthermore, the information that can be found within the pages described forthwith shall be considered both accurate and truthful when it comes to the recounting of facts. As such, any use, correct or incorrect, of the provided information will render the Publisher free of responsibility as to the actions taken outside of their direct purview. Regardless, there are zero scenarios where the original author or the Publisher can be deemed liable in any fashion for any damages or hardships that may result from any of the information discussed herein.

Additionally, the information in the following pages is intended only for informational purposes and should thus be thought of as universal. As befitting its nature, it is presented without assurance regarding its prolonged validity or interim quality. Trademarks that are mentioned are done without written consent and can in no way be considered an endorsement from the trademark holder.

# Table of Contents

# Summary of the Book

# BOOK 2: *Python For Beginners*

## Introduction

## Chapter 1: Introduction to Python

What is Python?

Python and its History

Python and Its Features

First Python Program

Building Development Environment

Use of Interactive Command Line

Python Development Tools

Python Under Different Platforms

## Chapter 2: Variables and Constants in Python

Why Variables are needed?

Variable Naming and Assignment

Static Type and Dynamic Type

Python's Numeric Data Types

Decimal Module

Constant

Formatting Input and Output Function

Hands-on Practice Exercise

**Chapter 7: Files in Python**

What are Files in Python?

**Conclusion**

# BOOK 3: *Python Machine Learning*

**Introduction**

**Chapter 1: What is Data Science and Deep Learning?**

Why Data Science Is Important

What is Data Science?

Predictive casual analytics:

Prescription analytics:

Making predictions through machine learning:

Machine learning for the discovery of the pattern:

Data Science vs. Business Intelligence (BI)

Data Science Lifecycle

Phase 1 – Discovery:

Phase 2 – Preparation of data:

Phase 3 – model planning:

Phase 4 – Building the model:

Phase 5 – Operationalize:

Phase 6 – Communicate results:

Secret Sauces of Data Scientists

An In-depth Look into Deep Learning

**Chapter 2: Data Science and Applications**

Banking and Finance

   Fraud detection

   Customer data management

   Investment banks risk modeling

   Personalized marketing

Health and Medicine

   Analysis of medical image

   Genomics and genetics

   Drugs creation

   Virtual assistance for customer and patients support

   Industry knowledge

Oil and Gas

   Immediate drag calculation and torque using neural networks

   Predicting well production profile through feature extraction models

   Downstream optimization

The Internet

   Targeted advertising

   Website recommendations

   Advanced image recognition

# Chapter 5: Understanding the Fundamentals of Machine Learning

Prerequisites to start with machine learning

The semantic tree

Six Jars of Machine Learning

Learning

Loss

Task

Data

Evaluation

Model

Supervised learning

Machine Learning Roadmap

Linear Regression

Logistic Regression

Naive Bayes Classifier

K – Nearest Neighbors (KNN)

K – Means

Support Vector Machine (SVM)

Decision Trees

Random Forest

## Chapter 9: K – Nearest Neighbor Algorithms – K – Means Clustering

## Chapter 10: Neural Networks – Linear Classifiers

Neural Network Elements

Deep Neural Networks Key Concepts

Feedforward Networks

Multiple Linear Regression

Different Types of Classifiers

## Conclusion

# Step by Step Beginners' Guide to Learn Programming

*The Complete Introduction Guide for Learning the Basics of C, C#, C++, SQL, JAVA, JAVASCRIPT, PHP, and PYTHON.*

*A Pratical Programming Language Course*

By

Kevin Cooper

# Chapter One: Introduction to Programming

Thank you for buying this book because it is the best investment you will make in improving your skill as a programmer. The book contains information on the basics of programming in various programming languages including PHP, JavaScript, Java, Python, SQL, C+, C#, and C.

I am Kevin Cooper and if you are a beginner, do not worry because I started the same way as you are about to do. I will be your driver and guide for this wonderful journey of the beginners' guide to learning programming.

The book is geared towards you understanding the aforementioned programming languages in its simplicity. I will teach you in a way that you will not forget. The book contains exercises, which is important for you to practice if you want to be a productive and successful programmer.

Today, we have seen hundreds of programming languages created for different purposes. However, we have also seen some of these programming languages gaining more popularity over others.

No matter what your quest is, welcome to the world of programming where everything is possible. Programming is simply the act or process of writing programs to instruct the computer what actions to perform or not. These programs use various series of instructions in a particular language (all language have different instruction). Nevertheless, in this book, you learn the fundamentals of seven programming languages. These languages include C, C++, C#, SQL, Java, PHP, and Python.

Programming isn't complicated as many try to portray it. If that has been your perception, this step by step beginners' guide to learn programming will change that perception. It is surely going to be a fun ride as long as you stick to what is contained in this book. I am confident this book contains everything you need as a beginner, who is looking forward to going into advanced coding. Let's crack the nuts together.

## What is a Programming Language?

In layman's term, this is an artificial language aimed at controlling the operation and functionality of a computer. It is akin to our English language, which we use to express our ideas. Just like there are rules in the English language, so it is with programming languages. They have rules (syntactic and semantic rules), which programmers must adhere to

To understand it better, an example will clarify everything. Assuming you met someone on the way and he/she asked for the nearest bank. What would be your response to the person? How will you describe the direction in such a way that the person never forgets? Obviously, you will do something like this:

- Take the straight path towards you for 1 kilometer
- Take the right turn at the traffic light
- Then drive for another half kilometer
- At your right-hand side is the bank

This is an instruction in the English language and it followed a particular sequence for the person to follow in order to get to the bank. For a moment, what will be the situation if the same case scenario is a computer program? As simple as the direction is, you can write programs for this example using any programming language of your choice. However, you won't use your daily English language words but those understood by the computer.

A program, also called software sometimes contains a couple of lines to millions of lines with each providing different instructions. The instructions are called source code whereas the act of writing codes is known as program coding. It doesn't matter how the body of a system looks, without a program, the computer can do nothing. The program gives life to the computer when you power it on.

Just as we have different languages in the world, computer scientists have developed various languages but with the primary purpose of writing computer programs. There are over a hundred programming languages available for anyone to learn. It is hard to learn everything but it is important to have basic knowledge of the important once.

## Building a Foundation for Writing Codes

Programming languages are geared towards solving a particular problem. Yes, you want to be a problem solver by creating important product and services but irrespective of how you practice, there are essential skills you must possess. Learning programming will offer you numerous job opportunities and increase your wages while working for fewer hours. Coders or developers spend time making applications, websites, and systems work together in order to improve the experience of their employers and end-users. Welcome to the Programming industry where there is no impossibility as long as you can envision it. However, there are important skills you must have before starting this journey.

- **Self-Reliance** – This skill is huge because as a beginner, you may feel overwhelmed. You will be confronted with various decisions to make such as what language to learn? Should I focus on the back end or front end? Where do I start? At times, you will feel like giving up after hours of no sleep without any significant progress. However, you do not have to give up. Success doesn't come cheap, there is a price to pay. To be a successful programmer, you have to master distraction, frustrations, impatience, and be self-reliance to accept the responsibility at hand.

- **Attention to details** – If you want to excel as a beginner, you must have attention to the minimum detail. Everything matters in programming. A single spelling can cause your program to go wrong if you are not painstaking in paying attention to details. You don't have to work round the clock; take some time off and refresh yourself in you want to up and doing. Make your own research, make your own notes, and continue to improve yourself.

- **Abstract thinking** – Programmers are thinkers, who think outside the box. They are not confined to a particular solution. They have their perspective on a global level, seeing things from a different angle in order to find ways of improving on what already exists.

- **Patience** – Whoever tells you coding is easy is lying because you have to dedicate time, resource to come up with solutions. At some stage, you should expect some level of frustration because things may not go the way you wanted. At times, you may feel useless and the project isn't worth the time, however in such a situation, you have to be patient. Every successful programmer has undergone through these challenges. Patience is the key to writing codes. According to Steve Jobs, " It's worth waiting to get it right" Therefore, no matter the challenge, let patience be the key.

# Chapter Two: Learning C Programming Language

## Introduction

The C programming language is one of the most commonly used languages with various versions developed over the years. The C language is the fundamental language to understand before considering learning the C# and C++ language. My goal in this chapter is to enable you to have the fundamental knowledge concerning the basics of C programming language including the various data types.

Before starting, it is important to familiarize yourself with the language. The C programming language is also referred to as a general-purpose because programmers can use it for varieties of application. Its popularity is linked to its efficiency despite how old it has been in existence. Most C programs are portable, which means that a code written in a particular system can work in another operating system.

## Features of C Programming Language

It is significant to identify certain features of the C language.

- **Fast** – New programming languages including Java and Python provides more features than C language.

Nevertheless, in terms of performance, they are lower to C.

- **Modularity** – This feature is unique as you can store C code in the form of libraries for future purposes. The language comes with its own standard libraries that you can use to solve various problems. Assuming you want something to display on the screen, you can use the "studio.h" library, which enables you to use the print f() function.

- **Portable** – Have you heard the statement, "Write once, compile everywhere." Yes, it is true with C programs because a program written in one system with Mac OS can be compiled in another system for instance Windows 7 without any change to the program.

Other features include reliability, interactivity, efficiency, and effectiveness.

## Why Learn C Programming Language?

Perhaps, you are thinking, of what use is the C programming language today? Is it the only accessible programming language to users? Definitely, there are other languages you can learn, which are way higher and modern when compared to the C language.

However, there are important reasons most people choose to learn this programming language. Firstly, the C programming language preexisted before most of the computer languages you have thought about. There are unlimited resources to tap from the program with numerous functions to meet every programming need.

Secondly, most people still learn the language because it is hard for anyone not to get the solution they desire. It doesn't have to take you years to learn a particular programming language. The internet has even made it easier as there are thousands of free tutorials to learn the language.

Thirdly, the C programming language is the language used by UNIX. Interestingly, UNIX is one of the leading computer software in the world. Besides, other operating systems also take advantage of the simplicity of the programming language. Importantly, the way the language expresses ideas to make it easier for anyone to implement the language without requiring any aid.

If you are not still convinced, then it is imperative for me to indicate that the C programming language is the foundation for other programming languages, which is why we started this book with the language. For instance, there are certain commands and principles you will see here that are applicable to other programming languages.

For a newbie, C programming is the best to start your programming learning process. However, for an easier language to understand, you can go for Python, which I will talk about towards the end of this book.

## Uses of Programming Language

Interestingly, you can use the C language for creating various system applications, which is an integral aspect of several operating systems including Linux, Windows, and UNIX. The following are areas where C is used.

- Interpreters
- Network drivers
- Spreadsheets
- Graphic packages
- Operating system development
- Database systems
- Compiler and assemblers

## Setting Up the Environment

In learning a new language, you have to set up the environment to run the programs. In learning the C programming language, one should start from the basics before going to the complex aspects.

If you want to take this quest seriously, then you should begin by downloading and installing the C compiler. In computer programming, compilers are simply programs that read code and generate executable programs that a computer can understand. The compiler is necessary as it reads the code you input and converts it to a computer-friendly signal.

There is no universal compiler because some programs can work in a certain operating system while the same cannot be said for others. However, the following suggestions will help you. If you are using a Window computer, you can install MinGW or Microsoft Visual Studio Express. However, for Mac and Linux operating system, you can use XCode and GCC respectively.

Besides a compiler, you will need a text editor to start coding. The compiler and text editor has different roles.

The role of the text editor is for you to type your program. There are various text editors available such as notepad, Emacs, OS Edit, etc. if you use a text editor, you create a source file, which has the source code. C programs have their file extension as ".c"

Once you complete your program in the text editor, the next thing is to save it. After undergoing the compilation process, you can execute it. The role of the compiler is to make the file you created usably. The compiler will make the source code created in the text editor readable for human.

# Pre-requisite for Learning C

Unlike some programming languages that require you to study another language, C language is different. There is no prerequisite for learning the C programming the language. You don't require a preknowledge of data structures, algorithms, or even Boolean logic. However, with the basic knowledge of computers and logical skills, it is enough to begin your journey of learning C. Get the compiler installed on your computer and stay dedicated and surely you will be good at it over time.

As a professional programmer, I will advise you before beginning with this book, you should endeavor to understand basic computer programming terminologies as it will fast track your learning process.

## Understanding the Basics

It is essential to identify the structure of a C program because without that your foundation in this language will be shaky. Getting yourself set up with these basics will help you a lot, as it will be a reference point to certain things I will explain in this book. The following are the basic structures:

- **Documentation section** – This section provides comments concerning the program, the author's name, the date it was created, the modification date, etc.
- **Link Section** – This includes header files necessary to execute program
- **Definition Section** – In this section, variable declaration and assignment of values are done.
- **Global Declaration Section** – Global variables are usually highlighted here. When you want to use a variable

40

throughout the program, you define them at the global declaration section.

- **Function prototype declaration section** – This section gives details about the various function such as parameter names, return types used within the function
- **Main function** – All C programs must originate from the main function. Primarily, it comprises of two different sections – the execution and the declaration sections.
- **User-defined function** – These sections contain functions defined by the users to perform a certain task.

Don't worry because it may look "foreign" to you as a beginner. However, I like to use examples to highlight my points. Assuming you want to write "Hello, Welcome to C Programming Language for Beginners" what code will you use to produce these words?

| C Program Commands | Explanation |
|---|---|
| #include<stdio.h> | This preprocessor command contains the standard input-output header contained in the C library before the compilation of the program. |

| | |
|---|---|
| int main () | This function indicates where the program execution begins |
| { | This specifies the starting point of a function |
| /* comments*/ | Whatever is written between the /*...*/ is disregarded by the compiler because it serves as an explanation or comments. |
| Printf("Hello, Welcome to C Programming Language for Beginners"); | The Printf command displays "Hello, Welcome to C Programming Language for Beginners" to the screen |
| Getch(); | The command waits for the user to input any character of their choice from the console |

| Return 0; | This ends the main function of the program while returning 0 |
| --- | --- |
| } | The closing brace specifies the ending point of the main function |

Let's assume you want the following statement to show on the screen. "Hello, Welcome to C Programming Language for Beginners" on the screen, it will be as follow.

```
#include <stdio.h>
/* the int main () is the part where the execution of the program begins*/
Int main ()
{
        /* Performing the First Programming Sample in C language*/
        Printf("Hello, Welcome to C Programming Language for Beginners");
        Getch();
        Return 0;
}
```

Output

**Hello, Welcome to C Programming Language for Beginners**

To ensure you write a program in C language and get the output, there are important steps to follow. There is no exception to these steps as far as it is a C program. It doesn't matter if it is a small or large program. These involve the creation, compilation, execution (running), and outputting of the program. For you to do this there are certain prerequisites

- You must have a C compiler installed on your system. With this, you can execute programs.
- It is not compulsory to install one on your system as you can instead use an online compiler to compile and execute your programs. Just search for online compilers for C and you will get more details.

# Data Types

A data type is a very simple but important concept to understand in any programming language. It is a representation of a particular type of data, which is processed through a computer program. A particular data type determines a storage space along with the manner the bit pattern is understood when processing the data.

In C language, data types are categorized into four different groups

| Types | Data Types |
|-------|------------|
| Enumeration data type | Enum |
| Basic Data | Int, float, char, double |
| Derived data type | Pointer, array, union, structure |
| Void data type | Void |

## Basic Data Types

Integer Data Type

This data type enables a user to use a variable to store numerical values. It is represented by the keyword "int" with storage size ranging from 2, 4, or 8 bytes. However, the integer data type varies depending on the processor you are using. For instance, if the computer is a 16-bit processor system, the int data type will be allocated 2-byte memory.

Character Data Type

This type of data type allows the variable to store only a character. Unlike the int, the char data type has a storage size of 1. This means that you can only store a particular character for the data type. The character keyword is represented by the "char" keyword.

## Float Data Type

These comprise of two types – the float and double data type

**Float** – this allows you to store decimal values with a storage size of 4. However, the storage size varies from one processor of a computer to another. On the other hand, the double is identical to the float data type. After the decimal value, the double data type allows as far as -10 digits.

## Enumeration Data type

This data type comprises of named integer constants in the form of a list. By default, it begins with 0 with the value increasing by 1 for the consecutive identifies within its list. The syntax for Enum in C programming language is:

*enum identifier [{enumerator-list}];*

## Derived Data Type

These data types include array, structure, pointer, and union.

## Void data type

This type of data type does not have a value and used in pointers and functions.

## Keywords, Identifiers (Variables), and Literals

In C language, we have a character set, which includes a set of alphabets, letters, and some special characters. The alphabets comprise of those in upper and lower case. Note that the alphabets "A and a" are not the same – C language is case sensitive.

Keywords are reserved words in programming that has its own distinct connotation to the compiler. They are an integral aspect of the syntax of the language that cannot be used as an identifier. For instance:

int number;

In this example, the word "int" is a reserved keyword, which indicates that number is a variable of integer type. The table below shows the keywords allowed in C language

| volatile | void | unsigned | while |
|----------|------|----------|-------|
| typedef | struct | union | switch |
| size | signed | short | static |
| register | int | return | long |
| goto | for | float | if |
| enum | double | extern | else |
| default | continue | const | do |
| case | auto | char | break |

Identifiers are names given to entities like functions, variables, structures, etc. They are unique and created to an entity within the execution of the program. For instance,

```
int Money;
double accountBal;
```

In the example above, money and accountable are identifiers. Remember identifiers must not be the same as keywords. How then do you form an identifier?

- An identifier can have letters, digits, and underscore. Letters can be both lowercase and uppercase.
- The first letter for an identifier must be an underscore or letter.
- A keyword cannot be used as an identifier
- There is no particular length for an identifier

## Literals

These are values whose value cannot be changed in the course of the program. The term is used in place of constant, so when you see constant they mean the same thing. Constants comprise of various data types including integer, character, floating, and string.

An integer constant on no situation must have an exponential or fractional part. We have three integer literals in C programming. These are:

- Decimal (example: 54, -98, 11)
- Octal (example: 042, 089, 044)
- Hexadecimal (example: 0x9f, 0x345, 0x7a)

Floating-point literals are numerical literal with an exponent or fractional part. For instance, -4.0, 0.0000345, -0.44E-9.

Characters are literally formed by enclosing them with a single quotation mark. For instance: 't', 'h', '8', etc;

Finally, a string literal comprises of a sequence or collection of characters encircled in double quotation marks. For instance, "love", "C Programming", "Professional"

# Operators in C Programming Language

Operators are symbols, which tell the compiler what particular operation to carry on a particular variable. In C language, we have long-range operators, which are used to execute several operations on variables or operands. I will explain the basic operators you should know as a beginner learning programming.

## Arithmetic Operators

In C programming language, these operators perform mathematical operators namely addition, subtraction, division, multiplication. These can be executed on various numerical values.

| Operator | Meaning | Example |
|---|---|---|
| + | Addition | A + C = 50 |
| * | Multiplication | A * C = 10 |
| - | Subtraction | A – C = 20 |
| / | Division | A/C= 5 |
| % | Modulo division | C/A =0 |
| ++ | Increment by 1 | C++ |
| -- | Decrement by 1 | C-- |

Example 1

```
#include <stdio.h>
main()
{
int day1 = 31;
int  = day2;
int day3 ;
final = day1 + day2;
printf("First Line - Value of day3 is %d\n", day3 );
day3 = day1 – day2;
printf("Second Line - Value of day3 is %d\n", day3 );
day3 = day1 * day2;
printf("Third Line  - Value of day3 is %d\n", day3 );
day3 =  day1 / day2;
printf("Fourth Line - Value of day3 is %d\n", day3);
day3 = day1 % day2;
```

```
printf("Fifth Line - Value of day3 is %d\n", day3 );
day3 = day1 ++;
printf("Sixth Line - Value of day3 is %d\n", day3 );
day3 = day2--;
printf("Seventh Line  - Value of day3 is %d\n", day3);
}
```

If you compile this program and it executed successfully, your output will be as follows: First Line  - Value of day3 is 51

Second Line - Value of day3 is 11

Third Line  - Value of day3 is 620

Fourth Line  - Value of day3 is 1

Fifth Line  - Value of day3 is 5

Sixth Line  - Value of day3 is 32

Seventh Line  - Value of day3 is 19

## Relational Operators

The role of these operators is to verify the relationship or association that exists between two different operands. The table below shows the basic relational operators in the C language. Assuming the value for loss and profit are "25" and "35" respectively.

| Operator | Meaning | Example |
|----------|---------|---------|
| == | This operator evaluates whether the | loss==profit is evaluated as not true |

|  | value is equivalent or not to the second value on the right. If it is true, the condition turns out to be true. |  |
|---|---|---|
| > | The operator verifies if the left operand greater than that on the right side | From the value, loss >profit is false true |
| < | The operator verifies if the left operand is less than that of the right side | loss < profit is true |
| != | The operator verifies if the operand on the left side | loss !=profit returns true |

| | | |
|---|---|---|
| | fulfill the condition by not being equivalent to the one on right side | |
| >= | This verifies if the left operand is either greater or equivalent to the right operand | loss>=profit returns not true |
| <= | This verifies if the operand on the left is either less or equivalent to the right operand | loss<=profit is true |

The example below will make it clearer.

```
#include <stdio.h>
```

```
main()
/*Variable declaration and operations on the variables*
{
int days = 31;
int week = 20;
int month ;
if( day== week )
{
printf("First Line - day is equal to week\n" );
}
Else
/*This evaluate the first condition*/
{
printf("First Line - day is not equal to week\n" );
}
if ( day < week )
{
printf("Second Line - day is less than week\n" );
}
else
{
printf("Second Line - day is not less than week\n" );
}
if ( day > week )
{
printf("Third Line - day is greater than week\n" );
}
else
{
printf("Third Line - day is not greater than week\n" );
}
```

```
/* Lets change value of day and week */
day = 5;
week = 20;
if ( day <= week )
{
printf("Fourth Line - day is either less than or equal to week\n" );
}
if ( day >= week )
{
printf("Fifth Line - y is either greater than or equal to week\n" );
}
}
```

Program output:

```
First Line - day is not equal to week
Second Line - day is not less than week
Third Line  - day is greater than week
Fourth Line - day is either less than or equal to week
Fifth Line  - day is either greater than or equal to week
```

# Logical Operators in C Programming Language

There are three basic logical operators used in C. The purpose of this operator is to evaluate variables and returns either a 0 or 1 depending on whether an expression is false or true. If you want to write a program that requires making decisions, then you have to use the logical operators.

| Operator | Meaning | Example |
|----------|---------|---------|
| && | Logical AND. This operator evaluates to true only when both expressions or conditions on the operands are true. | If a =4 and b = 2; the expression ((a==4) && (a<4)) is equivalent to 0. |
| \|\| | Logical OR. This evaluates to true if one condition operated on the operands is also true. | If a =4 and b = 2; the expression ((a==4) && (a<4)) equals to 1. |
| ! | Logical Not. This returns true only if the operand | If a=5 then, the expression! holds true. |

| | is 0 | |
|---|---|---|

## Bitwise Operators

These special operators are used in manipulating data at the bit level. It is used to shift bits from the right position to the left. Nevertheless, they don't work with double float variables.

| Bitwise Operator | Meaning |
|---|---|
| \| | OR |
| ^ | Exclusive OR |
| & | AND |
| << | Left Shift |
| >> | Right Shift |

Truth Table for bitwise operator

| Y | Z | Y ^ Z | Y \| Z | Y & Z |
|---|---|---|---|---|
| 0 | 1 | 1 | 1 | 0 |
| 1 | 0 | 1 | 1 | 0 |
| 0 | 0 | 0 | 0 | 0 |
| 1 | 1 | 0 | 1 | 1 |

The table above to explain the bitwise operator will make no sense if you are a beginner; the following explanation will clarify it for you. For instance, Y = 60 and Z = 13, the binary format of Y and Z will be 0011 1100 and 0000 1101 respectively

Y = 0011 1100

Z = 0000 1101

From the truth table,

Y | Z = 0011 1101

Y&Z = 0000 1100

Y ^ Z = 0011 0001

I know you may be thinking about how we came about the values below; well it is very simple to understand. Using the Y & Z as an example, the value for Y is 0011 1100 while that of Z is 0000 1101. From the truth table, we go under the Y & Z section. When Y is 0 and Z is 1, what is the value under Y & Z (What you are doing is matching the first binary number of Y with that of Z? obviously, you get a 0. If you continue with that patter, you will get 0000 1100 for Y & Z.

## Assignment Operators

The table below will give a better view of what assignment operators work in C programming.

| Assignment Operators | Meaning | Example |
|---|---|---|

| | | |
|---|---|---|
| = | This allocates the value of the right operand to left operand | V = B + D In his situation, the value of B + D will be assigned to V |
| *= | The left operand gets multiplied by the right operand. furthermore, the product is then allocated to the left operand. | V* = B is equal to V= V*B |
| -= | This deducts the value of operand on the right from the left before assigning it to the left. | V -=B This is equivalent to V=V-B |
| += | This adds the | V+= is |

|  | value of the right operand from the left before allocating the value to the content on the left | equivalent to V=V+B |
|---|---|---|
| /= | In this, the value of the operand on the left is divided by the right before assigned to the left | V/= is equivalent to V = V /D |

## Decision Making in C

It is hard to write a complete program without using decision in C language. What do you think decision-making involves in the context of programming? Well, it is a way of executing certain statements as long as they meet the laid down conditions. However, you will learn the statement, format, and an example to explain the decisions. The diagram below shows a typical decision-making process in C.

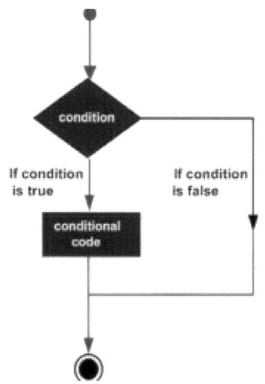

## If Statement

This mentions a particular condition and specifies a particular thing will happen if the stated condition or statement becomes true. However, if the condition doesn't turn out true, then the thing suggests will not happen.

Format:

```
if (boolean_condition){
/* expression (s) that will perform the action if the
Boolean condition stated is true */
}
```

## Diagrammatic representation

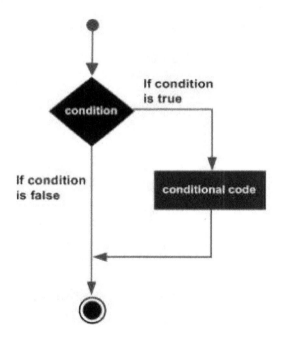

Program to exemplify the "If Statement"

```
#include <stdio.h>
/* Beginning of the main program*/
```

```
int main ()
{
/* Definition of local variables in the program */
int x = 15;
/* Evaluates the boolean condition */
if( y < 30 )
{
/* if the condition (y < 30) is true then display the
outcome */
printf("y is less than 30\n" );
}
printf("value of y is : %d\n", a);
return 0;
}
```

Once you finish and the program is executed, your output will
look like this:

```
x is less than
```

## If ... else Statement

This decision making statement uses an If, which is
accompanied by an optional statement that performs the action
when the "IF" condition turns false.

Format:

```
if(expression or condition){
/* this statement here will be executed as far as the
condition is met */
}
Else{
/* expression (s) will be implement if the expression is
not true */
}
```

## Diagrammatic Representation

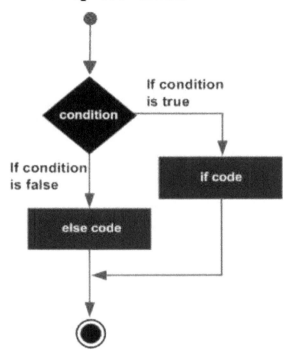

Sample Program for If…else Statement

```
#include <stdio.h>
/* beginning of the execution of the program*/
int main ()
{
/* definition of local variable */
int length = 200;
/* Evaluates the expression or statement*/
if( length< 40 )
{
```

```
/* if the expression or statement is true then display the
output as stated */
printf("length is less than 40\n" );
}
else
{
/* if  the condition is not true (false) then display the
output as stated */
printf("length is not less than 40\n" );
}
printf("value of length is : %d\n", length);
return 0;
}
```

Output:

```
length is not less than 40;
value of length is: 200
```

## If...else if...else statement

This decision is similar to a situation where you have to make a decision after another decision.

Format:

```
if(Statement1)
```

```
{/* if statement1 is evaluated as true, then evaluate the
statement */}
else if( statement 2)
{ /* Evaluates statement when statement 2 is true */}
else if( statement 3)
{/* Evaluate when statement 3 is true */}
else
{/* Evaluate all conditions are false */}
```

Let's consider a program

```
#include <stdio.h>
int main ()
/* Program execution starts here*/
{
/* Definition of variable */
int x = 90;
/* verify the expression */
if( x == 9 )
{
/* if the expression above is true then print what is
requested */
printf("Value of x is 9\n" );
}
else if( x == 15 )
{
```

```
    /* if else if condition is true */
    printf("Value of x is 15\n" );
    }
    else if( x == 60 )
    {
    }
    else
    {
    /* if none of the conditions is true */
    printf("The values don't match\n" );
    }
    printf("The Precise value of x is: %d\n", x );
    return 0;
    }
```

Once executed, the output is:

```
    The values don't match
    The Precise value of x is: 90
```

# Conclusion

The c programming language is not a hard language to learn because it is fundamental for any beginner. If you have completed reading this chapter, I can guarantee that you have the basic knowledge of C programming. However, it is important to dive deeper if you want to perfect your skill with this language.

# Chapter Three: C# Programming

## Introduction

Did you know that C# is an object-oriented language? Actually, Microsoft developed the language as part of its inbuilt .NET initiative. This programming guide on C# will take you through the basics of C# while equipping you with every concept, you need to understand and relevant programs to explain the language better.

## Prerequisite for Learning C#

While there is no standard prerequisite when it comes to learning C#, it is important that as a beginner you have a basic knowledge of computer and programming. However, if you already have previous knowledge on C or C++ language, it will be great. Importantly, before beginning, you have to install Visual Studio. If you are considering space in your system and looking for a way to overcome the hassles of installing the Visual Studio IDE, why not opt to use online compilers.

## Features of C# Language

While C# is narrowly similar to various high-level languages such as C and C++ with strong resemblance with Java, however, it does still have a strong programming feature that makes it popular among many programmers in the world. The features include:

- Integration with Windows
- Indexers
- Simple multithreading
- Standard library
- Boolean conditions
- Easy to use generics
- Properties and events
- Assembly versioning
- Automatic garbage collection

# Understanding the Basics of C#

To begin, let us start with the simplest program you will come across in any programming language. Yes, it's the simple "Hello World!" program. This involves displaying some text directly to the output screen. The primary aim of this program is to familiarize you with the requirement and syntax of C#.

```
// Hello World! Beginners' Program
namespace Hello
{
  class World {
    static void Main(string[] args)
    {
      System.Console.WriteLine("Hello World, Welcome
```

```
        to My First C# Programming!");
           }
         }
       }
```

Output

Hello World, Welcome to My First C# Programming!

## *Explanation of the Hello World program*

*// Hello World! Program*

Whenever you see a line beginning with "//", it indicates the starting point of a comment in C#. These comments are exempted when the compiler executes the codes in the program. The purpose of comments is to make developers have a better understanding of their codes.

*namespace Hello{...}*

This line uses the keyword "namespace" to define our own unique namespace. In the example above, our namespace is Hello. Perhaps, it looks abstract. Well, consider namespace as a container that comprises of methods, classes, and other namespace.

class World{...}

The statement above creates a new class "World." Creating a class is compulsory in C# because the language is object-oriented.

*static void Main(string[] args){...}*

This line must be included in every single program. Main() is a method of class World. The program begins execution from the beginning of the Main() method. Therefore, all programs in C# must contain have a Main() method.

*System.Console.WriteLine*("Hello World Welcome to C# Programming Language!");

This prints the word in quotes to the screen.

### Points to remember

- There must be a class definition for every C# program
- Execution of the program begins from the Main() method
- Comments are not compulsory but necessary

The program above is an introduction for beginners. Later in this chapter, you will see other programs that may seem complex. However, the secret is compiling them on your own while making some changes. If nothing makes sense so far, don't worry with time, everything will be clearer.

# Data types

Nothing should be new to you at this point, because some of these terms have been explained in previous chapters. However, it is important to throw more light on them once a while. The C# language has its own basic data types, which we will discuss in this section. You can use data types in C# to build values that will be used in the course of the program or application. Let us expound on these data types with example.

## Integer

Integer data types work with numbers, which are normally whole numbers. C# uses the reserves word "Int32" to declare a variable as an integer type. For instance, if I declare the variable number1 as an integer. After this, I will further allocate a numerical value to number1

```
using System;
namespace DemoProgram
{
 class Program
//This part creates a new class, which we call Program
 {
  static void Main(string[] args)
  {
   Int32 number1=50;
   Console.Write(number1);
```

```
        Console.ReadKey();
    }
    }
}
```

The outcome of the program above will be:

50

**Explanation**: We declare the variable "number1" to be of integer type (Int32) with the value "50" assigned to the variable. Then the result is displayed to the console.

## Double

This data type is used when decimal numbers are involved. Examples include 10.58, 25.98, or 45.01. In C#, the keyword "Double" is used to denote a double data type. In the example below, the variable "number1" is defined as double and a value assigned to it.

```
using System;
namespace DemoProgram
{
class Program
// This part creates a new class, which we call Program
{
```

```
        static void Main(string[] args)
        {
        // Declaration of the variable "number" to be of double
        data type
          double number1=45.01;
          Console.Write(num);

          Console.ReadKey();
        }
        }
        }
```

The output of the program will display

45.01

## Boolean

The Boolean data type works with Boolean values, which can only be false or true. The keyword "Boolean" is used to declare this kind of datatype. For instance, the program below declares "OFF" as Boolean with the value "False" assigned to it. Eventually, the console display "False" as the output.

```
        using System;
        namespace DemoProgram
        {
```

```
class Program
// We create a new class call Program
 {
   static void Main(string[] args)
   {
// Here is the declaration of the variables as Boolean
     Boolean OFF=false;
     Console.Write(status);

     Console.ReadKey();
   }
 }
}
```

## String

At times, when writing a program, you may choose to write a specific message shown on the screen. To do this, the "string" data type allows text to be displayed. It uses the keyword "String"

```
using System;
namespace DemoProgram
// The goal of this program is to display a string on the
screen
{
 class program
```

```
// We create a new class called Program
{
  static void Main(string[] args)
  {
    String statement1="This is C# Programming for
Beginners'.";
    Console.Write(statement1);

    Console.ReadKey();
  }
}
}
```

The output will be:

This is C# Programming for Beginners'.

# Variables

In C#, it is a memory location that contains a data type that determines the kind of value to store in the variable. Variables are declared in the format below:

[modifiers] data type identifier;

The modifier in the format above represents an access modifier. On the other hand, the identifier represents the variable name. The first example below shows a variable declaration where the public is the modifier, number1 is an identifier name, and int is the data type. However, the second example indicates that the second variable type is a local variable.

Public int number1; // First example

Int number1; // second example

## Variable Modifiers

A modifier allows a programmer to specify some features, which is applied to the identifier. A local variable has a scope, which is defined within the block in the program.

| Modifier | Meaning |
| --- | --- |
| Internal | Accessible only by the current program |
| Public | Accessible as a field anywhere in the program |
| Protected | Accessible within the class it is defined |
| Private | Accessible within the type in which it is defined |

## Constants

Constants are values whose values don't change throughout the program time frame. C# uses the keyword "const" and it always comes before the data type and variable. If you decide to allocate value to a particular constant, it will return compilation error. For instance,

const int number1 = 45;

number1 = 89;

// This will be a compilation error because the assignment towards the left side has to be an indexer, variable or property.

Note that local variables can be declared as constants. These constants are usually static, even if they don't use any static keyword.


# Operators in C#

You should be familiar with operators even if you are a beginner. These are symbols used in programming to perform various operations on an operand. Operands can be either constants or variables. For instance, in 3 * 6, * is an operation used to perform multiplication operation whereas 3 and 6 are the operands. You can use operators in C# to manipulate values and variables in the course of a program. However, C# supports numerous operators depending on the operation type they perform. Without much time, let us begin with the operators in C#.

## Arithmetic Operators

These operators are used for various numeric data types, which includes arithmetic operations including addition (+), subtraction (-), multiplication (*), and division (/). Furthermore, C# has another unique arithmetic operator known as the %, which is the remainder after a division operation is performed.

Importantly, unlike other languages, the operator + (addition) operate differently when used with string and number types. For instance, the result of the expression 7 + 4 is 11. However, when used with strings, the result of the expression, "7 +4" is "74". Therefore, with the number type, it acts as an addition whereas with strings, it is a concatenation operator. A simple program can be helpful to set things in order.

```
using System;

namespace Oper
{
```

```csharp
class ArithmeticOper
{
// Always remember you have to create a new class by
using the class statement
    public static void Main(string[] args)
    {
        double income = 12.20, expenses =
2.30, res;

        int loss = 21, profit = 4, ; dem
        // Addition operator (+)
        res = income + expenses;
        Console.WriteLine("{0} + {1} = {2}",
income, expenses, res);


        res = income - expenses;
        Console.WriteLine("{0} - {1} = {2}",
income, expenses, res);


        res = income * expenses;
        Console.WriteLine("{0} * {1} = {2}",
income, expenses, res);
```

```
                        res = income / expenses;
                        Console.WriteLine("{0} / {1} = {2}",
        income, expenses, res);


                        dem = loss % profit;
                        Console.WriteLine("{0} % {1} = {2}",
        loss, profit, dem);
                            }
                }
        }
```

12.2 + 2.3 = 14.5

12.2 − 2.3 = 9.9

12.2 * 2.3 = 28.06

12.2 / 2.3 = 5.30434782609

21 % 4 = 1

When you properly compile this program without any error, you will get the following output.

## Logical Operators

You can use these operators to perform logical operations and they include AND, OR. These operators operate on Boolean expression and return the same Boolean values. The result can only be true (T) or false (F) as illustrated in the table below.

| Operand Y | Operand Z | AND (&&) | OR (\|\|) |
|---|---|---|---|
| T | T | T | T |
| F | T | F | T |
| T | F | F | T |
| F | F | F | F |

From the table, the OR operator evaluates to true (T) only in a situation where one operand is true (T). However, for the AND operator, once one operand is false (F), the operation is also False.

Sample program

```
using System;

namespace Operator
{
        class Logical
// Here, we name the class we created as Operator
        {
```

```
            public static void Main(string[] args)
            {
// Declaration and giving variables values
                bool outcome;
                int income = 20, expenses = 30;
                // OR operator
                outcome = (income == expenses) ||
(income> 5);

                Console.WriteLine(outcome);
                // AND operator
                outcome = (income == expenses) &&
(incomeb > 5);

                Console.WriteLine(outcome);
            }
        }
}
```

The outcome of the program above should be:

True

False

**Note**: These programs are for explanatory purposes. It is important for you to try it on your own. If you want to learn to program effectively, you must be ready to practice frequently and this is a way to improve your programming skill.

# Relational Operators

These operators in C# return either a true or a false result. If you want to compare variables or expression, the best option is the relational operator. Additionally, they have a lower priority in comparison with arithmetic operators. Besides this, you can use them in loop and decision-making. The table below shows the basic relational operators in C#.

| Relational Operators | Name of Operator | Example |
|---|---|---|
| == | Equal to | 6 == 7 return false |
| != | Not equal to | 5 != 7 return true |
| > | Greater than | 7 > 5 returns true |
| < | Less than | 8 < 9 evaluates true |
| <= | Less than or (equivalent) equal to | 9<= 7 evaluates true |
| >= | Greater than or equal to | 5 >= 7 returns false |

Sample Program

```csharp
using System;

namespace Oper
{
    class Relational
    {
        public static void Main(string[] args)
        {
// Declaration of variables
            int outcome;
            int day1 = 21, day3 = 23;
            outcome = (day1==day3);
            Console.WriteLine("{0} == {1}
returns {2}",day1, day3, outcome);
            outcome= (day1 > day3);
            Console.WriteLine("{0} > {1} returns
{2}",day1, day3, outcome);
            outcome = (day1< day3);
            Console.WriteLine("{0} < {1} returns
{2}",day1, day3, outcome);
            outcome = (day1 >= day3);
            Console.WriteLine("{0} >= {1}
returns {2}",day1, day3, outcome);
            outcome = (day1 <= day3);
```

```
                    Console.WriteLine("{0} <= {1}
returns {2}",day1, day3, outcome);
                         outcome = (day1 != day3);
                         Console.WriteLine("{0} != {1}
returns {2}",day1, day3, outcome);
                    }
               }
          }
```

Output:

```
20 == 30 returns False
20 > 30 returns False
20 < 30 returns True
20 >= 30 returns False
20 <= 30 returns True
20 != 30 returns True
```

## Unary Operators

These operators unlike the ones we have discussed so far operate on one operand instead of both. The unary operators in C# include

| Operator | Name | Description |
|----------|------|-------------|
| - | Unary Minus | Inverts the operand sign |

| + | Unary Plus | Leaves the operand to sign the way it is |
|---|---|---|
| -- | Decrement | Decreases value by 1 |
| ++ | Increment | Increase value by 1 |
| | | |

Sample Program for Unary Operator

```
using System;

namespace UnaryOperator
{
    class UnaryOpe
    {
        public static void Main(string[] args)
        {
// Declaration of variables in the program
            int num = 25, outcome;
            bool flag = false;
            outcome = +num;
            Console.WriteLine("+num = " +
outcome);
```

```
                    outcome = -num;
                    Console.WriteLine("-num = " +
outcome);

                    outcome = ++num;
                    Console.WriteLine("++num = " +
outcome);

                    outcome = --num;
                    Console.WriteLine("--num = " +
outcome);

                    Console.WriteLine("!flag = " +
(!flag));
            }
        }
}
```

The output is as follows:

```
    +num = 25
    -num = -25
    ++number = 26
    --number = 25
    !flag = True
```

## Bitwise Operators

In our last operators in C# is the bitwise operator, which performs bit manipulation similar to what I have explained in the preceding chapter. Since you are familiar with the operation, I will simply highlight the operators and a simple program to demonstrate how they work. For more, you can check "Chapter Two" to refresh your memory.

| Operator | Operator Name (Bitwise) |
|----------|-------------------------|
| & | AND |
| ^ | Exclusive OR |
| \| | OR |
| ~ | Complement |
| << | Left Shift |
| >> | Right Shift |

Look at the program below.

```
using System;

namespace OperBit
{
// Creating a new class known as BitOpe
```

```
class BitOpe
{

    public static void Main(string[] args)
    {
// Declaration of variables with values
        int income = 20;
        int expenses = 30;
        int outcome;
        outcome = ~income;
        Console.WriteLine("~{0} = {1}",
income, outcome);
        outcome = income&expenses;
        Console.WriteLine("{0} & {1} = {2}",
income,expenses, outcome);
        outcome = income | expenses;
        Console.WriteLine("{0} | {1} = {2}",
income,expenses, outcome);
        outcome = income ^ expenses;
        Console.WriteLine("{0} ^ {1} = {2}",
income,expenses, outcome);
        outcome = income<< 2;
        Console.WriteLine("{0} << 2 = {1}",
income, outcome);
        outcome = income>> 2;
```

```
                    Console.WriteLine("{0} >> 2 = {1}",
    income, outcome);
                }
        }
    }
```

If the program doesn't contain any error, your output should be as follows:

```
    ~20 = -21
    20 & 30 = 0
    20 | 30 = 50
    20 ^ 30 = 50
    20 << 2 = 40
    20 >> 2 = 2
```

## Ternary Operator

This operator will be strange because it is the first time I am mentioning it in this book. The ternary operator "?" operates on three operands and functions like the "if... then... else" statement.

Format:

*Variable = condition? Statement1: statement2;*

The operation works this way. If the condition stated is true, then the outcome of statment1 is allocated to the variable. However, if it turns out to be false, the value is allocated to statement2. Consider the program below.

```
using System;

namespace OperTer
{
        class Ternary
// The new class name for this program is Ternary
        {
                public static void Main(string[] args)
                {
// Declaration of variables as integer and string
                        int num = 21;
                        string outcome;
                        outcome = (num % 2 == 0)? "Even
Number" : "Odd Number";
                        Console.WriteLine("{0} is {1}", num,
outcome);
                }
        }
}
```

The output will be:

With this, I believe you have an excellent understanding of operators in C#. You are surely making progress in your quest to be an around programmer.

## Array

An array in C# is simply a data structure, which stores a group or sequence of fixed-size elements. All elements have the same size. In a simple way, it is a storage position for a sequence of data, which is considered as a group or collection of variables having a similar data type.

For instance, you intend to have array but with an integer value, you have to first declare it.

Int [5];

In the example above, the total number of elements will be 5 i. An array is very efficient, especially when you need to store a group of values with a similar data type. Therefore, rather than declaring the variable one after the other, you can decide to use one declaration for them all. The variable will reference the list of array elements in the program. An example will make things easier for you.

95

```
namespace demoProgram {
    class programArray
{
// Study the program carefully how the array is declared
    Static void main (string[] args)
    Int [] Table;
        }
    }
}
```

In the example above, you have an idea of the line – Int []
numbers;

So far, you should know that we are using an integer data type.
The [] is the placeholder, which specifies the array rank. It
identifies the exact number of elements contained in that array
we want. Lastly, the array has a name, which in this example is
"Table"

Let's go further with this example, consider the next line of
codes.

```
using System;

namespace demoApplication {
```

```
    class ArrayProgram
{
    Static void main (string[] args)
   Int [] Table;
    Table = new Int [5];
    Table [0] = 8;
    Table [1] = 9;
    Table [2] = 10;
    Table [3] = 11;
    Table [4] = 12;
    Table [5] = 13
      }
    }
}
```

What we did here is to initialize the array by specifying the number of "Table" the array will accommodate. Furthermore, I assigned values to each array element. In array, the index position always begins at 0.

Let us assume you want to display the full content of the program. It will look like this.

```
namespace DemoApplication
{
 class ArrayProgram
 {
 static void Main(string[] args)
 // Declaration of variables begins here
  {
   Int[] Table;
   Table=new Int[3];

 Table [0] = 8;
   Table [1] =9;
   Table [2] = 10;
   Table [3] = 11;
   Table [4] = 12;
   Table [5] = 13;

   Console.WriteLine(Table[0]);
   Console.WriteLine(Table[1]);
   Console.WriteLine(Table[2]);
   Console.WriteLine(Table[3]);
   Console.WriteLine(Table[4]);
   Console.WriteLine(Table[5]);

   Console.ReadKey();
```

```
        }
      }
    }
```

In C# programming language, you can declare the array as fixed or dynamic length. For the static length, you can store array on a pre-defined number of items as shown in our examples above. However, a dynamic array doesn't have predefined size rather the size increases as new items are added. It is also possible to alter a dynamic array after defining it.

## Arrays Definition for Different Data Type

In our previous examples, all the arrays are of integer type. However, it is not limited to an integer data type as you can use various data types including string, character, and double. Importantly, arrays are objects in C# language. This signifies that after the declaration of the array, it doesn't mean that the array is now created. You have to instantiate the array through the "new" operator.

Check out the examples below to know how to define arrays of string, char, and double.

```
using System;
```

```
namespace demoProgram {
  class program
// Beginning of the program
{
    Static void main (string[] args)
// Declaration of elements in the array
    string [] stringArray = new string [20];
    bool [] boolArray = new bool [2];
    char [] charArray = new char [7];
    double [] doubleArray = new double [4];
      }
    }
  }
```

# Categories of Array in C#

You can categorize arrays into four groups. These include single-dimensional arrays, rectangular arrays or multidimensional arrays, jagged, and mixed arrays. My focus will be on the first two arrays because jagged and mixed arrays will be complicated for you to understand as a beginner.

## Single-Dimensional

These set of arrays are the simplest and easiest to understand in C#. You can use single-dimensional arrays to store items of an array with an already predefined data type. The items in the array are stored continuously beginning from 0. So far, all the arrays I have explained in this chapter are single-dimensional arrays.

The code below declares and sets an array containing five items, with all having an integer data type. First is to declare the array before instantiating the array using the new operator.

```
int [] numberArray;
numberArray = new int [5];
```

C# uses a straightforward way of declaring arrays by putting the items in curly braces. Note that if a program forgets to initialize the array, the items are inevitably initialized to its definite original value for that array type. The code below should explain it better.

| 1 | int [] staticIntArray = new int [5] {2, 4, 6, 8, 10}; |
|---|---|
| 2 | string [] strArray = new string [4] {"Johnson", "Mikel, "Frederick", "Mahesh"}; |
| 3 | string [] strArray = {"Johnson", "Mikel, "Frederick", "Mahesh"}; |

From the three different codes, you will observe that the first example declares an array with 5 items. The second declares an array with string data type having 4 string items. However, the second and third examples are the same with the only difference being that we directly assigned the values to the array without using the new operator.

## Multi-Dimensional

This kind of arrays contains more than one dimension. Most beginners tend to run away from this kind of arrays because they look complex. It has the form of a matrix. This type of array can be of fixed or dynamic size. However, to declare a multi-dimensional array, the format is as follows:

*string [,] mutliDimStringArray*

### Initializing multi-dimensional arrays

The code below shows two different multi-dimensional arrays. It defines an array with a matric of 3x2 and 2x2 respectively. It is possible to store 6 items in the first array while 4 on the second. You should initialize both arrays during declaring it.

```
int[,] Mynumbers = new int[3, 2] { { 4, 2 }, { 5, 2 }, { 1, 3 }
};
string[,] names = new string[2, 2] { { "Queen", "Ben" }, {
"Paul", "Irene" } };
```

What if you are unsure the items the array will contain?. The code below clarifies that by creating two-dimensional arrays without any limit to the number of items.

```
int[,] numbers = new int[,] { { 4, 2 }, { 5, 2 }, { 1, 3 } };
string[,] names = new string[,] { { "Queen", "Ben" }, {
"Paul", "Irene" } };
```

Similar to the single-dimensional array where we omit the new operator, you can also do the same in multi-dimensional arrays by directly assigning the values.

```
namespace demoApplication {
    class programArray
{
// Don't forget we always have to create a new class
    Static void main (string[] args)
  int[, ] MyTable = {
{
  4,
  2
```

```
        },
        {
            5,
            2
        },
        {
            1,
            3
        }
    };
    string[, ] names = {
        {
            "Queen",
            "Ben"
        },
        {
            "Paul",
            "Irene"
        }
    };
            }
          }
        }
```

The code above may look complicated but we can make it simpler by initializing the array items one after the order. Look at the code below

```
int [, ] numb = new int [3, 2];
numb [0, 0] = 4;
numb [1, 0] = 2;
numb [2, 0] = 5;
numb [0, 1 ] = 2;
numb [1, 1] = 1;
numb [2, 1] = 3;
```

To access a multi-dimensional array items, you have to specify the dimension of the matrix. For instance, item (1, 2) exemplifies an array item on the second row and third column of the matrix. For you to access the "numb" array, you have to use the "Console.Writeline"

```
1.    Console.WriteLine(numb[0, 0]);
2.    Console.WriteLine(numb[0, 1]);
3.    Console.WriteLine(numb[1, 0]);
4.    Console.WriteLine(numb[1, 1]);
5.    Console.WriteLine(numb[2, 0]);
6.    Console.WriteLine(numb[2, 2]);
```

**Note:** You can perform various manipulations on arrays such as sorting, searching, reversing, and clearing an array list. So far, you have learned the basics of arrays including their various types. Don't forget to try some exercises on your own.

# Chapter Four: Beginners Guide to Learning C++

Yes, you have graduated after finishing your first course in this "Step by Step Beginners' Guide to Learn Programming" book. If you did go through the C programming language explained in the previous chapter, give yourself a treat because you have accomplished what many cannot do in a lifetime.

Welcome back from your treat. It is time to improve yourself in diversifying your programming skill in key languages. By the time you are through with this chapter, you will be better equipped to write codes using C++ language. In the end, you will roll your sleeve and program like a "badass" programmer.

C++ will help you understand the modern approach to software development. For a new developer, the essential thing is to understand the theories of programming, which will help you by not wasting your precious time with the technical details of the language.

## Brief History

In 1979, Bjarne Stroustrup developed C++ Programming language. Originally, the language was known as "C with classes" before the name was changed to C++ in 1983. The name is a demonstration that the language comes from the C programming language. Today, the language has evolved with C++14 as the standard C++. This version comes with added feature including the fixing of some bugs. The introduction of the C++14 took place on March 2014.

## Is there anyone using C++?

The language is relevant in various sectors in the software industry. it may surprise you to know that the OS of your favorite Apple laptop is written in C++. Besides it, operating systems such as Windows 95, 98, Me, 2000, and the once-popular Window XP were also written in this language. Applications such as Internet Explorer, Microsoft Office, applications of Adobe Systems (Illustrator, ImageReady, Flash, Photoshop, Acrobat, etc.) are developed using C++. Furthermore, not forgetting the renowned Chromium Web Browser, and Google Search engine, these are just a few to mention.

## Why use C++ today?

Today, many software developers use C++ when the application requires efficiency and high performance. This has made many recognize C++ as a flexible and efficient language. Additionally, if you want to develop a big application but want less resource to use, then C++ is the best option.

# Difference between C and C++

Hardly can you talk about C++ without considering the difference with C programming language. Most beginners tend to find out what makes these two languages differ. C is a procedural language but doesn't support classes and objects. However, C++ is not only a procedural programming language but also an object-oriented language. There are other differences that exist between these two languages, which are shown below in the tabular form.

| Differences | C Programming Language | C++ Programming Language |
|---|---|---|
| Developers | AT&T Bell Labs by Dennis Ritchie in 1969 | Bjarne Stroustrup in 1979 |
| Division | Subset of C++ | Superset of C. This means you can run C programs in C++ environment |

| Language support | Procedural language | Procedural and Object-oriented language |
|---|---|---|
| Multiple Declaration | Multiple global declarations are allowed | Not allowed |
| Overloading support | Function and operator not supported | Supports operators and function overloading |
| Reference Variables | Not supported | Supported |
| Namespace feature | Not available | Available |
| Inheritance | Not possible | Allowed |
| Exception handling | Not supported | Supported |
| Input | Scanf | Cin |
| Output | Printf | cout |

# Structure of C++ Program

Since you already have a basic understanding of programming, I will teach you C++ by using a different strategy. Perhaps, the best way to learn any programming language is y writing a program. Does that sound interesting? Of course, I will start with a simple program, which you can modify. If you want to learn to program faster, always experiment with some addition.

From the sample of this program, I will explain the structure of the C++ program. So let us begin with our first C++ program.

| | |
|---|---|
| // First Programming in C++<br>#include <iostream><br>using namespace std;<br>Int main ()<br>{ | Welcome to C++ Programming! |

The panel on the left side represents the source code while the right side shows the result of the program after compilation and execution.

## // First Programming in C++

Whenever you see a line starting with "//" in the C++ program, it indicates a comment line. They don't have any effect on the course of the program. however, the reason behind them is for the programming to make some observation or explanations. It allows you to make a short description of what the program is all about

### #include <iostream>

Lines starting with # are directives for the preprocessor. Although they are not normal code lines with expressions, however, are indications for the compiler's preprocessor. In the program above, the directive tells the preprocessor to add the iostream to the standard file.

### Using namespace std;

Every element in the standard C++ library is usually declared in a namespace. Therefore, for one to access its functionality, you must declare use this expression to do that.

### Int main ()

This line indicates the beginning of the main function definition. The main function is the starting point of any C++ programs and their execution begins here. For any program, a pair of parentheses () always follow the word "main" What differentiates a function from other types of expression is the parentheses that follow the name.

### cout << "Welcome to C++ Programming!";

This line is a C++ statement. The cout is a standard output stream in C++, which is followed by a sequence of characters enclosed in quotes. If you observe clearly, the statement ends with a semicolon (;).

***Return 0;***

The return statement makes the main function (int main ()) to terminate.

# Data Types, Variables and Operator

Perhaps, you will question the usefulness of the program above. We had to write some lines containing statements, compile and execute them to produce a simple output on the screen. Why even compile it when you can produce it quickly without having to run the program. Interestingly, C++ programming is not limited to printing text on the screen. You can perform other activities. In this section, I will introduce you to the concept of variables, data types, and operators in C++ language.

Assuming I ask you to store the number 9 in your memory. After a while, I ask you to memorize any number 8. With this, you have to store two different numbers in your memory. Let us assume that I ask you to add 3 to the first number I asked you to store. For now, you have to retain a new number, which is 10 (9

+1) in addition to the second number 3. Furthermore, subtract the first number from the second, which will be 7.

This whole process you have just completing using your memory is similar to what a computer with two variables. The same action can be executed using the following instruction.

```
A = 9;
B = 3;
A = a+1;
Result = a – b;
```

This is very simple, right. Assuming you have to store millions of numbers, can your brain accommodate it? Emphatically, No! However, a computer can store much more than that and perform sophisticated mathematical operations. A Variable is part of a memory that stores a determined value.

Every variable requires an identifier, which differentiates it from others. For instance, in the example above, the variable identifiers include a, b, and results. You can call the variable any name you like.

## Identifiers

An identifier is valid if it has a sequence of one or more letters, underscore character (_), or digits. However, there shouldn't be any symbols, punctuation marks or space when naming an identifier. The only valid characters are letters, digits and underscore. Additionally, every variable identifier must start with a letter. Besides this, you can also use an underscore; however, in certain situations, they are reserved as specific keywords.

When naming an identifier, another important thing to consider is that they should not be keywords. Keywords are specific words used only by the compiler.

The standard reserved keywords in C++ language include asm, auto, bool, break, case, catch, char, class, const, const_cst, continue, default, delete, do, double, dynamic_cast, else, enum, explicit, export extern, false, float, for, friend, goto, if, inline, int, ling, mutable, namespace, new, operator, private, protected, public, register, reinterpret_cast, return, short, signed, sizeof, static, static_cast, struct, switch, template, this, throw, true, try, typedef, typeid, typename, union, unsigned, using, virtual, void, volatile, wchar_t, while

**Note** – Like C language, the C++ language is case sensitive. This means that when you write an identifier in capital letters, it is not equivalent to another having the same name in small letters. For instance, the variable HOUSE is not the same as using "house" or "House" as a variable. The three examples are different identifiers.

# Data Types in C++ Programming Language

In programming, variables are stored in computer memory; however, the computer must know the particular data you want it to store because it is not going to be the same amount of memory using in storing a letter or a number. Besides this, they are not interpreted in the same way.

Memory is organized in bytes. A byte is the smallest amount of memory, which can be managed in C++. The table below highlights the basic data types available in C++ along with their size and range.

| Data Type | Description | Size (byte) * | Range * |
|---|---|---|---|
| Char | Character | 1 | -128 to 127 and 0 − 255 |
| Short int | Short integer | 2 | -32768 to 32767 for |

| | | | |
|---|---|---|---|
| | | | signed while unsigned is 0 to 65535 |
| Int | Integer | 4 | -2147483648 to 2147483647 for signed while unsigned is 0 to 4294967295 |
| Long int | Long integer | 4 | Signed -2147483648 to 2147483647 while unsigned is 0 to 4294967295 |

| Float | Floating point number | 4 | +/- 3.4e +/-38 |
|-------|----------------------|---|----------------|
| Bool | Boolean value | 1 | True or false |
| Double | Double precision floating point number | 8 | +/- 1.7e +/- 308 |
| Long double | Long double-precision floating-point number | 8 | /- 1.7e +/- 308 |
| Wchar _t | Wide character | 2 or 4 | 1 wide character |

** The values of the size and range of the data types depends on the preprocessor of the system that the program is compiled. However, the above table shows the values for a 32-bit system.

# Variable Declaration

You cannot use a variable in C++ unless you declare it. When you hear of variable declaration, it means stating the particular data type you want that variable to be. the syntax for variable declaration involves writing the particular data type and followed by a valid variable identifier. You must adhere to the rule of variable number in order not to have issues when writing your program.

For instance

```
Int abe;
Float newNumber;
```

In C++, these two are valid variables declared. The first one declares "ab" as a variable of integer type while the second declares the word "newNumber" as a variable type of float. Once these variables have been declared, you can use them within the program. however, instead of declaring a different variable of the same type on different lines, you can decide to put them on the same line and separate them using a comma.

For example, if you were to declare a, b, c, d, and e as an integer, you can declare them like this:

119

Int a, b, c;

Rather than

Int a;

Int b;

Int c;

Since you are new to the language, I will use an example to demonstrate with a variable declaration in a program.

```
// Declaring Variable
#include <iostream>
using namespace std;
int main ()
{
int A, B;
int Outcome;

// The Process of Variable declaration
A = 5;
B = 14;
A = A + 1;
Outcome = A * B;
// Print the outcome of the process
cout << Outcome;
// End the Program
```

```
    Return 0;
    }
```

Output

```
    84
```

Is there anything looking strange in the above program? Obviously, it shouldn't because we have covered most of the areas in the program. However, the only line that may look strange is the "A = A +1; else everything looks good.

# Variable Scope

A variable in C++ can be in a global or local scope. When you declare a variable within the body of the source code is it global; nevertheless, a local variable is one declared within the body of a block or function. If you look at our program above, you will observe that the variables were declared along with the data type was declared at the beginning of the main function (int main ()). Global variables can be referenced from anywhere in the program, it does not matter if it is inside a function. However, local variables are limited to enclosed braces {}. The diagram below is self-explanatory for you.

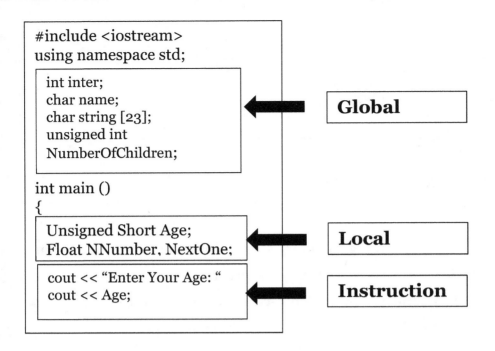

```
#include <iostream>
using namespace std;

    int inter;
    char name;
    char string [23];
    unsigned int
    NumberOfChildren;

int main ()
{
    Unsigned Short Age;
    Float NNumber, NextOne;

    cout << "Enter Your Age: "
    cout << Age;
```

**Global**

**Local**

**Instruction**

## Variable Initialization

When you declare local variables, by default its value is undetermined. However, you may decide to store a value when you are declaring the variable. For this to happen, you would have to initialize the variable. There are two ways of variable initialization in C++.

The first one involves appending and equal sign (=) followed by the value, which the variable will initialize. For instance, I want to declare a variable "A" of data type integer while initializing it to the value 5 at the moment. This will be:

Int A = 5;

The second means of initializing variables is through a process called "constructor initialization", which involves enclosing the initial value between parentheses (()). For instance,

Int A (0);

In C++, both ways of variable initialization are valid and acceptable.

```cpp
// Variable Initialization in C++
#include <iostream>
using namespace std;
int main ()
{
int A, B;
int Outcome;

// The Process of Variable declaration
A = 5; //initial value = 5
B  (14); // initial value = 14
A = A + 1;
result = A * B;
// Print the outcome of the process
cout << result;
// End the Program
Return 0;
}
```

84

# Strings in C++ Programming

Variables with non-numerical value and longer than a single character are known as a string. The C++ has its own standard library that allows strings operation. Although it is not a fundamental data type, it does behave in a similar fashion as data types.

To be able to use a string in C++, you have to include an additional header in your program.

```
// String Operation in C++
#include <iostream>
#include <string>
using namespace std;
int main ()
{
string myName = "My Name is
Johnbull Cosmos.";
cout << myName;

Return 0;
}
```

```
My Name is Johnbull
Cosmos.
```

This is quite enough to understand string, as I will not dive deep into its operation. With this, you can display a string with various characters. Remember, you have to declare the variable with the string keyword (string myName = "My Name is Johnbull Cosmos.";)

## Constants

By now you will understand what constants or literals are if you go through the C programming in chapter two. It has the same operation in C++; constants are used to express the value of a variable in the course of the program. Remember our previous program where we declare A = 5. In this situation, 5 is a literal constant. Literal constants are categorized as follows

## Integer numerals

These numerical constant specify integer decimal values. To use a numerical constant you don't require any special character or quote attached to them. Examples of integer numerals include

1176

45

-404

## Floating-point number

These numbers have decimal or exponents. They include a decimal point or e character or both attached together. For instance,

3.1578

2.25e23

16.5e-19

## Character and string Constant

At times, you may have non-numerical constants such as:

'e'

'Hello World'

'My C++ Programming Lesson'

# Defining Constant in C++

You may decide to define your own constant in the course of a process without having to consume memory. You can do this by using the #define preprocessor directive. The format is as follow

#define variable value

For example:

 #define Pi = 3.142

#define newline '\'

From the example above, the #define defines two new constants with variable name Pi and newline.

```cpp
// Example for Defining
Constants in C++
#include <iostream>
using namespace std;
#define Pi = 3.142
#define newline '\n'

int main ()
{
double r = 9.0
double circle;
circle = 2 * Pi * r;
cout << circle;
cout << newline;
Return 0;
}
```

```
56.556
```

# Operators in C++ Programming Language

Now you have the basic knowledge of data types, variables, and constants, it is time to start operating with them. C++ has its own integrated operators to perform such activity. Most programming languages have their operators as keywords but in C++, you can use your normal signs on the keyboard. It depends on English words to perform various operations. Additionally, you don't have to memorize anything in this section.

C++ offers various types of operators to use with literals and variables to get a result. Perhaps you know the basic operators from your C programming section. However, there are other operators that C++ language has. I will take them one after another while using examples to explain how they work.

## Arithmetic Operators

I don't have to explain much about this operator since you already know them. However, the basic arithmetic operators in C++ include +, -, *, /, and % (modulo). Modulo is the remainder when you divide two numbers. For instance, in a program, you wrote

```
b = 21 % 5;
```

The variable b will contain 1 since that is the remainder when you divide 21 between 5.

Besides this, there are two additional operators known as the decrement (--) and increment operators (++). These two operators can be used before (prefix) or after (postfix or suffix) a variable. In as much as expressions such as b++ and ++b have the same meaning; however, in a situation where the result of the decrease or increase is evaluated in as a value in an outer expression, the meaning will be different. In the scenario where the increment operator is the prefix (++b), the value of the variable "b" is increased before you evaluate the result of the expression

On the other hand, where the increment operator is the postfix (b++) the value of the variable "b" is increased after the evaluation of the operation. Does it sound confusing? Well, an example will make it clearer for you.

| Example 1 | Example 2 |
|---|---|
| B=4;<br>C = ++B;<br>//A contains 4 while B contains 4 | B=4;<br>C=++B<br>//C contains 3 while B contains 4 |

Does it make any sense now? Of course, it should be if you are not clear, here is the explanation.

In the first example, the content of B is first increased before the value is copied to A whereas in the second example, the value of B is copied A before the value of B is increased.

Study the Program below, what do you think will be the output?

```
int main()
{
```

```
        int i = 0;
        while(i < 10)
        {
                cout << i++; //post increment
        }
        cout << endl;
        i = 0;
        while(i<10)
        {
                cout << ++i; //pre increment
        }
        return 0;
}
```

## Logical Operators

There are three logical operators in C++, which are the conjunction (&&), disjunction (||), and the negation (!) operators. You can also refer to them as the AND, OR, and NOT operator.

The table below shows the AND and OR logical operators

| A | B | A&&B | A||B |
|---|---|------|------|

| True | True | True | True |
|------|------|------|------|
| True | False | False | True |
| False | True | False | True |
| False | False | False | False |

Table for NOT

| Logical Operator | NOT |
|------------------|-----|
| True | False |
| False | True |

# Relational Operators

The relational operator is used to evaluate a comparison between two values or expression. The result of the relational operation is normally a Boolean value, which can only be true or false (0 for true and 1 for false). The format is as follows:

Operand1 (operational operator) operand2

The operands can be a literal or a variable. The following are the relational operators in C++

| Relational Operators | Description | Meaning |
|----------------------|-------------|---------|
| == | Equal to | Returns true if both operand 1 and 2 are |

| | | equal |
|---|---|---|
| != | Not Equal to | Returns true if both operands are not equal |
| > | Greater than | Returns true if operand 1 is greater than operand 2 |
| < | Less than | Returns true if operand 1 is less than operand 2 |
| >= | Greater than or equal to | Returns true if operand 1 is greater than or equal to operand two, else it |

| | | is false |
|---|---|---|
| <= | Less than or equal to | Returns true if operand 1 is less than or equal to operand two, else it is false |

Example of Relational Operators

```
// Example of Relational Operators
#include <iostream>
using namespace std;
int main ()
{
int four = 4;
int six = 6;
cout << " 4 is equal to 6 = " << (four == six) << endl;
cout << " 4 is not equal to 6 = " << (four != six) << endl;
cout << " 4 is less than 6 = " << (four < six) << endl;
cout << " 4 is greater than 6 = " << (four > six) << endl;
cout << " 4 is not less than 6 = " << (four >= six) << endl;
```

```
cout << " 4 is not greater than  = " << (four <= six) <<
endl;
   return 0;
}
```

If you compile and execute this program properly, you will see the output as:

```
4 is equal to 6 = 0
4 is not equal to 6 = 1
4 is less than 6 = 1
4 is greater than 6 = 0
4 is not less than 6 = 0
4 is not greater than 6 = 1
```

## Bitwise Operators

This operator is similar to the logical operators we just discussed. However, it performs logical operations on bits. Unlike the logical operators, that use true or false, the bitwise operators return the output as either 0 or 1.

| Operator | ASM Equivalent | Description |
|----------|----------------|-------------|
|          |                |             |

| & | AND | Bitwise AND |
|---|---|---|
| ^ | XOR | Bitwise Exclusive OR |
| \| | OR | Bitwise Inclusive OR |

| A | B | A & B | A \| B | A ^ B |
|---|---|---|---|---|
| 0 | 0 | 0 | 0 | 0 |
| 0 | 1 | 0 | 1 | 1 |
| 1 | 1 | 1 | 1 | 0 |
| 1 | 0 | 0 | 1 | 1 |

Now, are you wondering how come about the 1's and the 0's? I didn't perform any magic here. Here is the secret. For the bitwise "&", the bit is 1 only when both variables (A and B) have 1 as their corresponding bit. For the XOR, the resulting bit is 1f only one variable has the corresponding bit whereas the OR must have at least a variable with 1 in its corresponding bit.

## Assignment Operators

The function of this operator is to assign a value on the right-hand side to the variable on the left. It uses the "=" as the operator in C++. You can also combine assignment operators with the different operators mentioned so far in this chapter. If you combine them, they form a composite or compound assignment operator. Composite operators include +=, -=, *=, /=, >>=, <<=, %=, |=, ^=, and &=.

Consider the following expression

| Expression | Meaning |
|---|---|
| Number1 += number2; | Number1 = Number1 + number2; |
| b-= 10; | b = b – 10; |
| cost *= profit + 2; | cost = cost * (profit +1); |

Example of all Composite Assignment operators

Let A = 20 initially for the below examples

| Composite Assignment Operator | Example | Is Equivalent to | Result |
|---|---|---|---|
| += | A += 2 | A = A + 2 | 22 |
| -= | A -= 2 | A = A - 2 | 8 |
| *= | A *= 2 | A = A * 2 | 20 |
| /= | A /= 2 | A = A / 2 | 5 |
| %= | A%= 2 | A = A % 2 | 0 |
| <<= | A <<= 2 | A = A << 2 | 40 |

| >>= | | A >>= 2 | A = A >> 2 | 2 |
|---|---|---|---|---|
| &= | | A &= 2 | A = A & 2 | 2 |
| ^= | | A ^= 2 | A = A ^ 2 | 8 |
| \|= | | A \|= 2 | A = A \| 2 | 10 |

Let's apply everything we have learned in this chapter by creating a Fibonacci program for up to 12 numbers.

```cpp
#include<iostream>

using namespace std;

main()
{
  int a, b, n1 = 0, n2 = 1, next;

  cout << "Enter the number of terms of Fibonacci series
you want" << endl;
  cin >> a;

  cout << "First " << a << " terms of Fibonacci series are
:- " << endl;

  for ( b = 0 ; b < a ; b++ )
```

```
    {
      if ( b <= 1 )
        next = b;
      else
      {
        next = n1 + n2;
        n1 = n2;
        n2 = next;
      }
      cout << next << endl;
    }

    return 0;
  }
```

Depending on your input, the result will differ. Run the program and discover what the output will look like.

## C++ Capabilities

Considering the uniqueness of the C++ programming language, it has the following capabilities

- An object-oriented language supports aggregation, multiple inheritance, and dynamic behavior.

- It is highly portable
- It supports operator overload to work naturally with user-defined classes
- It gives developers a whole lot of choices in terms of design and coding.
- It doesn't require any graphic environment
- It is compatible with C

# C++ Limitations

- It is difficult to debug when used for complex web application
- It does have security
- Normally used for specific platform application
- It doesn't support garbage collection
- Doesn't support built-in threads
- It is not secure because it has friend function, pointer, global variable

# Chapter Five: SQL

## Introduction

Structured Query Language (SQL) is a standard language designed for a relational database management system to help manage data effectively. It is a programming language precisely designed for the storage, retrieval, managing, and manipulation of data relational database management system (RDBMS).

It is hard to perform any database activity without using SQL because it is supported by various prominent relational database systems such as Oracle, SQL Server, and MySQL. Furthermore, some features available in the standard SQL are implemented differently in various database systems.

IBM developed this query language originally in the early 1970s. Originally, it wasn't called SQL but SEQUEL (Structured English Query Language) before it was changed to SQL. You are in for a wonderful adventure because this aspect of this book will help you learn and understand the basics of SQL.

## Pre-requisites for Learning SQL

Since this book is for beginners, I am assuming that you don't have any knowledge about the database. My goal is to help you understand the basic concepts of SQL Languages. however, SQL is a declarative query language used for creating and manipulating databases. It doesn't require rocket science to understand the basic concepts because its syntax is simple and easy to understand when compared to other programming languages.

Nevertheless, foundational knowledge of relational database management system and a keen interest to study the language is my own prerequisites you need to start your journey of learning SQL.

## What can you do with SQL?

You can use SQL for a whole lot of things, which includes:

- Create a database
- Create tables in a database
- Request or query information from a database
- Insert records
- Update or modify records in a database
- Delete records from a database
- Establish permissions or full control access in the database

The list below is just the tip of the iceberg of what you can do with SQL.

# Topics to Cover in SQL

This chapter covers all fundamental concepts of SQL language like creating database and table, adding records to tables, using constraints, selecting records from tables, updating and deleting records in a table. The list is endless.

Once you have familiarized yourself with the basics, you will learn the methods of retrieving records by searching records, joining multiple tables, etc. In the end, I will highlight some advance concept in SQL such as performing aggregations and modifying an existing table structure.

# What is SQL?

SQL is a computer language used for storing, manipulating, and retrieving of data stored in a relational database management system. A query language as stated earlier is used for accessing and modifying data in a database.

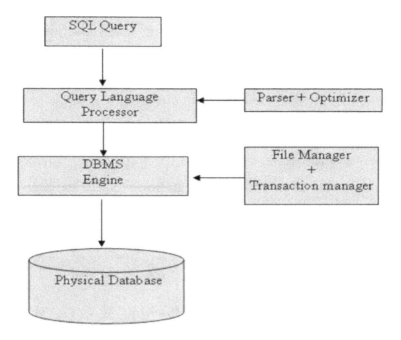

Before you can begin experimenting with SQL, you must have access to a database system. There are various online SQL editors you can use to evaluate or test SQL statements I have provided as examples in this book. However, you need a full-fledged database management system in order to execute SQL statements.

# Basic Terms

## What is Relational Database?

A relational database is a type of database categorized into tables with each table relating to another within the database. It allows data to be divided into smaller, logical, and manageable units for better performance and easier maintenance. To relate one table to another, you need to create a common field or key in a relational database system.

## Definition Data

Data is a fact that relates to a particular object under consideration. For instance, your name, weight, height, weights are unique to you. You can also consider a file, image, or picture as data.

## Definition Database

A database is a systematical collection of data. Through a database, you can manipulate and manage data easily. For instance, your electricity supply has a database to manage your billing, address, and other relevant information. Another example is your famous Facebook account; it contains information relating to your friends, messages, member activities, pictures, etc.

## Definition Database Management System

DBMS is a collection of programs enables users to access database, report, manipulate, and represent data. Furthermore, it allows users to control access to the database. DBMS is not a new concept and was first implemented in the 1960s.

## Types of Database Management System

- **Hierarchical DBMS** – this uses a "parent-child" relationship in storing data. People hardly use them nowadays. However, it has the structure of a tree with nodes representing records. An example of this type of DBMS is the registry used in Windows XP

- **Network DBMS** – This DBMS allows many-to-many relationship. For beginners, this is a complicated database structure. An example is the RDM server.

- **Relational DBMS** – This kind of DBMS defines a database relationship in terms of tables. Unlike the network DBMS, relational DBMS doesn't allow many-to-many relationship. Example of relational DBMS includes a Microsoft SQL Server database, Oracle, and MySQL.

- **Object-Oriented Relation DBMS** – This allows the storage of new data types. Data are stored in the form of objects

# Setting Your SQL Work Environment

Peradventure you don't have any database management system in your computer, you can opt for various free open source database management system. You can decide to opt for the famous MySQL, which can be downloaded for both Windows and Linux operating systems.

Furthermore, you can install SQL Server Express, which is a free version of Microsoft SQL Server. Otherwise, you can decide to install XAMPP or WampServer. The WampServer is a Windows web development environment that allows you to create a MySQL database, PHP, and Apache2.

## SQL Syntax

**SQL Statements** – These statements are simple and straightforward like your normal English language. However, they have specific syntax. Don't form your own meaning when you see some of the common English words you are conversant within this chapter.

An SQL statement comprises of a series of keywords, identifiers, etc. and ends with a semicolon (;). The following is an example of a SQL statement:

```
SELECT stu_name, DoB, age FROM studentFile Where
age > 20;
```

The statement may look clumsy but for better readability, you can rewrite it in this format.

```
SELECT stu_name, DoB, age
FROM StudentFile
WHERE age > 20;
```

The purpose of the semicolon is to submit the statement to the database server or terminates the SQL statement.

## Case Sensitivity in SQL

Keywords in SQL are not case sensitive like the previous languages discussed in this book. For instance, the keyword SELECT is the same as the select. However, depending on the operating system, the table names and database can be case-sensitive. Generally, Linux and UNIX platforms are case-sensitive, unlike Windows platforms that are not case-sensitive.

The example below retrieves records from the studentFile table

| SELECT stu_name, DoB, age FROM studentFile; |
| --- |
|  |
| select stu_name, DoB, age from studentFile; |

The first one capitalizes the keywords whereas the second isn't capitalized. It is better to write SQL keywords in uppercase in order to differentiate it from other text.

## SQL Comments

Similar to other programming languages, SQL comments are ignored and provide quick explanations concerning the SQL statements. You can either use a single-line or multi-line comments when writing comments in SQL. The two examples below will distinguish both comment writing formats.

```
--Select all the students
SELECT *FROM studentFile;
```

To write a multi-line comment, you use the /* with the statements followed by the */.

```
/* Select all the students
 whose age is greater than 20*/
SELECT *FROM studentFile
WHERE age > 20;
```

## Database Creation

Before you can work with data, the first thing to do is to create a database. I am assuming you have installed the SQL Server or have MySQL in your system. Furthermore, ensure to allow every necessary privilege needed.

There are two ways of creating a database

- Using the simple SQL query
- Using MySQL

**Simple SQL Query**

The syntax for creating a database in SQL is

```
CREATE DATABASE databaseName;
```

For the examples illustrated earlier, to create the table, we have to use:

> *CREATE DATABASE studentFile;*

**Note:** You can also use CREATE SCHEMA rather than using CREATE DATABASE to create a database. Additionally, creating a database doesn't make it available for use. To select the database, you have to select the database using the USE statement. For instance, the USE studentFile; command will set the StudentFile database as the target database.

**MySQL Database Creation**

I will use a command line tool to create a database in MySQL.

**Step 1:** Invoking the MySQL command-line tool

To do this, you have to log into your MySQL server. You have to log in as a root user and enter your password when asked. If everything goes right, you will be able to issue SQL statements.

**Step 2:** Creating the database

To create the database "studentFile", you have to execute the following command.

> mysql> CREATE DATABASE studentFile;

If the database was successful, you will see – Query OK, 1 row affected (0.03 sec). However, if the database already exists, an error message will display. Therefore, to avoid such situation, you can include an optional clause – IF NOT EXISTS. To apply it to the example, it will be written as:

```
mysql> CREATE DATABASE IF NOT EXISTS
studentFile;
```

**Step 3:** Selecting the Database

If the database already exists and you use the IF NOT EXISTS statement, to select this new database as the default database, you have to select it.

```
mysql > USE studentFile;
```

**Tip** – in order to see all the list of existing databases when using MySQL server, you can use the "SHOW DATABASES" keyword to execute it.

# Creating Tables in SQL

So far, I am convinced you now know how to create a database. It is time to upgrade your knowledge in SQL by creating a table inside our database. The table will hold the data in the database. The purpose of the table is to organize your data or information into columns and rows.

The syntax for table creation

150

*CREATE TABLE tableName (*

>*Column1_name data_type constraints,*
>
>*Column2_name data_type constraints,*
>
>*Column3_name data_type constraints,*

*);*

For better understanding, I will create a table in our studentFile database using the MySQL command-line tool. The code below simplifies that.

```
-- Syntax for MySQL Database
CREATE TABLE studentRecord (
  id INT NOT NULL PRIMARY KEY
AUTO_INCREMENT,
  Studname VARCHAR(50) NOT NULL,
  DoB DATE,
  phoneNum VARCHAR(15) NOT NULL UNIQUE

-- Syntax for SQL Server Database
CREATE TABLE studentRecord (
  id INT NOT NULL PRIMARY KEY IDENTITY(1,1),
  Studname VARCHAR(50) NOT NULL,
  DoB DATE,
  phoneNum VARCHAR(15) NOT NULL UNIQUE
);
```

The code above creates a table named studentRecord with five columns id, Studname, DoB, and phoneNum. If you observe, a data type declaration succeeds each column name.

In a database table, every column must have a name followed by a data type. The developer decides on the particular to use, depending on the information to store in each column. From the example above, some statement looks "foreign" and requires explanations. Later, I will talk about the various data types but to familiarize yourself with them, they include:

- Exact numeric
- Approximate numeric
- Date and time
- Character strings
- Unicode character strings
- Binary strings
- Other data types

Besides the data type, there are constraints used in the code. Constraints are rules defined concerning the values permitted in columns. The following constraints were mentioned.

- The PRIMARY KEY constrains, which marks the corresponding field as the primary key for the table
- The NOT NULL constraints, which make sure fields cannot accept an unacceptable value

- The AUTO_INCREMENT attribute, which automatically assigns a value to a field left unspecified. It increases the previous value by 1 and only available for numerical fields.
- The UNIQUE constraint ensures every single row contains a unique value in the table

In a similar fashion, you can use the IF NOT EXIST statement we used when creating a database to overwrite an existing table. This is important as it avoids any already existing table. Alternatively, if you want to display available tables, you can use the SHOW TABLES statement.

```
CREATE TABLE IF NOT EXISTS studentRecords (
    id INT NOT NULL PRIMARY KEY
AUTO_INCREMENT,
    Studname VARCHAR(40) NOT NULL, DoB,
    phoneNum VARCHAR(25) NOT NULL UNIQUE
);
```

# Constraints In SQL

As the name implies, it is a restriction or limitation imposed on a column (s) of a table in order to place a limitation on the type of values the table can store. They provide a better mechanism to retain the reliability and accuracy of the data contained in the table. We have several categories of constraints, which includes:

**NOT NULL Constraint** – This statement states that NULL values will not be accepted at the column. What it means is that a new row cannot be added in a table without the inclusion of a non-NULL value for such a column.

For instance, the statement below creates a table "studentRecords" with four columns and three of these columns (id, Studname, and phoneNum) do not accept NULL Values.

```
CREATE TABLE studentRecords (
    id INT NOT NULL,
    Studname VARCHAR(30) NOT NULL,
    DoB DATE,
    phoneNum VARCHAR(15) NOT NULL
);
```

**Tip:** A null value is not the same as blank, zero (0), or a zero-length character string. The meaning of a NULL is that there hasn't been any entry made in that field.

- **PRIMARY KEY Constraint** – This classifies a column (s) with values that distinctively recognize a row in the table. You cannot have two rows simultaneously in a particular table having the same value for its primary key. The example below shows a SQL statement creating a table named "studentRecords" and identify the id column as the primary key.

```
CREATE TABLE studentRecords (
```

```
id INT NOT NULL PRIMARY KEY,
Studname VARCHAR(30) NOT NULL,
DoB DATE,
phoneNum VARCHAR(15) NOT NULL
);
```

- **UNIQUE Constraint** – if you want to restrict a column (s) to contain unique values in a table, the UNIQUE statement is used. While the PRIMARY KEY and UNIQUE constraint enforce uniqueness in a table; however, the UNIQUE constraint is used when your goal is to enforce the exclusivity on a particular column (s). I will use our previous example to specify the phone column as unique. With this, the phone column won't allow duplicated values.

```
CREATE TABLE studentRecords (
   id INT NOT NULL PRIMARY KEY,
   Studname VARCHAR(30) NOT NULL,
   DoB DATE,
   phoneNum VARCHAR(15) NOT NULL UNIQUE,
   country VARCHAR(30) NOT NULL DEFAULT
'England'
);
```

- **FOREIGN KEY Constraint** – This particular kind of constraint is a column (s) used to set up and implement a relationship among data in two different tables.

- **CHECK constraint** – The purpose of this statement is to restrict values in a column. For instance, the range of student age column can be restricted by creating CHECK constraint, which allows values only 16 to 45. This hinders ages entered from exceeding the age range. Here is an example to illustrate it.

```
CREATE TABLE studentRecords (
    stu_id INT NOT NULL PRIMARY KEY,
    stu_name VARCHAR(55) NOT NULL,
    stu_date DATE NOT NULL,
    age INT NOT NULL CHECK (age >= 16 AND age <= 45),
    dept_id INT,
    FOREIGN KEY (dept_id) REFERENCES departments(dept_id)
);
```

# Inserting Data in Tables

In previous examples, I created a table with the name "studentRecords" in our "studentFile" database. Now, we need to add information into the table. To do this, SQL has a unique keyword, which is the "INSERT INTO" statement.

Format:

INSERT INTO NameOfTable (columnA, columnB, columnC,...)
VALUES (value1, value2, value3,...);

The syntax is self-explanatory but if you are unclear, the tableName is the name of your table. In our examples so far, we have used "studentRecords." However, the column1, column2, column3,... represents the name of the table columns with value1, value2, value3 the parallel values for the columns.

To insert records to our "studentRecords" table, we will use the following statement.

INSERT INTO studentRecords (FullName, Age, Sex, PhoneNum) ;
VALUES ('Donald Williamson', '30', 'Male', '0722-022569') ;

If you observe, there is no value inserted for the id field. Do you remember when we created the table (studentRecords), we mark the id field with an AUTO_INCREMENT flag. Let's add another record to our table.

INSERT INTO studentRecords (FullName, Age, Sex, PhoneNum) ;
VALUES ('Jefferson Peterson', '45', 'Male', '0252-027948') ;

Why don't you add another one?

INSERT INTO studentRecords (FullName, Age, Sex,

PhoneNum) ;

VALUES ('Mariah Lawson', '50', 'Female', '0722-457906')

;

If you were to display the output of this table, it will look like this

| id | FullName | Age | Sex | PhoneNum |
|----|----------|-----|-----|----------|
| 1 | Donald Williamson | 30 | Male | 0722-022569 |
| 2 | Jefferson Peterson | 45 | Male | 0252-027948 |
| 3 | Mariah Lawson | 50 | Female | 0722-457906 |

So far, I am convinced without any doubt that creating a database shouldn't be an issue. The same applies to create a table and inserting records. However, what if you want to retrieve the content of a table, how will you go about that? The next section will clarify that.

## Selecting Data in a Table

If you want to retrieve data in a table, the "SELECT" statement is what you will use. This statement can retrieve all information in the rows in one time as long as it satisfies the condition stated.

Format

SELECT column1_name, column2_name, FROM tableName;

Note: This system is for specific columns. However, if your goal is to select the entire, consider the syntax below:

SELECT *FROM tableName;

**Note**: Whenever you see an asterisk (*) in SQL, just know it is a wildcard character, which signifies everything. It copies all the content.

Let's use the information we inserted when we used the "INSERT INTO" statement.

| id | FullName | Age | Sex | PhoneNum |
|---|---|---|---|---|
| 1 | Donald Williamson | 30 | Male | 0722-022569 |
| 2 | Jefferson Peterson | 45 | Male | 0252-027948 |
| 3 | Mariah Lawson | 50 | Female | 0722-457906 |

If we use the "SELECT *FROM studentRecords;" it will display the following information.

| id | FullName | Age | Sex | PhoneNum |
|---|---|---|---|---|
| 1 | Donald Williamson | 30 | Male | 0722-022569 |
| 2 | Jefferson Peterson | 45 | Male | 0252-027948 |
| 3 | Mariah Lawson | 50 | Female | 0722-457906 |

Perhaps, you only need certain information in the table, you use specific columns. Assuming we want to select only the id, FullName, and sex. It will look like this.

```
SELECT id, FullName, Sex
FROM studentRecords;
```

After executing this statement, the output will be

| id | FullName | Sex |
|---|---|---|
| id | FullName | Sex |
| 1 | Donald Williamson | Male |
| 2 | Jefferson Peterson | Male |
| 3 | Mariah Lawson | Female |

# SQL WHERE Statement

By now, I know you can fetch records in a table column or all the records in the table. However, in a real-world situation, we need to delete, update, or select records that fulfill certain criteria such as those in a particular age, country, or group. In this section, I will expound how we can use the "WHERE" clause.

Syntax

SELECT columnList FROM tableName WHERE condition;

The columList include fields/column like name, country, age, phone, etc. of a table. Furthermore, if you want all the values of the various columns, you can use the syntax below.

SELECT * FROM tableName WHERE condition

Let me use an example to explain the SELECT statement assuming the table name is "studentRecords."

| id | FullName | Age | Sex | PhoneNum |
|----|----------|-----|-----|----------|
| 1 | Donald Williamson | 30 | Male | 0722-022569 |
| 2 | Jefferson Peterson | 45 | Male | 0252-027948 |
| 3 | Mariah Lawson | 50 | Female | 0722-457906 |

| 4 | Jackson Fred | 32 | Male | 0721-487924 |
| 5 | Venus Sean | 38 | Female | 0787-972853 |
| 6 | Merkel Hassan | 36 | Female | 0978-216597 |

# Filtering records using WHERE clause

Using the table above, I want to return all students whose age is above 30. We can use the WHERE clause to remove unwanted data.

```
SELECT *FROM studentRecords WHERE age >35;
```

After executing this statement, the output will look like this:

| id | FullName | Age | Sex | PhoneNum |
|----|----------|-----|-----|----------|
| 2 | Jefferson Peterson | 45 | Male | 0252-027948 |
| 3 | Mariah Lawson | 50 | Female | 0722-457906 |
| 5 | Venus Sean | 38 | Female | 0787-972853 |
| 6 | Merkel Hassan | 36 | Female | 0978-216597 |

The statement below will fetch all the record of the student with id 4

| SELECT *FROM studentRecords WHERE id = 4; |
|---|

The output will be:

| id | FullName | Age | Sex | PhoneNum |
|---|---|---|---|---|
| 4 | Jackson Fred | 32 | Male | 0721-487924 |

You can combine certain operates with the "WHERE" clause. The table below summarizes the important operators used in SQL.

| Operator | Description | Example |
|---|---|---|
| = | Equal | WHERE id = 4 |
| > | Greater than | WHERE age > 30 |
| < | Less than | WHERE age < 25 |
| <= | Less than or equivalent to | WHERE price <= 900 |
| >= | Greater than or equivalent to | WHERE age >= 15 |
| **LIKE** | Simple pattern matching | WHERE name LIKE 'Dav' |
| **IN** | Check whether a specified value matches any value in a list or subquery | WHERE Country IN ('BRAZIL', 'SWEDEN') |
| **BETWEEN** | Check whether a specified value is within a range of values | WHERE age BETWEEN 3 AND 5 |

# The AND operator

The SQL language gives developers the opportunity to use the AND and OR operators to fetch specific records from a table. The AND operator is used to combine two conditions while returning true only when both conditions are true.

Format:

SELECT columnName1, columnName2 FROM tableName WHERE condition1 AND condition2;

The example below will demonstrate how the AND operator works.

| id | FullName | Age | Sex | PhoneNum | Dept_No |
|----|----------|-----|-----|----------|---------|
| 1 | Donald Williamson | 30 | Male | 0722-022569 | 0101 |
| 2 | Jefferson Peterson | 45 | Male | 0252-027948 | 0102 |
| 3 | Mariah Lawson | 50 | Female | 0722-457906 | 0103 |
| 4 | Jackson Fred | 32 | Male | 0721-487924 | 0104 |
| 5 | Venus Sean | 38 | Female | 0787-972853 | 0105 |
| 6 | Merkel Hassan | 36 | Female | 0978-216597 | NULL |

```
SELECT *FROM studentRecords
WHERE age > 30 AND Dept_No = 0104;
```

After execution, the output will look like this:

| id | FullName | Age | Sex | PhoneNum | Dept_No |
|----|----------|-----|-----|----------|---------|
| 4 | Jackson Fred | 32 | Male | 0721-487924 | 0104 |

## The OR Operator

This operator combines two different conditions; however, if one or both conditions are true, it returns true. Assuming you want the record of students whose age is greater than 40 or the Dept_No is equal to 0104.

```
SELECT *FROM studentRecords
WHERE age > 40 OR Dept_No = 0104;
```

The output will be:

| id | FullName | Age | Sex | PhoneNum | Dept_No |
|----|----------|-----|-----|----------|---------|
| 2 | Jefferson Peterson | 45 | Male | 0252-027948 | 0102 |
| 3 | Mariah Lawson | 50 | Female | 0722-457906 | 0103 |
| 4 | Jackson Fred | 32 | Male | 0721-487924 | 0104 |

Furthermore, you can combine the "AND" and "OR" operator to create compound expressions. Consider the statement below.

```
SELECT *FROM studentRecords
WHERE age > 40 AND (Dept_No = 102 or
Dept_No=103);
```

After execution, the output will be:

| id | FullName | Age | Sex | PhoneNum | Dept_No |
|----|----------|-----|-----|----------|---------|
| 2 | Jefferson Peterson | 45 | Male | 0252-027948 | 0102 |
| 3 | Mariah Lawson | 50 | Female | 0722-457906 | 0103 |

# SQL UPDATE STATEMENT

You have learned how to insert data including selecting a particular data from a table under certain condition (s). However, over time students or employee information may require updating such as location, phone number, address, etc. SQL has a unique statement that allows you to update your table without having to create a new table.

Format:

```
UPDATE tableName
SET column1Name = value1, column2Name = value2,...
colunmNamen = valueN
WHERE condition;
```

In the syntax above, column1_name, column2_name are the names of the fields or columns of a table whose value you want to update. You can also use the combination of the "AND" and "OR" operator to update statements in the table. Let me use an example to demonstrate the update statement.

| id | FullName | Age | Sex | PhoneNum | Dept_No |
|----|----------|-----|------|----------|---------|
| 1 | Donald | 30 | Male | 0722- | 0101 |

| | | | | | |
|---|---|---|---|---|---|
| | Williamson | | | 022569 | |
| 2 | Jefferson Peterson | 45 | Male | 0252-027948 | 0102 |
| 3 | Mariah Lawson | 50 | Female | 0722-457906 | 0103 |
| 4 | Jackson Fred | 32 | Male | 0721-487924 | 0104 |
| 5 | Venus Sean | 38 | Female | 0787-972853 | 0105 |
| 6 | Merkel Hassan | 36 | Female | 0978-216597 | NULL |

To update the student record of Venus Sean to Venus Williams Sean, the statement will be

UPDATE studentRecords SET FullName = "Venus Williams Sean"
WHERE id =5;

The output will be:

| id | FullName | Age | Sex | PhoneNum | Dept_No |
|---|---|---|---|---|---|
| 1 | Donald Williamson | 30 | Male | 0722-022569 | 0101 |
| 2 | Jefferson Peterson | 45 | Male | 0252-027948 | 0102 |

| 3 | Mariah Lawson | 50 | Female | 0722-457906 | 0103 |
| 4 | Jackson Fred | 32 | Male | 0721-487924 | 0104 |
| 5 | Venus Williams Sean | 38 | Female | 0787-972853 | 0105 |
| 6 | Merkel Hassan | 36 | Female | 0978-216597 | NULL |

# SQL DELETE

Finally, you have learned how to insert, select, and update information in a table. However, it is important to know how to delete a specific field or entire table especially if the table has fulfilled its purpose.

Format:

*DELETE FROM table_name WHERE condition;*

Using the table below, let us delete some records from the student's record created.

| id | FullName | Age | Sex | PhoneNum | Dept_No |
|----|----------|-----|-----|----------|---------|
| 1 | Donald Williamson | 30 | Male | 0722-022569 | 0101 |
| 2 | Jefferson | 45 | Male | 0252- | 0102 |

| | | | | 027948 | |
|---|---|---|---|---|---|
| | Peterson | | | | |
| 3 | Mariah Lawson | 50 | Female | 0722-457906 | 0103 |
| 4 | Jackson Fred | 32 | Male | 0721-487924 | 0104 |
| 5 | Venus Sean | 38 | Female | 0787-972853 | 0105 |
| 6 | Merkel Hassan | 36 | Female | 0978-216597 | NULL |

DELETE FROM studentRecords WHERE id >4;

After execution, the outcome will be as follow:

| id | FullName | Age | Sex | PhoneNum | Dept_No |
|---|---|---|---|---|---|
| 1 | Donald Williamson | 30 | Male | 0722-022569 | 0101 |
| 2 | Jefferson Peterson | 45 | Male | 0252-027948 | 0102 |
| 3 | Mariah Lawson | 50 | Female | 0722-457906 | 0103 |
| 4 | Jackson Fred | 32 | Male | 0721-487924 | 0104 |

However, to delete the entire data in a table, there isn't any need to use the WHERE clause. To delete all records in the "studentRecords" table, you have to use the statement below.

```
DELETE FROM studentRecords;
```

# Chapter Six: Introduction to Java Programming

Welcome to your fifth programming course in this book. Indeed, you have progressed beyond your expectation. Did you think you could do it at the beginner? Nobody is born a programmer rather by learning and putting it to practice, they become good at it.

Welcome to Java Programming. I will introduce you to Java in its simplicity. Java is one of the most interesting and practicable programs to learn as a beginner. At the end of this chapter, you will become a professional computer programmer.

As I always tell beginners, programming is easy. At first, many consider Java as a hard language to understand but after familiarizing themselves with the environment, they discover it is quite easy to learn. It doesn't matter your programming experience or level, this chapter was written putting various things into consideration. As you expand your programming knowledge, you will discover that you will be a top-notch programmer in all areas.

In spite of the numerous programming languages in the world, Java is one of the languages in high demand. If you dedicate your time into studying the environment, you are literally setting yourself into a fast-growing career in the next few years.

Java programming skills are sought after because of its flexibility, readability, and simplicity. Presently, if you are a Java programmer or developer in the United States of American, you will be earning nothing less than $85k annual salary. Do you still think Java programming is worth learning?

# Pre-requisite for Learning Java

You must know the basics of how to use a computer system. However, if you are a beginner to programming, then you need to understand the fundamental to programming. If you already know programming languages like C, C++ or any object-oriented language, then Java should be an easy language for you to learn.

# Concepts of Java Programming

Since the demands for breaking through various hurdles of coding extremely large projects, we have seen the advent of object-oriented programming. This has led to the combination of some of the best methodologies of structured programming along with new concepts. In this section, I want to briefly explain some of these programming concepts in Java Programming.

## Encapsulation

From the name, you can have an idea of what encapsulation entails. Encapsulation in a layman term is a method that binds the programming code along with data it operates while keeping them safe from exterior interference. An object is formed when these data and code are connected with each other. This object can be private or public; if it is private, the data or code will be inaccessible by any program that exists out the object. However, if it is public, it can be accessible by other programs even if they are not within the object.

## Polymorphism

Another important concept of Java Programming is polymorphism, which involves creating a particular interface for several methods. The significance is that it reduces program complication by permitting the same interface.

## Inheritance

This concept involves an object receiving the same features or properties of another object that supports it. For instance, you have a watermelon, which is of the classification of watermelon. It also belongs to a fruit class that is part of a larger class known as food. This food class has features that make it nutritious and edible. Additionally, the fruits can be sweet and juicy. Therefore, combining these features and other things makes up the watermelon.

# Understanding the Java Environment

It is important to understand the Java environment and I will start by telling you how you can install the software on your computer. After installation, you can start with the basic "Hello World" program.

Before starting up, you need to be sure that your computer has what it takes to write Java programs. It is advisable to check websites that offer the language free. You can visit **www.oracle.com/technetwork/java/javase/downloads** or **www.java.com** to install the software on your system.

Basically, what you will need to write Java programs include

- JDK (Java Development Kit)
- Text Editor (NotePad, TextPad, Atom, Sublime for windows; for Mac – gEdit, jEdit, Atom while for Ubuntu, you can use gEdit)

The language is a high-level programming language, which means you cannot run it on your computer directly. For you to run the program on your system it needs to be translated to the language the computer understands and this is where the javac compiler comes to play. The compiler takes the java code and translates it to machine code.

Java Virtual Machine is a virtual machine that resides on your computer. Its role is to make it easier for the compiler to generate byte code for the machine. JVM is a program that makes it easier to run a java platform independently.

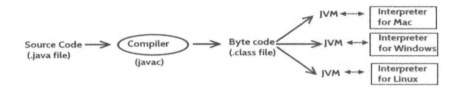

# Running Your First Java Program

Tighten your seat belt because here is where the real thing starts. In this aspect, I will show you the easiest way to write java programs, compile them, and finally execute them. let's start with the simple program.

```
public class BeginnersProgram {
  public static void main(String[] args){
    System.out.println("Hello World, This is my first
programming practice in java.");
  }//End of main
}//End of FirstJavaProgram Class
```

Output

```
Hello World, This is my first programming practice in
java.
```

Explanation

*public class MyFirstJaveProgram {*

this is the beginning of a java program. All java application must have at least a class definition, which comprises of the class keyword accompanied by the class name. From the first line, you can see that the class is public

*public static void main(String[] args){*

This statement makes the main method to be "public". What it means is that you can call the method from outside the class. The void in the statement signifies that it doesn't return anything whereas *main* is a method name. It is the starting point where the program begins execution. Additionally, the (String[] args) is a command line argument

*System.out.printlin ("Hello World, This is my first programming practice in java.")*

This statement prints out the content of what is in the quotes to the console while inserting a newline.

## Variables

I believe you know what a variable is as you have gone through various programming languages in this book. The variable is allocated a value during the program. Its value changes in the course of the program. For instance,

int number1 = 12;

In this example, number1 is a variable name where 12 is the value assigned to it. On the other hand, int is a data type that declares "number1" as a variable.

## Declaring Variables in Java

Syntax:

*data_type variableName = value;*

It is compulsory in Java to have the data type and variable name but the value is optional you can allocate value to a variable after declaring it. For instance, in the previous example, I declared number1 as a variable with data type as an integer. In the next section, I will talk more about data types.

## Convention in Variable naming in Java

- Variable names are case sensitive
- Variable names can start with special characters such as underscore and dollar sign ($)
- Variable names cannot contain whitespace. For instance, int student = 40; this is not valid because of the space the variable contains
- Variable names must start with a small letter. For instance number1; however, if the variable is lengthy, you can use capital little like this – numberStudent1, NewBus, etc.

## Types of Variables

Variables are of three types in Java.

### Local Variable

You declare these variables inside the method of a class. Furthermore, the scopes of these variables are limited to the method. Their values cannot be changed and accessed outside the method. From the example below, the instance variable is declared having the same local variable name. The essence of this is to show the scope of the local variable scope. Study the program properly because missing any step here will affect you later.

```java
public class VariableExa {
    // I want to declare the instance variable at this point
    public String myVar="instance variable";
// declaration of instance variable done
    public void myMethod(){
        // Here I am declaring our local variable
        String myVar = "Inside Method";
        System.out.println(myVar);
    }
    public static void main(String args[]){
        // This area creates the object
        VariableExa obj = new VariableExa();
```

```
        /* we call the variable name, which changes myVar
value.
        * Furthermore, myVar will be displayed after
        * the method call, to indicate that the
        * scope of the local variable is restricted to only the
method.
        */
        System.out.println("Calling Method");
        obj.myMethod();
        System.out.println(obj.myVar);
    }
}
```

The output of this program after execution will be:

```
Calling Method
Inside Method
instance variable
```

## Static Variable

Some programmers refer to it as a class variable because of its association with the class. For instance, if you create four different objects; however, these objects have the same class with access to the static variable, the static variable will be common for all object. In order words, an alteration to the variable through the use of a single object will literally imitate

180

others when accessed through the other objects. Consider the program below that illustrates the use of a static variable.

```java
public class StaticExa {
    public static String ClassVar="class or static variable";

    public static void main(String args[]){
        StaticExa obj = new StaticExa();
        StaticExa objA = new StaticExa();
        StaticExa objB = new StaticExa();

        //The three objects will display "class or static variable"
        System.out.println(obj.ClassVar);
        System.out.println(objA.ClassVar);
        System.out.println(objB.ClassVar);

        //altering the static variable value through objA
        objA.ClassVar = "Text Changed";

        //The three objects will display "Text Changed for object"
        System.out.println(obj.ClassVar);
        System.out.println(objA.ClassVar);
        System.out.println(objB.ClassVar);
```

```
        }
    }
```

The output of the program will be:

```
        class or static variable
        class or static variable
        class or static variable
        Text Changed for object
        Text Changed for object
        Text Changed object
```

## Instance Variable

This variable is the opposite of the static variable because every single object within a class contains its own duplicate, unlike the static variable that contains the same object. From the example below, the value of the instance variable (obj2) is changed and when displayed with other objects, others remained unchanged, unlike the obj2.

```
public class InstanceExa {
    String InstanceVar="My Instance variable";

    public static void main(String args[]){
```

```
            InstanceExa obj = new InstanceExa();

            InstanceExa objA = new InstanceExa();

            InstanceExa objB = new InstanceExa();


            System.out.println(obj.InstanceVar);

            System.out.println(objA.InstanceVar);

            System.out.println(objB.InstanceVar);



            objA.InstanceVar = "Text Changed for Variable";



            System.out.println(obj.InstanceVar);

            System.out.println(objA.InstanceVar);

            System.out.println(objB.InstanceVar);
        }
    }
```

The output of the program will be:

```
My Instance variable

My Instance variable

My Instance variable

My Instance variable

Text Changed for Variable

My Instance variable
```

Now, observe the difference between the static variable and the instance variable. Did you notice any major difference? Let us move into something more important – data types.

# Data Types

The meaning of data type is the same whether it is Java, C, C++, or SQL. The data type defines that particular value a variable can accommodate. For instance, a variable of integer data type has the capacity of only accommodating integer values. Nevertheless, data types are of two types in Java. These are primitive and non-primitive. Notwithstanding, my focus in this book is on the primitive data types. For clarity purpose, you should know that non-Primitive data types include strings and arrays.

# Java Programming Primitive Data Types

Generally, Java has eight primitive data types and these include int, short, Boolean, char, long, byte, double and float. These data types are the same irrespective of the operating system you are using.

## Int

This data type is used to hold integer variables and ranges from -2,147,483,648 up until 2,147,483,647. It has a default size and value of 4 bytes and 0 respectively. The example below shows the variable "number1" declared as an integer data type and printed out.

```
class DataTypeExample {
    public static void main(String[] args) {
// Declaration of variables
        number1 = 1250;
        System.out.println(number1);
    }
}
```

Outcome:

```
1250
```

## Byte

A byte data type can only hold numbers between -128 and 127. It has a data size and value of 1 byte and 0 respectively. Study the program below.

```
class DataTypeExample {
    public static void main(String[] args) {
```

```
        // declaration of NewNum as byte
        byte NewNum;

        NewNum = 80;
        System.out.println(NewNum);
    }
  }
```

Output:

```
    80
```

Now, let us consider another example of the byte data type.

```
    class DataTypeExample {
      public static void main(String[] args) {

        byte NewNumber;

        NewNumber = 180;
        System.out.println(NewNumber);
      }
    }
```

What will be the result now? If your answer is 180, you are obviously wrong. Are you surprised? Do you remember the byte data type range is between -128 and 127? Therefore, if you

186

execute the above program, you will get a type mismatch error because 180 is beyond the range data type.

## Short

In terms of size, it is greater than the byte data and has a default size of 2 bytes. It has a data range of 32,768 to 32767.

```
class DataTypeExample {
    public static void main(String[] args) {
        // Declaration of the variable
        short number1;

        number1 = 18000;
        System.out.println(number1);
    }
}
```

The output will be:

18000

## Long

You can use this data type when the int data type isn't big enough to accommodate the value you want to use. It ranges from -9,223,372,036,854,775,808 to 9,223,372,036,854,775,807 and has a size of 8 bytes.

```
class DataTypeExample {
    public static void main(String[] args) {
// declaration of the variable to demonstrate long data
type
        long number1= -48972698741L;

        System.out.println(number1);
    }
}
```

Output

-48972698741

**Double**

This holds up to 15 decimal numbers and has a size of 8 bytes.

```
class DataTypeExample {
    public static void main(String[] args) {
//declaration of variable

        double number1 = -789874437.9d

        System.out.println(number1);
    }
}
```

What will be the Output:

-4.145898371E7

## Char

This holds characters and has a size of 2 bytes.

```
class DataTypeExample {
    public static void main(String[] args) {
        // declaration of variable Myname as char
        char Myname = 'Johnson';

        System.out.println(Myname);
    }
}
```

Output

Johnson

## Boolean

This either holds true or false value.

```
class DataTypeExample {
    public static void main(String[] args) {
        // performing Boolean operation using true and false

        Boolean light = True;

        System.out.println(light);
    }
}
```

The Output will be:

True

**Float**

This holds 6 to 7 decimal number and has a size of 4 bytes.

```
class DataTypeExample {
    public static void main(String[] args) {
float number1 = 20.70f;
            System.out.println(number1);
    }
}
```

Output

20.70

| **Summary of primitive data types** |
|---|
| • If you want to store whole numbers, you can use long, short, byte, and int data types |
| • char is used for storing letters |
| • double and float for fractional numbers |
| • Boolean for variables that hold true or false |

# Operators in Java Programming

This section describes available operators you can use in the course of your coding. You can use them to manipulate variables or create complex programs. Normally, you can use these operators to compare, modify, and control data within the Java environment. The basic operators in Java include:

## Arithmetic Operators

You are already familiar with these operators and they include addition (+), subtraction (-), multiplication (*), division (/), and modulo (%). I will use a simple program to illustrate these operators.

```java
public class ArithmeticOperator {
    public static void main(String args[]) {
// declaration of profit and loss as integer to perform the
arithmetic operation
    int profit = 250;
    int loss = 70;

    System.out.println("profit + loss: " + (profit + loss) );
    System.out.println("profit – loss: " + (profit–loss) );
    System.out.println("profit * loss: " + (profit * loss) );
    System.out.println("profit/ loss: " + (profit / loss) );
    System.out.println("profit % loss: " + (profit % loss) );
    }
```

```
            }
```

The Output of this program will be:

```
        profit + loss: 320
        profit- loss: 180
        profit * loss: 22400
        profit / loss: 3.5714
        profit % loss: 60
```

## Assignment Operator

These operators include =, +=, -=, *=, /=, and %=

Income=expenses this assigns the value of the variable expenses to Income

Income +=expenses is equivalent to Income = Income + expenses

Income -=expenses is equivalent to Income = Income - expenses

Income*=expenses is equivalent to Income = Income * expenses

Income/=expenses is equivalent to Income = Income/expenses

Income%=expenses is equivalent to Income = Income % expenses

Consider the program above to illustrate the use of assignment operators

```java
public class AssignOpe {
  public static void main(String args[]) {
    int income  = 10;
    int expenses = 20;

expenses += income ;
    System.out.println("+= Output: "+expenses);

expenses = income ;
    System.out.println("= Output: "+expenses);

    expenses -= income ;
    System.out.println("-= Output: "+expenses);

expenses /= income ;
    System.out.println("/= Output: "+expenses);

    expenses *= income ;
    System.out.println("*= Output: "+expenses);


    expenses %= income ;
```

```
                System.out.println("%= Output: "+expenses);
    }
}
```

The output of the program will be:

```
    += Output: 20
    = Output: 10
    -= Output: 10
    /= Output: 10
    *= Output: 100
    %= Output: 0
```

## Logical operator

These are used for conditional statements and loops to evaluate a condition. These operators are &&, !, and ||.

| Operator | Meaning | Example |
|----------|---------|---------|
| ! | Logical Not. This evaluate true only if the operand is 0 | If a=5 then, the expression! holds true. |

| && | Logical AND. It returns true only when all the operands are true. | If a =4 and b = 2; the expression ((a==4) && (a<4)) equals to 0. |
|---|---|---|
| \|\| | Logical OR. This evaluates to true when one operand returns true | If a =4 and b = 2; the expression ((a==4) && (a<4)) equals to 1. |

Consider the program above.

```
public class LogicalOperator {
  public static void main(String args[]) {
// Declaration of variables
boolean No = false;
boolean Yes = true;


  System.out.println("Yes && No: " + (Yes&&No));


  System.out.println("!(Yes && No): " + !(Yes&&No));
```

```
                System.out.println("Yes || No: " + (Yes||No));
    }
    }
```

Output will be:

```
    Yes && No: false
    !(Yes && No): true
    Yes || No: true
```

# Conclusion

There are other operators available in Java; however, with the aforementioned operators, you can start programming. Finally, you have gotten to the end of the basics of Java programming. Don't stop here, put to practice everything you have learned and considered moving to advanced programming.

# Chapter Seven: JavaScript Programming for Beginners

If there is anything I want you to hold at the end of this programming guide for JavaScript is the fact that:

- JavaScript is the HTML and web language
- It is easy to Learn

If you can do that, then at the end, you will smile your way to programming for the web. However, your speed in learning JavaScript and other programming language is very dependent on you. If you find yourself struggling, don't feel demoralized rather take a break and reread the material after you have settled down. Remember, this chapter gives you the basics of JavaScript as a beginner to familiarize yourself with the language.

## Introduction

This JavaScript guide is written with the intention to help both beginners and professionals understand the programming language for the web more efficiently. JavaScript is a solution aimed at performing various actions dynamically. The JavaScript translator, which is rooted in the web browser such as Firefox, Google Chrome, Internet Explorer, Safari, etc., allows the interpretation of the JavaScript code.

JavaScript is an object-oriented scripting language, which is lightweight and works in cross-platform such as Mack, Linux, or Windows. If you want to create an interactive website for users, the place of JavaScript cannot be overemphasized.

## What is JavaScript?

It is a scripting language created in 1995 by Netscape as a means of validating forms while offering interactive content for websites. The language has evolved over time with it being used by various web browsers.

## Why should I Study JavaScript?

You should study JavaScript because it is among the three fundamental languages every web developer must learn and understand. With HTML, you can define your web page contents whereas CSS allows you to identify your web page layout; however, with JavaScript, you can program the actions of these web pages. You see the important role JavaScript plays in web pages.

## Importance of JavaScript for Websites

- Displaying time and date
- Client-side validation of controls
- Displaying clocks

- Displaying popup windows and dialog boxes such as a prompt dialog box, confirmation dialog box, and an alert dialog box
- Display times such as online test
- Displaying animations

If you judiciously follow this guide, by the end, you will be a master of the art programming web pages.

## Pre-requisites for learning JavaScript

Although, you will hear many developers educating beginners about the fact that there are no prerequisites to learning JavaScript. That is true because you can learn the language without having any programming foundation or knowledge. However, to expedite your learning process, you can improve yourself on basic courses such as:

- Discrete mathematics
- Algebra
- Algorithms in Data structures
- Learn a static language like C++ as it will give you the cutting-edge

## Variables in JavaScript

Variables shouldn't be new if you went through Chapter two to Chapter six of this book. In a layman term, a variable is a memory location designed to store different values and assigned with a name. JavaScript uses the "var" keyword, accompanied by the variable name. For instance, to a name as a variable, you will use the statement below.

```
var exam = 50;
var test = 12;
var score = exam * test;
```

In the example above, exam, test, and score are variables given values with the value stored. We can perform various operations in JavaScript including multiplication, subtraction, addition, subtraction, and division. Variables and values can be declared as a number, string, or letter.

```
var name = "insert your name";
var number = '45';
```

From the example, you can enclose string with a single or double quote because they work exactly the same way.

## JavaScript Identifiers

Every variable in JavaScript must have a unique name, which is used to identify it. These unique names are called identifiers. Identifiers have certain rules, which include:

- Every identifier must begin with a letter

- They can contain digits (0-9), letters (a-z), dollar signs ($), and underscores (_)
- Reserved words are not accepted
- Variable names are case sensitive
- An identifier can begin with a dollar sign or underscore.

# Scope of JavaScript Variable

JavaScript allows two types of variable scope, which includes global and local variable scope. A variable is said to be global if it is declared outside the function body. With this, every statement has access to the variable within the same document. However, a local variable scope has its scope within the function. With this, the variable is only available to statements within the same function.

# Data Types in JavaScript

Data types are important in JavaScript because it determines the type of value assigned to an identifier. Without data types, hardly can your computer solve any problem safely. JavaScript has two types of data types, which are:

Primitive data types

These are the primary blocks of any JavaScript program and includes:

- Numeric – You can use both floating numbers and integer in JavaScript. However, it doesn't support the use of decimal numbers.

- Strings – This is a group of characters encircled in either a single or a double quote. Every string must end with its corresponding quote – a single quote must always end with a single quote.

- Boolean – This involves logical values, whose value is either true or false. Boolean data type uses conditional statements.

- Null – this represents no value, which means strings are empty

The other data type used in JavaScript is the compositive data type. It is imperative to note that JavaScript data types are dynamic, that is, the same variable can be used to hold different data types. For instance,

```
var a;          // Now a is undefined
a = 89;         // Now a is a Number
a = "Germany";  // Now a is a String
```

The program below demonstrates the use of data type in JavaScript. The first one shows a JavaScript program that shows the summation of two floating numbers (test and exam) while the second one illustrates the use of Boolean data type.

```html
<html>
<head>
<script language="javascript">
function showAlert()
{
var test=22.50;
var exam=50.50;
var score=0;
score=test+exam;
document.write(" score= "+score);
document.write("\t\tHello\nworld!\n");
document.write('\nWelcome to JavaScript');
}
</script>
</head>
<body>

<script language="javascript">

showAlert();

</script>

</body>
</html>
```

The program below illustrates the use of Boolean expression. First, I allocate the value "o" to the variable "number." Then the user is prompted to enter a number, which must be within the range of 1 and 500. Nonetheless, If the user entered a number above the stated range (500), a message will be displayed on the screen indicating an error.. However, if the number falls within the 500 range, it will determine if the figured inputted is either equal or greater

```html
<html>
<body>
<script type="text/javascript">
var number=0;
number=prompt("Enter a number");
document.write("Your entered number is :"+number);
if (number>=1 && number<10)
document.write("Your entered number is greater than 1
and less than 10");
else if(number>=10 && number<20)
document.write("Your entered number is greater than 10
and less than 20");
else if(number>=20 && number<30)
document.write("Your entered number is greater than 20
and less than 30");
else if(number>=30 && number<40)
document.write("Your entered number is greater than 30
```

```
and less than 40");
else if(number>=40 && number<100)
document.write("Your entered number is greater than 40
and less than 100");
else if(number>=100 && number<=500)
document.write("Your entered number is greater than
100 or less than 500");
else
document.write("You did not enter any number!")
</script>
</body>
</html>
```

# Operators in JavaScript

Operators are functions with arithmetic, bitwise or logical property. JavaScript also has its own operators to perform various operations. In this unit, I will explore the basic operators you can use as a beginner in JavaScript.

### Arithmetic Operators

| Operators | Meaning |
|-----------|-------------|
| + | Addition |
| - | Subtraction |
| / | Division |

| | |
|---|---|
| * | Multiplication |
| = | Assignment |
| % | Mod |
| -- | Decrement |
| ++ | Increment |

You should be conversant with some of these operators if you have gone through this book. However, I am not going to explain anything but illustrate each operator using a JavaScript program.

## Addition

```
var number1 = 105;
var number2 = 25;
var total = number1+number2;        //total = 130
```

## Subtraction

```
var number1 = 105;
var number2 = 25;
var total = number1-number2;        //total = 180
```

## Multiplication

```
var number1 = 105;
var number2 = 25;
var total = number1*number2;        //total = 2625
```

# Division

```
        var number1 = 105;
        var number2 = 25;
        var total = number1/number2;        //total = 4.2
```

# Mod

```
        var number1 = 105;
        var number2 = 25;
        var total = number1%number2;        //total = 5
```

Assignment

```
        var number1 = 105;
        var number2 ;
        number2 = number1;              //total = 105
```

Increment

```
        var number1 = 105;
        var number2 = number1++;     // number2 = 106
```

Decrement

```
        var number1 = 105;
        var number2 = number1--;     // number2 = 104
```

String Operators

The string operator uses the sign "+" to concatenate two or more strings.

```
        var FirstName = "Fname"';
```

```
var LastName = "Lname";
var FullName = FirstName + "" + LastName;
```

| Operator | Meaning |
|----------|---------|
| != | Not Equal to |
| == | Equal to |
| === | Equal to and equal type |
| < | Less than |
| > | Greater than |
| <= | Less than equal to |
| >= | Greater than equal to |

Comparison Operator in JavaScript

Logical Operators in JavaScript

| Operator | Property |
|----------|----------|
| ! | Logical not |
| \|\| | Logical or |
| && | Logical and |

# Basic JavaScript on the Browser side

When you hear about JavaScript on the browser side, it refers to the client-side, which means the code is run on the machine of the client – the browser. The browser-side components comprise of JavaScript, JavaScript libraries, CSS, images, HMTL, and whatever files downloaded to the browser.

# Browser-Side JavaScript Features

JavaScript is important for the web as it is likely to use it to write programs that execute arbitrary computations. You have the opportunity of writing simple scripts such as the search for prime numbers or Fibonacci numbers. However, in the context of web browser and the Web, JavaScript enables programmers to program with the capability of computing sales tax, based on the information provided by the users through an HTML form.

The truth about JavaScript language is in the document-based objects and browser that the language is compatible with. This may sound complex, however, I will explain the significant capabilities of JavaScript on the browser side along with the objects it supports.

- **Controls the Browser** – There are various JavaScript objects that permit the control of the browser behavior. Furthermore, the Window object support means of popping up dialog boxes that display messages for the users. Additionally, users can also input messages. Besides this, JavaScript doesn't provide a method that gives users the opportunity to directly create and manipulate frames inside the browser window.

Notwithstanding, you can take advantage of the ability to make HTML animatedly by creating the particular frame layout you want.

- **Interact with HTML Forms** – another significant part of the JavaScript on the browser side is its capability to work together with HTML forms. The ability comes because of the form element and its objects, which contains Text, submit, select, reset, radio, hidden, password, and text area objects. With these elements, you can write and read the values of the elements in the form.

- **Interact with Users** – JavaScript has another feature, which is its ability to define event handlers. Most times, users initiate these events. For instance, when someone moves the mouse through a hyperlink, clicks the submit button, or enters a value. The capability to handle such events is important because programming with graphic interfaces requires an event-driven model.

In addition to these aforementioned features, JavaScript on the browser side has other capabilities such as:

- Changing the displayed image by using the <img> tag to generate an animation effect and image rollover
- It has a window.setTimeout () method, which allows some block of random source code to be performed in the future within a split of a second

- It streamlines the procedure of working and computing with times and dates

# JavaScript Framework

Take a moment and consider creating a web application and websites like constructing a house. In building a house, you can decide to create every material you need to start the house from scratch before building without any plans. This will be time-consuming and won't make much sense. One thing you may likely do is to buy pre-manufactured materials such as bricks, woods, countertops, etc. before assembling them based on the blueprint you have.

Coding is like taking it upon yourself to build a house. When you begin coding a website, you can code all areas of the site from scratch without. However, there are certain website features, which gives your website more sense by applying a template. Assuming you want to buy a wheel, it will make to look for one that you can reinvent. This is where JavaScript Frameworks come to the scene.

JavaScript Framework is a collection of JavaScript code libraries, which gives website developers pre-written JavaScript codes to use for their routine programming tasks and features.

You can also refer to it as an application framework, which is written in JavaScript where the developers can manipulate the functions of these codes and reuse them for their own convenience. They are more adaptable for website designing, which is why many developers use them in building websites.

## Top JavaScript Framework

### Vue.js

This is one of the JavaScript frameworks, which was created to make the user interface development more organized. Created by Evan You, it is the perfect JavaScript framework for beginners because it's quite easy to understand. Furthermore, it focuses on view layers. With Vue.js, you don't need Babel. A Babel is a transpiler with the responsibility of converting JavaScript codes to the old version of ES5 that can run in all browsers. All templates in the Vue.js framework are valid HTML, which makes their integration easier. If you want to develop lightweight apps as a beginner, it is best to start with Vue.js.

### Next.js

Another important JavaScript Framework is the Next.js framework, which is an additional tool for server-side rendering. The framework allows developers to simplify the developing process similar to the Vue.js framework.

The features of this JavaScript Framework include page-based client-side routing and automatic splitting of codes. The framework also comes with a full CSS support, which makes styling of the user's interface easier for beginners and professionals.

## Ember.js

This framework, which was created a few years ago, is among the most sought JavaScript framework in the web industry. Famous companies such as LinkedIn, Heroku, and Kickstarter use the Ember.js framework in the design of their websites. It also comes with regular updates and offers a complete feature for users. Unlike the Vue.js framework, it is effective for developers who want to develop complex web applications. The focus of this framework is on scalability, which allows developers to use it for both web and mobile projects.

## Angular

Google released this JavaScript Framework in 2010 with regular updates and improvements taking place. It is one of the most sought after the framework for many developers because it simplifies the development of websites and apps. For other developers, it is because of its ability to create dynamic web apps.

# Chapter Eight: Introduction to PHP

PHP is an acronym for Hypertext Preprocessor. The language is a server-side HTML embedded scripting language. For beginners, it is hard to understand the aforementioned statement, however, let me break it down. When I say the langue is a server-side, I mean the execution of the scripts takes place on the server where the website is hosted. By HTML embedded, it means PHP codes can be used inside HTML code. Alternatively, a scripting language is a programming language, which is interpreted instead of being compiled like C++ and C programming language. Examples of scripting languages include Java, Python, Perl, and Ruby.

You can use PHP language on several platforms including UNIX, Linux, and windows and it supports many databases including Oracle, Sybase, MySQL, etc. furthermore, PHP files contain scripts, HTML tags, and plain text with extensions such as PHP3, PHP, or PHTML. Finally, the software is an open-source program, which is free.

## Pre-requisite for learning PHP

If you want to know if there is anything special necessary to know before learning PHP, then the answer to this question is no. Going through the documentation section gives you the necessary information you need. One major reason many find it easy to learn PHP is due to its documentation that every concept is explained in its simplicity.

Additionally, PHP is a simple and straightforward language for anyone to learn. However, if you want to learn web language effectively, it is important to learn the basics of the following languages:

- HTML – This is what PHP sends to the web browser
- MySQL – You need a database to store data
- CSS – You need this to add style to your HTML pages
- JavaScript – To make your pages interactive with the users

If you can equip yourself with these languages, then you can learn PHP effectively.

## Getting Started

Before starting this lesson, you should have the following:

- PHP and MySQL installed
- Web Server (Apache)

With these two programs, you can successfully write and execute PHP codes. You can purchase an inexpensive hosting plan that supports MySQL and PHP. However, if you want to save some cash, you can decide to install it on your system. To do this, you have to install WAMP server on your machine for Windows users. After the installation, you can access it through http://localhost in your browser. Ensure you have this set up before starting this course.

## PHP Syntax

When I started, I indicated that PHP codes are executed on the server-side. However, every PHP statement begins with <?PHP while ending with ?>. Let us begin with a simple program. You can copy and paste the program below using any text editor before saving it with the file name – index1.php

I named the file to "index1.php" because some root folder already has an index filename as shown in the image below.

| Name | Date modified | Type | Size |
|------|---------------|------|------|
| This PC > Local Disk (C:) > wamp > www | | | |
| elijahdokubo | 12/10/2018 5:17 PM | File folder | |
| greaterlight | 11/29/2018 10:08 ... | File folder | |
| mysite | 11/7/2018 2:21 AM | File folder | |
| SpredMax | 4/11/2019 11:41 AM | File folder | |
| wamplangues | 3/11/2018 6:21 PM | File folder | |
| wampthemes | 3/11/2018 6:21 PM | File folder | |
| wordpress | 2/14/2019 8:33 AM | File folder | |
| wordpress-5.0 | 2/14/2019 8:22 AM | File folder | |
| add_vhost | 11/5/2016 3:44 PM | PHP File | 20 KB |
| favicon | 2/4/2019 6:48 AM | Icon | 198 KB |
| index | 8/31/2017 6:26 PM | PHP File | 31 KB |
| test_sockets | 9/21/2015 6:30 PM | PHP File | 1 KB |
| testmysql | 12/13/2016 2:50 PM | PHP File | 1 KB |
| wordpress-5.0 | 12/10/2018 4:54 PM | Compressed (zipp... | 11,108 KB |

```
<html>
<head>
</head>
<body>

<?php
    /* This line contains a comment
    Which span to
    several lines */

    //This comment is a line comment

    //echo prints the statement onto the screen
    echo "Hello World, Welcome to PHP Programming!"
?>

</body>
</html>
```

When executed, you should have the output as:

# Variables in PHP Programming

I will go directly into the PHP variable declaration statement as we have dealt with variables in different chapters in this book. Every variable in PHP normally begins with the dollar ($) sign. Most beginners make the mistake of not including the dollar ($) at the beginner. I know you won't make that mistake.

```
<?PHP
    $variable1 = 280;
    $variable2 = "PHP Programming";
?>
```

We first declare variable1 with the value 280. However, the second is a string variable with value as "PHP Programming"

It is important to note that every statement n PHP ends with a semicolon. You will get an error whenever you don't include a semicolon to indicate the ending of a statement.

## Variable Rules in PHP

- A variable name always begins with an underscore (_) or a letter
- A variable name must not include a space (s)
- Variable names can only have an underscore or alpha-numerical character

String Variables

String variables are important especially if you want to manipulate and store text in your program. The code below assigns the text "Welcome to PHP Programming" to the variable beginner and prints out the content to the screen.

```php
<?php
    $beginner = 'Welcome to PHP Programming';
    echo $beginner;
?>
```

Output

Welcome to PHP Programming

Strlen () function

Perhaps you want to determine the string length of a word or sentence, the strlen function is what you need. Consider the example below.

```php
<?php
    echo strlen("Today is the best day of your life.
    Programming is a lifelong skill and PHP is all your
    need");
```

```
        ?>
```

The outcome will be the string length of the text including the signs, space, characters). In this situation, the result will be 92 as shown below.

# Operators in PHP Programming

In this segment, I will rundown through the basic operators in PHP. I will look at the assignment, arithmetic, comparison, logical, and concatenation operators.

## Assignment operators

| Operator | Examples | Large notation |
|----------|----------|----------------|
| %= | p%=q | p=p%q |
| *= | p*=q | p=p*q |
| .= | p.=q | p=p.q |
| /= | p/=q | p=p/q |

| += | p+=q | p=p+q |
|----|------|-------|
| = | p=p | p=q |
| -= | p-=q | p=p-q |

## Logical Operators

| Operator | Description | Example |
|----------|-------------|---------|
| ! | not | p=9<br>q=9<br>!(p==q) returns false |
| && | and | p=9<br>q=9<br>(p < 10 && q> 1) returns true |
| \|\| | or | p=9<br>q=9<br>(p==5 \|\| q==5) returns true |

## Arithmetic Operators

| Operator | Description | Example | Result |
|----------|-------------|---------|--------|
| + | Addition | a=8<br>a+5 | 13 |

| | | | | |
|---|---|---|---|---|
| – | Subtraction | a=17<br>20-a | 3 |
| / | Division | a = 40<br>40/2 | 20 |
| * | Multiplicati<br>on | a=7<br>a*5 | 35 |
| ++ | Increment | a=9<br>a++ | a=1<br>0 |
| -- | Decrement | a=14<br>a-- | a=13 |
| % | Modulus<br>(division<br>remainder) | 56%6 | 2 |

## Comparison Operator

| Operator | Description | Example |
|---|---|---|
| == | is equal to | 48==49<br>returns false |
| != | is not equal | 48!=49<br>returns true |
| < | is less than | 48<49<br>returns true |
| <= | is less than or<br>equal to | 48<=49<br>returns true |

| | | |
|---|---|---|
| <> | is not equal | 48<>49 returns true |
| > | is greater than | 48>49 returns false |
| >= | is greater than or equal to | 48>=49 returns false |

# Conditional Statements in PHP Programming

At times, you may want to make decisions that require different actions when writing a program, conditional statement plays a huge role to perform some decision. In PHP language, we have the if statement, if... else statement, the if...elseif... else statement. In this section, I will expand on these statements including their syntax.

## If Statement

The statement is required to execute a line of code as far as the condition stated is true. Consider the example below.

```php
<?php
    $number= 23;
    if($number='23')
echo "Wake up! Time to begin Your Programming lesson.";
```

```
        ?>
```

In the statement above, we first declare allocate the value 23 to the variable "number". The if statement now evaluates if the variable "number" is equal to 23 since it is true, it will return:

Wake up! Time to begin Your Programming lesson.

## The If...else statement

This condition examines two different statements and evaluates one depending on the condition specified. A simple English illustration will be: buy a donut if there is no pizza available.

```php
<?php
    $decision1='Donut';
    if($decision1 == 'Donut') {
        echo 'Buy Donut when coming';
```

```
        } else {
            echo 'Buy Pizza when coming';
        }
    ?>
```

The output will be:

← → C ⌂ ⓘ localhost/index1

Buy Donut when coming

Let's twist the same code and consider the output.

```
    <?php
        $decision1='Donut';
        if($decision1 == 'Don') {
            echo 'Buy Donut when coming';
        } else {
            echo 'Buy Pizza when coming';
        }
```

```
            ?>
```

The output will be:

Buy Pizza when coming

It doesn't work on string alone but you can also use it on number operations.

## The if ... else if...else statement

You can use this statement to select a single option from a different line of codes. The example below will explain better.

```php
<?php
$number1=10;
$number2=10;
if($number1 == 8) {
    echo 'The expression is true';
} elseif($number2 == $number2) {
    echo 'The second expression is true';
} else {
    echo 'The two if statements are true';
```

```
        }
    ?>
```

## The output:

Switch Statement

The statement allows you to change the course of the program flow. It is best suited when you want to perform various actions on different conditions. Consider the example below.

```
<html>
<body>
<?php
    $a=2;
    switch ($a)
```

227

```php
        {
                case 1:
                        echo 'The number is 10';
                break;
                case 2:
                        echo 'The number is 20';
                break;
                case 3:
                        echo 'The number is 30';
                break;
                default:
                        echo 'There is no number that
match';
        }
?>
</body>
</html>
```

Output:

**Explanation**

In the example above, we declare the variable "a" to be 3. The switch statement has some block of codes, with case or default. If the value of the case is equivalent to the variable $a, it will execute the statement within that line and then break. However, if the value of the case is not equivalent to any of the variable, it will break from the case before executing the default code block.

# Conclusion

PHP language isn't restricted to professional web browsers alone. You don't have to be an IT administrative professional to learn it. Similar to any scripting language, it may seem complicated at the first time; however, if you preserver, you will discover it is an interesting language to learn. Learning PHP programming is the perfect way of understanding the server-side world.

Writing PHP code is not something intimidating if you start from the foundation as I have done in this book. PHP language is one of the languages you don't need anyone to teach you as long as you are ready to learn everything. In this book, you have learned everything you need to get your environment ready, variables, conditional statements, and much more.

# Chapter Nine: Python Programming Language

## Introduction

Python Language is one of the easiest and straightforward object-oriented languages to learn. Its syntax is simple, thereby making it simple for beginners to learn and understand the language with ease. In this chapter, I will cover several aspects of the Python programing language. This programming guide is for beginners who want to learn a new language. However, if you are an advanced programmer, you will also learn something.

Guido Van Rossum developed the Python language but the implementation began in 1989. Initially, you could have thought, it was named after the Python snake; however, it was named after a comedy television show called "Monty Python's Flying Circus."

## Features of Python

There are certain features that make the python programming language unique among other programming languages. The summary is displayed in the diagram below.

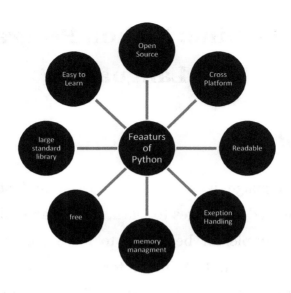

1. **Easy to learn** – Because python is a high-level and expressive language, it is easy for everyone – including you to learn and understand irrespective of their programming level – beginners to advanced programming

2. **Readable** – It is quite easy to read the language

3. **Open source** – The language is an open-source language

4. **Cross-platform** – This means it is available and you runnable on different operating systems including UNIX, Linux, Windows, Mac, etc. This has contributed to its portability.

5. **Free** – The language is downloadable without paying anything. Furthermore, not only can you download it, you

can it for various applications. The software is distributable freely.

6. **Large standard library** – Python has its standard library, which contains various functions and code, which you can add to your code.

7. **Supports exception handling** – Most programming languages have this exception handling feature. However, an exception is a situation that takes place in the course of program execution and has the tendency to disrupt the flow of the program. With python exception handling feature, you can write less error code while testing various situation that may lead to an exception in the future.

8. **Memory management** – The language also supports automatic memory management, which means it clear and free memory automatically. There is no need for clearing the memory on your own when you remember.

## Uses of Python

Most beginners before choosing to learn a programming language first consider what the uses of such language are. However, there are various applications of the python language in a real-world situation. These include:

1. **Data Analysis** – You can use python to develop data analysis and visualization in the form of charts

2. **Game development** – Today, the game industry is a huge market that yields billions of dollars per year. It may interest you to know that you can use python to develop interesting games.

3. **Machine learning** – We have various machine learning applications that are written using the python language. For instance, products recommendation in websites such as eBay, Flipkart, Amazon, etc. uses a machine-learning algorithm, which recognizes the user's interest. Another area of machine learning is a voice and facial recognition on your phone.

4. **Web development** – You didn't see this coming. Well, web frameworks such as Flask and Django are based on the python language. With Python, you can write backend programming logics, manage database, map URLs, etc.

5. **Embedded applications** – You can use python to develop embedded applications

# How to Install Python Programming Language

It is very easy to install python on your system. Since it is cross-platform, you don't need to crack your brain. By cross-platform, I mean you can install it on Ubuntu, Mac, UNIX, Windows, etc. To install it on your system, you can visit this link https://www.python.org/downloads. You can download it here and it comes with the option of choosing your particular operating system. So the installation process is not complicated. After downloading the software according to your operating system, follow the onscreen instruction to complete the process.

Since you are a beginner, I will teach you how to install the PyCharm, which is a common IDE used for python programming. IDE stands for an integrated development environment. The IDE contains a debugger, interpreter or compiler, and a code editor.

## Installation of PyCharm IDE

First, go to this address – https://www.jetbrains.com/pycharm/download/ to download the edition you want. After this, install the downloaded file. If you are using a MAC system, you have to double click the .dmg file before dragging PyCharm to the application folder. However, for windows users, you have to open the .exe file before following the direction on the screen.

## Launching PyCharm

For windows users, after installing the .exe file, you will see the PyCharm icon on the desktop depending on the option you selected during installation. You can also go to your program files > Jetbrains >PyCharm2017 and look for the PyCharm.exe file to launch PyCharm.

# Python Program Beginning

Once you open the IDE and give a name to your project, you can start programming. You can begin with this simple program

```
# This Python program prints Welcome to Python
Programming on the screen
print('Welcome to Python Programming')
```

If you did that, you should have the following

```
Welcome to Python Programming                    .
```

# Comments in Python

If you observe from the first line, I began with "#" whenever you see that it is a comment and in Python, it doesn't change the program outcome. Comments are very important because it helps you to easily read the program by providing further explanation of the codes in English for everyone to understand.

Comments can be written in two ways in Python. This could be single or multiple line comments. The single-line comment uses the #, which is an example of the previous code. However, the multiple line comment uses three single quotes (''') at the beginning and end respectively.

```
'''
Example of multiple line comment
```

```
'''
```

Let me use a real example to explain both the single and multiple line comment.

```
'''
Sample program to illustrate multiple line comment
Pay close attention
'''
print("We are making progress")

# Second print statement
print("Do you agree?")

print("Python Programming for Beginners") # Third
print statement
```

Output:

```
We are making progress
Do you agree?
Python Programming for Beginners
```

# Python Variables

We use variables to store data in programming. Variable creation is very simple to implement in Python. In python, you have to declare the variable name and value together. For instance

Number1 = 140 #number1 is of integer type

str = "Beginner" #str is of string type

## Variable Name Convention in Python

Another name for a variable name is an identifier. Python has some laid down rules when it has to do with naming variables. These rules differ from other programming languages.

1. Variable names must always start with an underscore (-) or a letter. For example, _number1, number1,
2. Variable names cannot contain special characters such as #, %, $, etc. however, they can have underscore and alphanumeric characters
3. A variable name cannot begin with a number. For instance, 3number is invalid
4. It is case sensitive. For instance, number1 and NUMBER2 are entirely different variable names in python

## Python Variable examples

Number1 = 589

```
Str = "Python Programming"
Print (Number1)
Print (Str)
```

The output will be:

```
589
Python Programming
```

## Multiple Assignment

You can also allocate several variables to a single expression in python. Consider the example below:

```
Profit = returns = yields = 35
print (Profit)
print (yield)
print (returns)
```

Output

```
35
35
35
```

Let us consider another example

```
A, B, C = 35, 8, 90
print (A)
print (B)
print (C)
```

Output

```
35
8
90
```

Concatenation and plus Operation on variables

```
A = 44
B = 68
print (A + B)

c = "Welcome"
d = "Home"
print (c + " " + d)
```

Output

```
112
Welcome Home
```

However, if you decide to use the + operator in conjunction with a and c, it will display an error such as unsupported operand type (s) for +: 'int'

# Data Types in Python

The purpose is to define the type of data a variable accommodate. For instance, "welcome home" is a string data type while 234 is an integer data type. In Python, data types are divided into two different groups. We have the immutable data types, whose values are unchangeable. They include tuple, string, and numbers. The other group is the mutable data types, whose values are changeable and they include sets, dictionaries, and list. In this book, my focus will be on the immutable data types.

## Numbers

When working with numbers, python supports floats, integers, and complex numbers. Float numbers are those with decimal points such as 9.9, 4.2, 42.9, etc. An integer is the opposite of float because it does not have a decimal point attached to it. For instance, 3, 35, 89, etc. however, a compound number contain an imaginary and real part such as 7+10j, etc.

Let's demonstrate the use of numbers in a python program

```
# Python program to show how we can use numbers
```

```
# declaring the variables number1 and number2 as
integer
number1 = 78
number2 = 12
print(number1+number2)

# declaring a and b as float data type
a = 15.9
b = 5.8
print(a-b)

# declaring x and y as complex numbers
x = 5 + 2j
y = 9 + 6j
print(y-x)
```

Output

```
100
10.1
4 + 4j
```

## Strings

This is a series of characters enclosed within a special character.
In Python, you have the option of using a single or double quote

to represent a string. There are various means of creating strings in python.

- You have the option of a single quote '
- You can use a double quote "
- You can use a triple-double quotes """

```python
# Ways of creating strings in Python
str = 'single string example'
print(str)


str2 = "double string example"
print(str2)


# multi-line string
str3 = """ Triple double-quote string"""
print(str3)


str4 = '''This is Python Programming '''
print(str4)
```

```
Single string example
double string example
Triple double-quote string
   Beginnersbook.com
This is Python Programming
```

## Tuple

Tuple works like a list but the difference is that in a tuple, the objects are unchangeable. The elements of a tuple are unchangeable once assigned. However, in the case of a list, the element is changeable.

In order to create tuple in python, you have to place all the elements in a parenthesis () with a comma separating it. Let me use an example to illustrate tuple in python.

```
# tuple of strings
bioDate = ("John", "M", "Lawson")
print(bioData)

# tuple of int, float, string
Data_New = (1, 2.8, "John Lawson")
print(Date_New)

# tuple of string and list
details = ("The Programmer", [1, 2, 3])
print(details)

# tuples inside another tuple
```

```
# nested tuple
Details2 = ((2, 3, 4), (1, 2, "John"))
Print(details2)
```

Output will be:

```
("John", "M", "Lawson")
(1, 2.8, "John Lawson")
("The Programmer", 1, 2, 3)
((2, 3, 4), (1, 2, "John"))
```

# Control Statement in Python Programming

There are various control statements used in Python to make a decision.

## If Statement

The statement prints out a message if a specific condition is satisfied. The format or syntax is as follow:

*If condition:*

    *Line of codes*

```
flag = True
if flag==True:
    print("Welcome")
```

```
        print("To")
        print("Python Programming")
```

Output

```
    Welcome
    To
    Python Programming
```

Consider another example

```
    number1 = 180
    if number1 < 290:
        print("number1 is less than 290")
```

Output

number1 is less than 290

## If-else statement

in our previous example, we only test a particular condition, what if you want to test two different conditions. That is where the "if-else statement" comes to play. In Python, the statement executes a particular statement if it is true but if it's not true, it executes the other statement.

Syntax

*If conditions*

*Statement1*

*Else*

*Statement2*

Let us use our last example to illustrate this.

```
number1 = 180
if number1 > 290:
    print("number1 is greater than 290")
else
    print ("number1 is less than 290")
```

**Output**

number1 is less than 290

```
Number1 = 15
if number1 % 4 == 0:
    print("the Number is an Even Number")
else:
    print("The Number is an Odd Number")
```

Output:

```
The Number is an Odd Number
```

## Bonus Programs

```
# Program to display the Fibonacci sequence depending
on the number the user wants

# For a different result, change the values
numb1 = 12

# uncomment to take input from the user
#num1 = int(input("How many times? "))

# first two terms
a1 = 0
a2 = 1
count = 0

# Verify if the number of times is valid
if numb1 <= 0:
    print("Please enter a positive integer")
elif numb1 == 1:
    print("Fibonacci sequence up to",numb1,":")
    print(a1)
else:
    print("Fibonacci sequence up to",numb1,":")
    while count < numb1:
        print(a1,end=' , ')
```

```
nth = a1 + a2
# update values
a1 = a2
a2 = nth
count += 1
```

What do you think the output will be?

```
Fibonacci sequence up to 12 :
0, 1, 1, 2, 3, 5, 8, 13, 21, 34, 55, 89
```

# Conclusion on Python Programming

So far, you have learned the fundamentals of Python Programming. However, there are advanced topics such as functions, recursions, python OOP, python constructors, etc. My goal is that you have the basic knowledge of the language to equip you in other programming languages. Now you know how to write a program in Python and use the language conveniently. I am convinced that you can install Python on a different system. I have also covered how to use the control flow tools such as if statement and if...else statement.

Python is not a hard language and at that, you should invest your time to dive into advanced programming.

# Glossary

**Algorithm** – A series of instruction aimed at solving a single problem.

**Boolean** – An expression whose statements can only be true or false. It is sometimes used in combination with AND, OR, NOT, XOR, and NOR operators. They are also called comparison expression or relational expression.

**Class** – A set of related objects sharing the same features in the course of a program

**Code** – A program code or source code written as a set of instructions under a particular language

**Compilation** – A process of creating a program using code, which is written in a particular computer language. When a program undergoes the compilation process, the computer understands the codes and run the program without any programming software. C++ is an example of a compiler

**Compile** – The process of creating executable from code written in a particular language

**Compile-time** – The total time taken for the compiler to compile a particular program

**Compiler** - A software that converts codes written into programs

Constants – A constant is a term in the course of a program whose value does not change throughout the program execution. It is different from a variable whose value changes. Constants remain fixed and can be a character, number, and string.

**Data types** – This is a classification of a data type in a program. Data types include integers, String, Boolean, etc. Unlike humans, computers cannot differentiate between a number and a letter unless specified.

**Array** – This is a group or list of similar data values, which are categorized. Although the values are of the same data type, however, their position is not the same. For instance, the student of a particular class can be an array but their results after the exam will be different.

**Declaration** – A statement that describes a function, variable or any identifier in the course of a program

**Developer** – An individual whose job is to create or work on the development of a product or services. Developers use various programming languages to develop these products

**Exception** – An anomalous and unexpected condition encountered while executing a program. Another word for an exception is an error and it causes the code to execute.

**Expression** – A group of symbols, letters, and number that represent a variable. An expression is used in various programming languages with each having its own rules.

**False** – A Boolean value in programming that is used when the outcome of the local statement is not true

**Function** – A group of instructions used in programming languages to return a single or set of results.

**Immutable Object** – An object which is unchangeable after created. These are common in object-oriented programming languages like Java

**Increment** – In programming, the process of increasing the numerical value of a particular variable. It is the opposite of decrement.

**Inheritance** - This concept involves an object receiving the same features or properties of another object that supports it.

**Interpreter** – In programming, a programming language doesn't require undergoing the compilation process before its execution

**JavaScript** - A scripting language that allows developers to insert code into a website page. They are used to perform various advanced tasks such as creating a calendar, printing the time and date

**Keywords** – These are reserved words used by a programming language and have special meaning. Each programming language has its own reserved keywords, which must not be used as a variable name. For instance, "continue", "static," "if," "return," and "default" are some of the keywords reserved in C programming language

**Loop** – A series of instruction that repeats itself pending when a specific condition is met before stopping the process. Loop is one of the basic concepts in programming. Almost all programming language use loop to execute complete decisions.

**Object-Oriented Programming** (OOP) – A model with data structure with data in the form of fields and functions that can be applied to it

**Objects** – A combination of related constants, variables, and other data structures, which can be manipulated together. Example, the gender of students in a particular school

**Operand** – A term used to represent an object in which various manipulations can take place. For instance, in the expression "num1+num2+num3", num1, num2, and num3 are operands.

**Operators** – A term used to describe operations that can take place in n operand or object. For instance, "a*b+C" in the expression, * and + are operators, which perform a certain operation on the operands.

**Polymorphism** - The ability of a particular programming language to interpret objects in various ways depending on their data type or class.

**Program** – a collection of instruction that must be executed serially. The CPU process the program before its execution. A program, also called software sometimes contains a couple of lines to millions of lines with each providing different instructions. The instructions are called source code whereas the act of computer programming is program coding.

**Programming language** - This is an artificial language aimed at controlling the operation and functionality of a computer similar to the English language, they have rules (syntactic and semantic rules).

**Reserved Words** – These are unique words reserved for a particular programming language. Same as keywords

**Statement** – It represents a single line of code, which is written to express an action that must be carried out in that programming language. For instance, Q =R+8

**Syntax** – These are rules that a particular programming language has. Different programming languages may have the same functions, features, and capabilities; however, they may have different syntax. For instance, the syntax for display a text to the screen in C++ is different from that of a Java program

**Variable** – A storage location used to save temporary data during a program. Unlike constants, you can manipulate, store, and display a variable value. For instance, an integer variable "number1" stores a value like 45. However, if after this, you use the same name and store 67 as the value, it takes the new value and discards the old value (45)

# Exercises for all Languages

## SQL Test Questions

**Q 1** - Which of the SQL statements below is not true?

    A. SQL statements can be written on more than a single line.

    B. SQL statements are not case sensitive

    C. Clauses must be on a separate line

    D. Keywords cannot be split across lines

**Q 2** – Consider the code below

> STUDENTS (StudID, FirstName, LastName, Email, PhoneNum, DoB, Subject, Total_Score);

Which statement below will display the student full name with a column heading "Name"

    A. SELECT FirstName || LastName as "Name" from STUDENTS;

    B. SELECT FirstName, LastName FROM STUDENTS;

    C. SELECT Name FROM STUDENTS;

    D. SELECT FirstName, LastName FROM STUDENTS;

**Q3** – Consider the code below

> STUDENTS (StudID, FirstName, LastName, Email,
> PhoneNum, DoB, Subject, Total_Score);

Which of the query will display subjects from the table?

   A. SELECT ALL subjects FROM STUDENTS;
   B. SELECT Subjects FROM STUDENTS;
   C. SELECT * Subject FROM STUDENTS;
   D. SELECT Subject OR Total_Score FROM STUDENTS;

**Q4** – Consider the code below

> Students (StudID, FirstName, LastName, Email,
> PhoneNum, DoB, Subject, Total_Score);

Which of the query will display students offering only
"MTH112) subjects from the table?

   A. SELECT StudID, FirstName, LastName FROM Students
      WHERE Subject = "MTH112";
   B. SELECT StudID, FirstName, LastName FROM Students
      WHERE subject is "MTH112";
   C. SELECT StudID, FirstName, LastName WHERE subject
      = "MTH112";
   D. SELECT StudID, FirstName, LastName FROM Students;


**Q5** – Consider the Schema below

> Students (StudID, FirstName, LastName, Email,
> PhoneNum, DoB, Subject, Total_Score);

A. SELECT FirstName FROM Students WHERE FirstName like "A";

B. SELECT FirstName FROM Students WHERE FirstName like "%A%";

C. SELECT FirstName FROM Students WHERE FirstName like "%A";

D. SELECT FirstName FROM Students WHERE FirstName like "A%";

## C++ Test Question

**Q1** – A trigraph character starts with

A. #

B. ?

C. ??

D. ##

**Q 2** - The default access specifier for class members is

A. Private

B. Protected

C. Public

D. None

**Q3** – C++ doesn't support the following inheritance

A. Multilevel

B. Hierarchical

C. Hybrid

D. There is no answer

**Q4** – From the following statement, which of them is true concerning inline function?

A. It doesn't execute faster when compared to normal function

B. It executes faster due to its higher priority when compared to normal function

C. It performs faster because it is treated as a macro internally

D. None of the above

**Q5** – Which of the statement below is the true definition of an abstract class?

A. It is a class, which must have a pure virtual function defined outside the class

B. It is a class, which may not have a pure virtual function

C. It is a class, which must have at least a pure virtual function

D. It is a class, which must have all pure virtual functions

**Q 6** - Which of the following is not a reserved word in C++?

A. extends

B. friend

C. this

D. volatile

**Q7** – determine the output of the program

```cpp
#include<iostream>

using namespace std;
class ab {

    public:
       int p;

        ab(int p) {
           p = p;
        }
};

main() {
    ab c(5);

    cout<<c.a;
}
```

A. Garbage

B. 5

C. Compile error "a" declared twice

D. Error at the statement a = a;

# C Programming Test Questions

**Q1** – Consider the simple program below?

```
#include<stdio.h>

main()
{
   int const a = 8;
     p++;
   printf("%d",p);
}
```

A. 6

B. 9

C. Runtime error

D. Compile error

**Q2** – determine the program

```
#include<stdio.h>

main()
{
   char p[]="welcome", q[]="welcome";

if(p==q){
        printf("equal strings");
```

```
        }
    }
```

A. No output

B. Unequal strings

C. Equal string

D. Compilation error

Q3 - Consider the code snippet below, choose the right output.

```c
#include<stdio.h>
main()
{
   int p = 5, q = 3, r = 4;
      printf("p = %d, q = %d\n", p, q, r);
}
```

A. compile error

B. p=5, q=3

C. p=5, q=3, 0

D. p=5, q=3, c = 0

**Q4** - determine the output of the program

```c
#include<stdio.h>
main()
{
int p = 1;
double q;
float r = 1.3;
```

```
    q = p + r;
    printf("%.2lf", q);
}
```

A. 2.3

B. 2.0

C. 2.30

D. Error

**Q5** – determine the output

```
#include<stdio.h>
main()
{
    enum { Germany, is=9, Excellent };
    printf("%d %d", Germany, Excellent);
}
```

A. Compile error

B. 0 1

C. 0 2

D. 0 8

**Q6** – determine the output of the program

```
#include<stdio.h>
main()
{
    char p = 'B'+265;
```

```
    printf("%c", p);

}
```

A. Compile error

B. Overflow error during runtime

C. B

D. A

**Q7** – determine the output of the program

```
    #include<stdio.h>

    main()
    {
      short unsigned int a = 0;
      printf("%u\n", a--);
    }
```

A. 65568

B. 32789

C. Compile error

D. 0

**Q8** – determine the output of the program

```
    #include<stdio.h>
    main()
    {
      unsigned q = 5, n=&q, *p = n+0;
      printf("%u",*p);
    }
```

A. Address of p

B. Address of n

C. Address of q

D. 5

**Q9** – Consider the code below, determine the output of the program

```c
#include<stdio.h>
main()
{
  int p = 8;
    if(q==8)
  {
    if(p==8) break;
    printf("You are Right");
  }
  printf("Hello");
}
```

A. You are Right

B. You are RightHello

C. Hello

D. Compile error

**Q10** – Consider the code, determine the program output

```c
#include<stdio.h>

main()
```

```
{
    int a = 8;
    if(a=8)
    {
        if(a=8) printf("You Are Right");
    }
    printf("Hello");
}
```

A. Compile error

B. You Are RightHello

C. Hello

D. You Are Right

Q11 – Consider the code snippet, determine the output of the program

```
#include<stdio.h>
main()
{
    for(4;5;6)
        printf("Welcome");
}
```

A. Compile error

B. No output

C. Prints "Welcome" once

D. Infinite loop

**Q12** – Consider the code below, what will be the value of a?

```
int a = ~1;
```

A. 2

B. -1

C. 1

D. -2

## JavaScript Programming Test Question

**Q 1** –from the statement below, which is true concerning the features of JavaScript?

A. JavaScript is integrated with Java

B. JavaScript is a lightweight, interpreted programming language

C. All of the above

**Q 2** –identify the correct feature of JaveScript in the statement below?

A. JavaScript is corresponding to and embedded with HTML

B. Open and cross-platform

C. A and B are True

D. All of the above

**Q 3** - Which of the statement below is true of the advantage of JavaScript?

  A. Less server interaction

  B. Increased interactivity

  C. Immediate feedback to the visitors

  D. All of the above

**Q 4** - Which of the statement below is true about variable naming conventions in JavaScript?

**B** - Variable names are case sensitive.

**A** - JavaScript variable names must begin with underscore or letter.

**C** – A and B is True

**D** - None of the above

**Q 5** – Is it possible to access Cookie using JavaScript?

  A. True

  B. False

**Q 6** - Which statement below is true regarding cookie handling in JavaScript?

  A. JavaScript can modify, create, read, and delete the cookie (s) of a webpage

  B. JavaScript can control cookies via the property of the cookie.

  C. A and B is True

  D. None of the above

**Q 7** – Identify the correct syntax to redirect a url using JavaScript?

    A. browser.location='http://www.newlocation.com';

    B. document.location='http://www.newlocation.com';

    C. navigator.location='http://www.newlocation.com';

    D. window.location='http://www.newlocation.com';

**Q 8** – Choose the right syntax to print a page using JavaScript

    A. browser.print();

    B. document.print();

    C. navigator.print();

    D. window.print();

**Q 9** – Identify the valid type of function supported by JavaScript?

    A. anonymous function
    B. Both of the above
    C. named function
    D. None of the above

# Summary of the Book

In Java Programming, you will acquire every information you need concerning data types, object-oriented programming, and control structures in Java. You will learn more than the codes. However, the next chapter challenges you on learning JavaScript, one of the most common scripting languages in the world. Furthermore, PHP will help you master the art of writing quality code. You will discover the basic syntax when writing PHP programs. In the SQL chapter, you will learn the nitty-gritty of creating a database and table easily. Furthermore, you will learn how to insert, select, and perform various actions on a table. This book indeed is a must-have for any serious programmer. Polish your programming skill by buying this book. Invest in your future.

The book covers programming topics such as:

- Prerequisites for learning each language
- Features of the language
- The concepts of different programming language
- Variables of the different programming language
- Where the language is applicable in our today world

The book is well arranged for easy understanding. Indeed the book is a comprehensive guide to understanding eight programming languages to start coding your way to the top.

Don't forget to brush your knowledge by going through the exercise page. It contains serious of questions to test your knowledge of each programming topic you have covered. Before you know it, you have mastered and the results on the screen will tell your success story. So what are you waiting for? Let the programming begin!

# Python for Beginners

*Practical Introduction to Python Programming, Learn Fast and Well Python Programming Language With Examples and Practical Exercises*

By

Kevin Cooper

# Introduction

Congratulations on **purchasing** *Python for beginners,* and thank you for doing so.

The following chapters will discuss python programming language in detail with a lot of examples and hands-on exercises. We will also look at a lot of basic concepts in a way that beginners can understand and appreciate the robustness of Python when compared to other entry-level programming languages.

We will first start with a brief introduction that is followed by the installation of Python development environments in the native system. We will then introduce basic programming concepts like variables, operators, conditional and loop structures with a lot of examples to make the reader understand Python language in detail.

A lot of programming code is also given so that the reader can get a good idea on both theoretical and programmatical concepts.    Let us start our journey into the world of Python.

There are plenty of books on this subject on the market, so thanks again for choosing this one! Every effort was made to ensure it is full of as much useful information as possible. Please enjoy!

# Chapter 1: Introduction to Python

This chapter introduces a brief knowledge to Python along with its history. This is quite basic and may involve theoretical background to make things easy for the beginners. We will also introduce an example program so that we can get a good starting feel for Python environment. Let us start for our very first chapter in this book.

## What is Python?

Python is a dynamic explanatory programming language. Python is easy to learn and powerful and supports object-oriented and functional programming. Python can be used on multiple operating systems such as Windows and UNIX, while Python can be used on development platforms such as Java and. NET, so it is also called "beginners programming language." Python's simplicity and ease of use make the development process concise, especially suitable for rapid application development.

In the next section, we will discuss a few basic historical advancements that lead to the discovery of the Python programming language.

# Python and its History

Python was developed by Guido van Rossum in 1989 and finally published in early 1991. Guido van Rossum used to be a member of the CWI Company and used the interpretive programming language ABC to develop applications. This language has many limitations in software development. Because he wants to complete some tasks in system management, he needs to acquire the system call capability provided by the operating system of the Amoeba machine.

Although Amoeba's special language can be designed to accomplish this task, van Rossum plans to design a more general programming language. Python language has been born for more than 20 years and is gradually developing into one of the mainstream programming languages. TIOBE has long occupied the eighth position in the ranking of programming languages.

Due to the dynamic nature of Python, program interpretation and execution are slower than compiled languages. However, with the continuous optimization of Python language, the continuous development of some projects such as PyCharm, and the continuous development of computer hardware technology, dynamic language has received more and more attention in the industrial field.

The representative languages include Python, Ruby, SmallTalk, Groovy, etc.

As we all know, Java is a recognized development language in the field of industrial applications. Java is easier to use than C++, and its internal structure is relatively simple. Python's syntax makes programming easier. Python can be used to write code that is more readable than Java.

With the advent of interpreters such as Jython, Python can be run on Java virtual machines. This way, Python can use Java rich application packages. Python is very similar to JavaScript, which is well known to readers. It is interpreted and executed, and its syntax structure has many similarities. JavaScript is the client script language on the browser side, and Python can also be used for Web development.

Python, as a scripting language, absorbs the advantages of Perl, react and other languages, which makes Python have React extensibility and Perl text parsing and matching capabilities. Python and Lisp also have similarities. Python can implement a functional programming model.

## Python and Its Features

Programming languages are continuously developing, from the initial assembly language to the later C and Pascal languages, to the present C++, Java and other high-level programming languages. The difficulty of program design is decreasing. A set of standards has been formed for software development and design. Development is no longer a complicated task.

At first, only machine code can be used to write code, but now an IDE environment with good debugging function can be used to program. Python is developed in C, but Python no longer has complex data types such as pointers in C language. Python's simplicity greatly reduces software code and simplifies development tasks. Programmers no longer focus on grammatical features, but on the tasks that the program is to accomplish.

Python has many important features, and some of them are creative and paved for a boom in software development.

## 1. Object-oriented features

Object-oriented programming solves the complexity of structured programming and makes programming closer to real life. Structured programming mixes data and logic together, which is not convenient for program maintenance. Object-oriented programming abstracts the behaviors and attributes of objects and separates the behaviors and attributes but organizes them together reasonably.

Python language has strong object-oriented characteristics and simplifies the implementation of object-oriented. It eliminates object-oriented elements such as protection types, abstract classes, interfaces, etc., making the concept of object-oriented easier to understand.

## 2. Built-in data structure

Python provides some built-in data structures that implement functions similar to collection classes in Java. Python's data structure includes tuples, lists, dictionaries, collections, etc. The appearance of the built-in data structure simplifies the design of the program. Tuples are equivalent to "read-only" arrays, lists can be used as variable-length arrays, and dictionaries are equivalent to Hash Table types in Java.

## 3. Simplicity

Python has fewer keywords. It does not have semicolons, begin, end, etc. The code blocks are separated by spaces or tab indents. Python's code is simple, short, and easy to read. Python simplifies loop statements and can be read quickly even if the program structure is very complex.

## 4. Robustness

Python provides an exception handling mechanism that can catch exceptions in programs. In addition, Python's stack trace object can point out the location of the program error and the cause of the error. Exception mechanism can avoid unsafe exit and help programmers debug programs.

## 5. Cross-platform

Python is compiled into platform-related binary code before interpretation and execution. This approach is similar to Java, but Python's execution speed has increased. Python-written applications can run on different operating systems such as Windows, UNIX, Linux, etc. Python code written on one operating system can be ported to other operating systems with only a few modifications.

## 6. Scalability

Python is a language developed by C, so it can be extended by C, and new modules and classes can be added to Python. At the same time, Python can be embedded into projects developed in C and C++ languages to make the program have script language.

## 7. Dynamics

Python is similar to JavaScript, PHP, Perl, and other languages. It does not need to declare another variable. It can create a new variable by directly assigning a value.

## 8. Strongly Typed Languages

Python's variables are created to correspond to a type, which can determine the type of variables according to the content of the assignment expression. Python has built a mechanism to manage these variables internally. Different types of variables require type conversion.

**9. Wide usage**

Python language is applied to the database, network, graphic image, mathematical calculation, Web development, operating system expansion, and other fields. Python is supported by many third-party libraries. For example, the PIL library (now no longer maintained but replaced by Pillow) is used for image processing, the NumPy library is used for mathematical calculation, the WxPython library is used for GUI program design, and the Django framework is used for Web application program opening.

With this explanation, we can easily understand the advantages of python programming language offers. Next, we will give an example program that will let us introduce to Python language.

# First Python Program

Python's source code file has "py" as the suffix. Next, write a simple Python program to create a file named sampleprogram.py to output the string "This is a whole new world."

**Code is here:**

```
if __name__ =="__main__":
```

```
print ("This is a whole new world")
```

## Code Description:

The first line of code is equivalent to the main () function in C language and is the entrance of Python program. The second line of code uses the print statement to output the string "This is a whole new world."

## The output is shown below:

This is a whole new world

Python's print statement is used to output the contents of the string, that is, to output the contents in double quotation marks to the console. Python's input and output are realized through "stream." The above print statement outputs the contents of the string to the standard output stream, that is, to the console. Streams can also output results to files, printers, etc.

Python programs are very simple to run, and the command format is as follows.

## Command is here:

python filepath samplefilename.py

Where samplefilename.py represents python's source code file, filepath represents the path where samplefilename.py is located. Enter the command shown in the DOS window and run the file sample.py.

This mode of operation is not intuitive enough and is not convenient for program debugging. Later, we will explain how to run Python programs in editors like Edit Plus and development tool PyCharm.

In the next section, we will describe the python development environment in detail.

# Building Development Environment

The installation and configuration of Python development environment are very simple. Python can be installed and developed on multiple platforms. IPython is a very popular, powerful, and easy-to-use Python installation package. This section describes the installation of IPython and the use of Python interactive command lines.

### Python download and installation

Python is installed by default on UNIX systems, Python's executable files are installed in the /usr/local/bin directory, and library files are installed in the /usr/local/python directory.

Although Python2 and Python3 are installed by default, Python in the terminal defaults to Python2, which is currently generally Python2.7.5. To use Python3, you need to enter python3 in the terminal or modify the default version. In a Windows environment, Python can be installed in any directory.

Readers can download Python3.3 from the official website www.python.org, which provides Python installation software for different operating systems such as Windows and UNIX.

Users can also install IPython interactive shell, which is much easier to use than the default terminal, supports automatic indentation, and has many useful functions and functions built-in. The address of its official website is http://ipython.org. It can be used on any operating system.

Windows users need to install Anaconda before installing IPython. Anaconda is an installation management program, which can be used to complete Python upgrade and other operations easily, and it has a lot of Python libraries, and its download address can be easily found out from the internet. Select the appropriate version of the user's machine and install it.

After the installation is completed, the user will find that in addition to the system default cmd.exe, there are more Anaconda Command Prompt terminals. The user can directly use the terminal or use the system default cmd.exe. After opening the terminal, enter Python and press enter, you may find that python version is 2.7.5 or something other than Python3.X we want. It doesn't matter.

**Open any terminal and enter the following command:**

update anaconda

create –n py3k python=versionnumber anaconda

During the installation process, there will be some prompts. Enter Y and press Enter. At this point, you can see information about a series of Python libraries installed. After the installation is completed, reopen the terminal and enter the following command:

activate py3k # This activates the interpreter in your system

Then enter iPython in the terminal, and the python version information and IPython version information will be displayed, and an interactive command window will be launched.

Since the current version supported by Anaconda defaults to Python2.7, you need to switch to py3k every time you want to use Python3.3. You can enter help in the IPython interactive environment to view help information.

## Use of Interactive Command Line

After IPython is successfully installed, Anaconda can choose to use its own terminal or system terminal. After entering the terminal, input ipython to start the interactive environment. If you are using native python, you can start the command line program by simply entering Python and entering the command interface.

Through the command line, you can directly input statements to the interpreter and output the running results of the program. The Python program can be entered at the prompt in the command line window. The following uses the print statement to output the string "This is our world," as shown.

Of course, you can also enter multiple lines of Python code in the command line window. Next, enter the code in sampleexample.py into the command line window. After inputting the last line of the program, press enter twice to finish the program and output the running result of the program, as shown.

Note if you want to exit the interactive command line, enter exit and press enter. In the next section, we will introduce IDE tools such as Pycharm.

# Python Development Tools

Python is rich in development tools, with many powerful IDE (Integrated Development Environment) tools, such as Komodo, PythonWin, Eclipse, PyCharm, etc. These tools not only support graphical operations but also have editing, debugging, and other functions.

In addition, the text editor can also be used as a Python development environment, such as Edit Plus, Vi, etc. PyCharm is a Python IDE developed by JetBrains. It has powerful functions and recently released an open-source community version, which is very suitable for learning.

## Use of PyCharm

PyCharm is a cross-platform IDE that is very easy to use. It is developed in Java. It has a paid version and a community free version. This book will use the community free version. You can install it after downloading. After the installation is completed, running the program for the first time will require setting a theme, etc. You can choose to skip this step or choose yourself.

After setting up, restart, you can enter the program. Because it is an IDE, you first need to create a project, and then you will need to set up a Python path step by step, according to the requirements.

Note: If Anaconda is used, you need to select python.exe in py3k under envs directory. Otherwise, the default Python2.7 version 2.7 will be used.

PyCharm has its own Python command line interactive Terminal, which can easily run code and do related tests. Move the mouse to the lower-left corner and click the TERMINAL button to open it, which is very convenient.

Click the [File] | [New] menu and select the corresponding file type to create a new file and write a Python program in it. Now start to create hello_world.py file, select the Run command in the [Run] menu or press Alt+Shift after writing +F10 key combination can run the code.

In addition, PyCharm also supports advanced functions such as quick jump, code refactoring, code testing, version control, debugging, etc. Next, we will talk about the Eclipse development environment.

**Introduction of Eclipse IDE**

Eclipse is an integrated development environment for Java development and an open-source project. Eclipse is very extensible. Eclipse can not only be used as the IDE of Java but also develop a large number of plug-ins to support other applications.

For types of languages, such as C, C++, Python, PHP, etc., if you want to develop Python on the Eclipse platform, you need to download PyDev. The easy Eclipse website provides various plug-in downloads of Eclipse and can obtain Easy Eclipse for Python, which runs separately.

Eclipse is very powerful, and it realizes intelligent functions such as the syntax highlighting, code prompting, and code completion of Python code. In addition, Eclipse provides more powerful debugging capabilities than PythonWin, and also supports Jython, Pyunit, team development, and other functions.

In Eclipse, source code is organized into a project. The structure of the Eclipse user interface is divided into a View and an Editor. Examples of views and editors include source code outline view, Java source code editor, Python source code editor, and file system navigation view.

**Eclipse user interface package**

Views are a set of windows that are usually used when performing some type of activity. The standard views in Eclipse include Debug, Java Browsing, Java, Java Type Hierarchy, Plug-in Development, CVS Repository Exploring, Resource, and Install/ Update. Easy Eclipse for Python provides a Pydev view. When the debugging mode is started, Eclipse automatically switches to debug view.

**Note**

Python needs to be installed on your computer before Pydev can be installed.

**Configuration of Edit Plus Editor Environment**

Python can also be developed using an editor. For example, the text editing software Edit Plus can also become Python's editing and execution environment, and even be used for debugging programs. Edit Plus has functions such as syntax highlighting and code automatic indenting.

Here's how to configure it:

The development environment of Edit Plus editor.

## 1. Add Python Groups

a) Run Edit Plus, select [Tools] | [Configure User Tools] to open the [Parameters] dialog box. Click the [Add Tool] button and select the [Program] command in the pop-up menu. The name of the newly-created group is named python.

b) Enter Python in the [Menu Text] text box, enter the installation path of Python in the [Command] text box, enter $(FileName) in the [Parameters] text box, and enter $(FileDir) in the [Start Directory] text box.

c) Check the [Capture Output] option, and the output result of the Python program will be displayed in the output column of EditPlus. Otherwise, a command line window will pop up after running the Python program and output the result to the command line.

d) Click the [OK] button to create a new python file. Python options will appear under the [Tools] menu. Click this option, or use the shortcut ctrl+1 to transport

Line Python program.

## 2. Set Python Highlight and Auto Complete

Edit Plus can not only be used as Python's development environment but also supports Java, C#, PHP, HTML and other types of languages. Different languages have different forms of grammatical highlighting and automatic completion. In order to realize grammar highlighting and automatic completion, two characteristic files need to be downloaded.

After downloading, extract the files python.acp and python.stx to the installation directory of EditPlus. Files with acp suffix represent automatically completed feature files, and files with stx suffix represent feature files with syntax highlighted. These feature files need to be set in EditPlus before writing Python code.

(1) Select [File] | [Settings and Syntax] option, select [python] option in the [File Type] list, enter python in the [Description] text box, and click on

Enter py in the text box [extension].

(2) In the Settings and Grammar tab, enter the path of python.stx in the Grammar File text box and python.acp in the Auto Complete text box.

(3) Python syntax does not use begin, end or {,} to distinguish code blocks, but uses colon and code indentation to distinguish the hierarchical relationship between codes. Click the [tab/indent] button to open the [tab and indent] dialog box and set the indentation method of Python code.

When using IDE tools, entering colon codes will automatically indent, and this function can also be set with Edit Plus. Enter the number of spaces in the Tabs and Indents text boxes respectively, generally set to Select the [Start Auto Indent] option, enter ":" in the [Start Auto Indent] option, and click the [OK] button to save the settings.

(4) Click the [Function Model] button to open the [Function Model] dialog box, as shown. In the [Function Model Regular Expression] text box, enter [\t]*def[\t].+:. Click [OK] to save the settings.

At this point, the Python development environment for Edit Plus has been set up. Edit Plus can also create templates for Python files, and code can be written on the basis of the templates each time a Python file is created. Py's content is as follows.

#! /usr/bin/python

**[Code Description]**


The first line of code enables Python programs to run on UNIX platforms.

Note that in Edit Plus, you can view the list of functions in the current Python file by using the shortcut Ctrl+F11. You need to save the Python program before running it. Next, use Edit Plus to write a Python program and output the result.

# Python Under Different Platforms

Java and .NET are two mature development platforms in the industry. Python can be used on these two development platforms, and Python can also be extended with Java and C#.

## 1. Jython

Jython is a Python parser written entirely in Java. Although the implementation and performance of Jython interpreter are still somewhat different from Python interpreter, Jython makes Python fully applicable under the Java development platform.

Jython enables Python programs to run on Java virtual machines while Python can access libraries and packages under Java. Jython also provides a perfect scripting environment for Java. Python can be used as an implementation language for middle-tier services in Java applications. Jython enables Java to extend Python modules, which in turn can be used to write Java applications.

## 2. IronPython

Iron Python is a Python implementation on the .NET platform. Iron Python provides an interactive console that supports dynamic compilation. It enables Python programmers to access all. NET libraries and is fully compatible with the Python language. Iron Python must provide support for .NET version 2.0. The appearance of Iron Python makes it possible to write

Python code under the .NET platform and call the rich .NET class library framework.

By this, we have explained a lot of basic concepts about Python. This chapter explained Python's history, features, and development environment. This chapter focused on the settings of the Python development environment, the features of IDE tools such as PyCharm and Eclipse, and the settings of Edit Plus editor. The next chapter will learn Python's basic syntax, including Python's file types, coding rules, data types, expressions, etc.

Let us dive into the next chapter where we will start discussing variables and data types in detail which are called as basic building blocks of any programming language.

# Chapter 2: Variables and Constants in Python

This chapter on a whole level will introduce a lot of basic concepts that programming languages deal with. We will be discussing concepts like variables and data types with programmatical examples in the coming sections. Let us start diving into the world of variables in Python.

The most basic data processing objects in programming languages are constants and variables. Their main purpose is to store data for various calculations and processing in programs. In this chapter, we will discuss Python's basic data processing functions such as data types, variables, and constants, and introduce beginners to the basic syntax they need when writing small applications.

## Why Variables are needed?

For any programming language, the basic part is to store the data in memory and process it. No matter what kind of operation we are going to perform, we must have the object of operation. It is difficult for a skillful woman to cook without rice. In Python language, constants and variables are the main ones. In fact, both of them are identification codes used by program designers to access data contents in memory.

The biggest difference between the two is that the contents of variables will change with the execution of the program, while the contents of constants are fixed forever. In the process of program execution, it is often necessary to store or use some data. For example, if you want to write a program to calculate the mid-term exam results, you must first input the students' results, and then output the total score, average score and ranking after calculation. This chapter describes how to store and access this data.

# Variable Naming and Assignment

In a program, program statements or instructions tell the computer which Data to access and execute step by step according to the instructions in the program statements. These data may be words or numbers. What we call variable is the most basic role in a programming language, that is, a named memory unit allocated by the compiler in programming to store changeable data contents.

The computer will store it in "memory" and take it out for use when necessary. In order to facilitate identification, it must be given a name. We call such an object "variable."

**For example:**

> > firstsample = 3

>>>second sample= 5

> > > result = firstsample+secondsample

In the above program statement, firstsample, secondsample, result are variables, and number 3 is the variable value of firstsample. Since the capacity of memory is limited, in order to avoid wasting memory space, each variable will allocate memory space of different sizes according to requirements, so "Data Type" is used to regulate it.

**Variable declaration and assignment**

Python is an object-oriented language, all data are regarded as objects, and the method of an Object reference is also used in variable processing. The type of variable is determined when the initial value is given, so there is no need to declare the data type in advance. The value of a variable is assigned with "=" and beginners easily confuse the function of the assignment operator (=) with the function of "equal" in mathematics. In programming languages, the "=" sign is mainly used for assignment.

The syntax for declaring a variable is as follows:

variable name = variable value

**e.g.**

number = 10.

The above expression indicates that the value 10 is assigned to the variable number. In short, in Python language, the data type

298

does not need to be declared in advance when using a variable, which is different from that in C language, which must be declared in advance before using a variable. Python interpretation and operation system will automatically determine the data type of the variable according to the value of the variable given or set.

For example, the data type of the above variable number is an integer. If the content of the variable is a string, the data type of the variable is a string.

## Variable naming rules

For an excellent programmer, readability of program code is very important. Although variable names can be defined by themselves as long as they conform to Python's regulations, when there are more and more variables, simply taking variables with letter names such as abc will confuse people and greatly reduce readability.

Considering the readability of the program, it is best to name it according to the functions and meanings given by variables. For example, the variable that stores height is named "Height" and the variable that stores weight is named "Weight." Especially when the program scale is larger, meaningful variable names will become more important.

For example, when declaring variables, in order to make the program readable, it is generally used to start with lowercase letters, such as score, salary, etc. In Python, variable names also need to conform to certain rules. If inappropriate names are used, errors may occur during program execution. Python is a case-sensitive language. In other words, number and Number are two different variables. Variable names are not limited in length.

Variable names have the following limitations: the first character of a variable name must be an English letter, underlined "_" and cannot be a number. Subsequent characters can match other upper- and lower-case English letters, numbers, underlined "_," and no space character is allowed. You cannot use Python's built-in reserved words (or keywords).

Although Python version 3. X supports foreign language variable names; it is recommended that you try not to use words to name variables. On the one hand, it is more troublesome to switch input methods when inputting program code. On the other hand, the reading of program code will not be smooth. The so-called reserved word usually has special meaning and function, so it will be reserved in advance and cannot be used as a variable name or any other identifier name.

**The following is an example of a valid variable name:**

pageresponse

fileName4563

level

Number_dstance

## The following is an example of an invalid variable name:

2_sample

for

$levelone

The user name learning classroom uses the help () function to query Python reserved word. The help () function is Python's built-in function. If you are not sure about the method and property usage of a specific object, you can use the help () function to query.

The Python reserved words mentioned above can be viewed by using the help () function. As long as "help ()" is executed, the help interactive mode will be entered. In this mode, the instructions to be queried will be input, and the relevant instructions will be displayed.

We can continue to input the instructions we want to query in help mode. When we want to exit help interactive mode, we can input Q or quit. You can also take parameters when entering the help () command, such as help ("keywords "), Python will directly display help or description the information without entering help interactive mode. Although Python uses dynamic data types, it is very strict in data processing, and its data type is "strong type."

**For example:**

> > > firstsample = 5

>>> secondsample= "45"

> > > print (firstsample+secondsample) # shows that TypeError variable firstsample is of numeric type and variable secondsample is of string type.

Some programming languages will convert the type unconsciously and automatically convert the value A to the string type, so firstsample+secondsample will get 545. Python language prohibits different data types from operating, so executing the above statement obviously Indicates information about the wrong type.

There is a difference between "strongly typed" and "weakly typed" in the data types of strong and weak type programming languages in small classrooms. One of the trade-offs is the safety of data type conversion. The strong type has a strict inspection for data type conversion. Different types of operations must be explicitly converted, and programs will not automatically convert. For example, Python and Ruby prefer strong types.

However, most weak type programming languages adopt Implicit Conversion. If you don't pay attention to it, unexpected type conversion will occur, which will lead to wrong execution results. JavaScript is a weak type of programming language.

# Static Type and Dynamic Type

When Python is executed, the way to determine the data type belongs to "dynamic type."

### What is the dynamic type?

The data types of programming languages can be divided into "Statically-Typed" and "Dynamically-Typed" according to the type checking method.

**1. Static types** are compiled with the type checked first, so the variables must be explicitly declared before they are used. The types of variables cannot be arbitrarily changed during execution. Java and C are such programming languages. For example, the following C language program statement declares that the variable number is of int integer type, and the initial value of the variable is set to 10. When we assign "apple" to number again, an error will occur, because "apple" is a string, and compilation will fail due to type discrepancy during compilation.

int firstsample = 10

firstsample = "apple"

#Error:

Types do not match

**2. Dynamic types** are compiled without prior type checking, and data types are determined according to variable values during execution. Therefore, there is no need to declare types before variables are used. The same variable can also be given different types of values, and Python is a dynamic type. For example, the following program statement declares the variable number and sets the initial value to the integer 10. When we assign the string apple to number, the type will be automatically converted.

firstsample= 10

firstsample= "love"

Print (firstsample)

# output string love

Python has a Garbage Collection mechanism. When the object is no longer in use, the interpreter will automatically recycle and free up memory space. In the above example, when the integer object number is reassigned to another string object, the original integer object will be deleted by the interpreter. If the object is determined not to be used, we can also delete it by using the "del" command with the following syntax:

del object name

**For example:**

> > number = "apple"

> > > print(number) # output apple

> > > del number # deletes string object number

> > > print(number) #Error: number does not define the execution result.

Since the variable number has been deleted, if the number variable is used again, an undefined error message for the variable will appear.

# Python's Numeric Data Types

Python's numeric data types are integer (int), floating-point number (float), and bool. The usage of these numeric types is explained one by one below.

The integer data type is used to store data without a decimal point, which has the same meaning as mathematics, such as -1, -2, -100, 0, 1, 2, 100, etc.

There are two types of integers in Python 2.x, int (integer) and long (long integer). However, Python has only int integer type after Python 3.x, python's numerical processing ability is quite strong, and basically, there is no limit on the number of bits.

As long as the hardware CPU can support it, even larger integers can be processed. Sometimes, for readability, we can use different numerical systems to represent integer values. For example, the memory address where data is stored is often expressed in hexadecimal. Integers contain positive or negative integers, which can be expressed in binary, hexadecimal or octal in addition to decimal, as long as ob, ox, and oo are added before the numbers respectively to specify the binary system.

Refer to numbers with decimal points, that is, a real number in mathematics. In addition to the conventional representation method of the general decimal point, the scientific notation can also be used to represent it in an exponential form, such as 6e-2, where 6 is the significant number, and -2 is the exponent.

Numbers in computers are stored using IEEE 754 standard specification. Floating-point numbers in IEEE 754 standard cannot accurately represent decimals.

For example, num obtained from num = 0.1+0.2 is not equal to 0.3, but 0.30000000000000004. This is not a problem unique to Python. All programming languages have precision problems with floating-point numbers, so special care must be taken when performing floating-point numbers.

The following two decimal arithmetic methods are provided for readers' reference.

# Decimal Module

This is a Python standard module library. Before using it, you need to import this module with import instruction before using it. After correctly importing this module, we can use the decimal. Decimal class to store accurate numbers. If the parameter is not an integer, we must pass in the parameter as a string.

**For example:**

import decimal

Num = decimal.decimal ("0.1")+decimal.decimal ("0.2")

And the result will be 0.3. Use the round () function to force the specified number of decimal places round(x[, n]) to be a built-in function, which returns the value closest to parameter x, and n is used to specify the number of decimal places returned.

**For example:**

result = 0.1+0.2

The program statement above print (round(num, 1)) takes the variable num to one decimal place, thus obtaining a result of 0.3. 2.2.3 Boolean Data Type (bool) is a data type that represents the logic and is a subclass of int, with only True value (true) and False value (false). Boolean data types are commonly used in program flow control. We can also use the value "1" or "0" to represent true or false values.

For example, the string and integer cannot be directly added, and the string must be converted to an integer. If all the operations are of numeric type, Python will automatically perform type conversion without specifying the forced conversion type.

**For example:**

num = 5+0.3

# Result num=5.3 (floating-point number)

Python will automatically convert an integer to floating-point number for operation. In addition, Boolean values can also be calculated as numeric values. True means 1, False means 0.

**For example:**

num = 5+True

# result num=6 (integer).

If you want to convert strings to Boolean values, you can convert them by bool function. Use the print () function in the following sample program to display Boolean values.

[sample procedure: bool.py]

converts bool type

print(bool(0))

print(bool("") )

```
print(bool(" ") )

print(bool(1) )
```

The execution results of the 05 print(bool("ABC ") sample program are shown. Program Code Resolution: Line 02: An empty string was passed in, so False was returned. Line 03 returns True because a string containing a space is passed in. When using Boolean, it values False and True, pay special attention to the capitalization of the first letter.

## Constant

Constant refers to the value that the program cannot be changed during the whole execution process. For example, integer constants: 45, -36, 10005, 0, etc., or floating-point constants: 0.56, -0.003, 1.234E2, etc. Constants have fixed data types and values.

The biggest difference between variable and constant is that the content of the variable changes with the execution of the program, while the constant is fixed. Python's constant refers to the literal constant, which is the literal meaning of the constant. For example, 12 represents the integer 12. The literal constant is the value written directly into the Python program.

If literal constants are distinguished by data type, there will be different classifications, for example, 1234, 65, 963, and 0 are integer literal constants. The decimal value is the literal constant of the floating-point types, such as 3.14, 0.8467, and 744.084. As for the characters enclosed by single quotation marks (') or double quotation marks ("), they are all string literal constants. For example," Hello World "and" 0932545212 "are all string literal constants.

# Formatting Input and Output Function

In the early stage of learning Python, the program execution results are usually output from the control panel or the data input by the user is obtained from the console. Before, we often use the print () function to output the program's execution results. This section will look at how to call the print () function for print format and how to call the input () function to input data.

**The print format**

The print () function supports the print format. There are two formatting methods that can be used, one is print format in the form of "%" and the other is print format in the form function. "%" print format formatted text can use "%s" to represent a string, "%d" to represent an integer, and "%f" to represent a floating-point number.

**The syntax is as follows:**

PRINT (formatted text (parameter 1, parameter 2, ..., parameter n))

**For example:**

score = 66

Print ("History Score: %d"% score")

**Output**

Result: History Score: 66

%d is formatted, representing the output integer format.

The print format can be used to control the position of the printout so that the output data can be arranged in order.

**For example:**

print("%5s history result: %5.2f"% ("Ram,"95))

The output results of the sample program

print("%5s history results: %5.2f"% ("Raj,"80.2))

The formatted text in the above example has two parameters, so the parameters must be enclosed in brackets, where %5s indicates the position of 5 characters when outputting, and when the actual output is less than 5 characters, a space character will be added to the left of the string.

%5.2f represents a floating-point number with 5 digits output, and the decimal point occupies 2 digits. The following example program outputs the number 100 in floating-point number, octal number, hexadecimal number and binary number format using the print function, respectively.

**You can practice with this example program:**

[Example Procedure: print_%.py]

Integer Output

visual = 100 in Different Decimal Numbers

print ("floating point number of number %s: %5.1f"% (visual,visual))

print ("octal of number %s: %o"% (visual,visual))

print ("hex of number %s: %x"% (visual,visual))

The execution result of the print ("binary of number %s: %s"% (visual,bin(visual))) will be displayed.

**Program code analysis:**

Lines 02-04: output in the format of floating-point number octal number and hexadecimal number.

Line 05: Since binary numbers do not have formatting symbols, decimal numbers can be converted into binary characters through the built-in function bin () and then output.

**2. The output**

Print format of the format () function can also be matched with the format () function. Compared with the% formatting method, the format () function is more flexible. Its usage is as follows: print("{} is a hard-working student ... ."format ("First ranker ")).

Generally, the simple FORMAT usage will be replaced by the braces "{}," which means that the parameters in FORMAT () are used within {}. The format () function is quite flexible and has two major advantages: regardless of the parameter data type, it is always indicated by {}.

Multiple parameters can be used, the same parameter can be output multiple times, and the positions can be different.

For example: print("{0} this year is {1} years old ... ."format ("First ranker ,"18)), where {0} means to use the first parameter, {1} means to use the second parameter, and so on. If the number inside {} is omitted, it will be filled in sequentially.

We can also use the parameter name to replace the corresponding parameter, for example: print("{name} this year {age}.."format(name=" First ranker ,"age=18)) can specify the output format of the parameter by adding a colon":" directly after the number.

**For example:**

print('{0:.2f}'.format(5.5625)) means the first parameter takes 2 decimal places.

In addition, the string can be centered, left-aligned, or right-aligned with the "<" ">" symbol plus the field width.

**For example:**

print("{0:10}

score: {1: _ 10}." format ("Ram," 95))

print("{0:10}

results: {1:>10}."format("Raj," 87))

The output of the print("{0:10} result: {1:*<10}."format("Ram," 100)) program is shown. {1: _ 10} indicates that the output field width is 10, and the following line "_" is filled and centered. {1:>10} indicates that the output field is 10 wide and aligned to the right, and the unspecified padding characters will be filled with spaces. {1:*<10} indicates that the output field is 10 wide, filled with an asterisk "*" and aligned to the left.

**Input Function:**

Input() input is a common input instruction, which allows users to input data from "standard input device" (usually refers to keyboard) and transfer the numerical value, character or string entered by users to the specified variable. For example, if you calculate the total score of history and mathematics for each student, you can use the input command to let the user input the results of Chinese and mathematics, and then calculate the total score.

**The syntax is as follows:**

variable = input (prompt string) when data is Entered, and the enter key is pressed, the entered data will be assigned to the variable.

The "prompt string" in the above syntax is a prompt message informing the user to enter, for example, the user is expected to enter height, and the program then outputs the value of height.

**The program code is as follows:**

height =input ("Give exact your height:")

For example, score = input ("Give exact your math score:")

The output of the print("%s' math score: %5.2f"% ("ram,"float(score)))

When the program is executed, it will wait for the user to input data first when it encounters the input instruction. After the user completes the input and presses the Enter key, it will store the data input by the user into the variable score. The data input by the user is in string format. We can convert the input string into an integer, floating-point number, and bool type through built-in functions such as int (), float (), bool ().

The format specified in the example is floating point number (%5.2f), so call float () function to convert the input score value into floating point number. The next section will introduce more complete data type conversion. If we use an integrated development environment such as Spyder, don't forget to switch the input cursor to Python console before inputting when the program is executed to input prompt information. Let's practice the use of input and output again through the sample program.

[Example Procedure: Format. Py] format.py】

name = input ("Give exact Name:")

che_grade = input ("Give a language score:")

math_grade = input ("Give Math Score:")

print("{0: 10} {1: > 6} {2: > 5}." format ("name," "language," "mathematics"))

The execution results of the 06print ("{0: < 10} {1: > 5} {2: > 7}." format (name, che _ grade, math _ grade)).

**Program Code Analysis:**

Lines 01-03: Require users to enter their names, Chinese scores, and math scores in sequence.

Lines 05 and 06: output the names, Chinese and math headers in sequence, and then output the names and results of the two subjects in the next line.

Data type conversion requires operations between different types in expressions. We can convert data types "temporarily," that is, data types must be forced to be converted.

There are three built-in functions in Python that cast data types.

**1. int ():**

Cast to integer data type

For example: x = "5"

num = 5 + int(x)

Print(dude) # Result: The value of 10 variable x is "5" and is of string type, so int(x) is called first to convert to integer type.

**2. float ():**

Cast to floating point data type

For example: x = "5.3"

dude = 5 + float(x)

Print(dude) # Result: The value of 10.3 variable X is "5.3" and is of string type, so float(x) is first used to convert to floating point type.

**3. str ():**

Cast to string data type

For example: first = "5.3"

dude = 5 + float(first)

Print ("The output value is"+str(dude)) # Result:

The output value is 10.3.

In the above program statement, the string of words "the output value is" in the print () function is a string type, the "+"sign can add two strings, and the variable dude is a floating point type, so the str () function must be called first to convert it into a string.

[sample procedure: conversion.py]

data type conversion

str = "{1}+{0} = {2}"

first = 150

second = "60"

The execution result of 04 print(str.format(first, second, first+int(second))) program

Line 01:

Since B is a string, specify its display format first. Note that the numerical numbering sequence of braces' {}' is {1}, {0}, {2}, so the display sequence of variables A and B is different from the parameter sequence in Format.

Line 04:

First, call int () to convert b to an integer type, and then calculate.

# Hands-on Practice Exercise

-The pocket money bookkeeping butler designed a Python program that can input the pocket money spent seven days a week and output the pocket money spent every day. The sample program illustrates that this program requires the user name to be entered, and then the sum of spending for each day of the week can be entered continuously, and the pocket money spent for each day can be output.

Program code shows that the following is the complete program code of this example program.

[example program: money.py]

pocket money bookkeeping assistant

```
# -*- coding: utf-8 -*-
"""
```

You can enter pocket money spent 7 days a week and output the pocket money spent every day.

```
"""
name = value ("Give name:")
```

working1 = value ("Give the total amount of pocket money for the first working:")

working2 = value ("Give the total amount of pocket money for the next working:")

working3 = value ("Give the total amount of pocket money for the third working:")

working4 = value ("Give the total amount of pocket money for the fourth working:")

working5 = value ("Give the total spending of pocket money for the fifth working:")

working6 = value ("Give the total spending of pocket money for the sixth working:")

working7 = input ("Give the total allowance for the seventh working:")


```
print("{0:<8}{1:^5}{2:^5}{3:^5}{4:^5}{5:^5}{6:^5}{7:^5}." \

format("name,""working1,""working2,""working3," \

"working4,""working5,""working6," \

"working7"))
print("{0:<8}{1:^5}{2:^5}{3:^5}{4:^5}{5:^5}{6:^5}{7:^5}." \

format(name,working1,working2,working3,working4,working5,
working6,working7))
```

```
ave=total/7
```

```
print("total cost: {0:<8} average daily cost {1: 5}." format (total,
ave))
```

With this, we have completed a brief explanation regarding python and its basic concepts that are necessary for understanding traditional programming methodology. In the next chapter, we will discuss in detail about Operators and other moderate level topics that are necessary for a clear understanding of programming.

# Chapter 3: Operators in Python

In this chapter, we will explain about operators in detail. Operators are very necessary for programming knowledge. We will look at about them in detail in the next sections that follow.

**Why are Operators Necessary?**

One of the main characteristics of a computer is that it has strong computing power. It inputs the data obtained from the outside into the computer, carries out operations through programs, and finally outputs the desired results. In this chapter, we will discuss various types and functions of operators in Python and how to use Python to design expressions for arithmetic calculation and logical judgment.

No matter how complex the program is, the ultimate goal is to help us complete all kinds of operations, and the process must rely on one expression to complete. The expression is just like the usual mathematical formula,

For example: first=(second+third)*(first+10)/3.

The above mathematical formula is an expression; the =,+,* and/sign are operators, and variables first, second, three, and constants 10 and 3 are operands. An expression consists of an operator and an operand.

## What are Operands and Operators?

From the following simple expression (which is also a program statement): first = second+5 the above expression contains three operands first, second, and 5, an assignment operator "=," and an addition operator "+." In addition to arithmetic operators, Python also has comparison operators and logical operators applied to conditional judgment expressions.

In addition, there is an assignment operator that assigns the result of the operation to a variable. Operator if there is only one operand, it is called "unary operator," such as "-23" which expresses negative value. When there are two operands, they are called "binary operators." Arithmetic operators such as addition, subtraction, multiplication, and division are called "binary operators," such as 3+7. These various and fully functional operators have different operation priorities. This chapter will introduce the usage of these operators in detail.

## Arithmetic operator

This is the most frequently used operator in programming languages. It is commonly used for some four operations, such as addition operator, subtraction operator, multiplication operator, division operator, remainder operator, division operator, exponent operator, etc. The +, -, *, and/operators are the same as our common mathematical operation methods, while the sign operator is mainly used to represent the positive/negative value of operands.

Usually, the + sign can be omitted when the constant is set to a positive number.

For example, "first=5" and "first=+5" have the same meaning. In particular, we should remind everyone that negative numbers are also represented by the "-" operator. When negative numbers participate in subtraction, in order to avoid confusion with subtraction operators, it is better to separate negative numbers with small brackets "()."

"/"and "//"are both division operators. The operation result of "/"is a floating-point number. The "//"will remove the decimal part of the division calculation result and only takes the integer. The "%" operator is the remainder.

**For example:**

first= 5

second= 2

Print(first/second) # result is floating-point number 2.5

Print(first// second) # result is integer 2

Print(first% second) # Result Is Remainder 1

If the result of the operation is not assigned to other variables, the data type of the operation result will be dominated by the variable whose data type occupies the largest memory space in the operand. In addition, when the operands are integers, and the operation result will produce decimals, Python will automatically output the result as decimals. We do not need to worry about the conversion of data types.

However, if the operation result is to be assigned to a variable, the memory space occupied by the variable must be large enough to prevent the excessively long part of the operation result data from being discarded. For example, if the result of the operation is a floating-point number and is assigned to an integer variable, the decimal part of the operation result will be truncated.

The division "/"operator in the arithmetic operator is a conventional division. The quotient obtained after the operation is a floating-point number. If the quotient is expressed as an integer, the int () function can be called.

Int(15/7) # Output 2 "* *" is a power operation, for example, to calculate the fourth power of 2:

print(7** 4) # The result is 28

Note that the priority of arithmetic operators +, -, *, and/is "multiply and divide first, then add and subtract." The following example illustrates that the operation result of the above formula of 10+2*3 is 16. In the expression, the precedence of parentheses is higher than in multiplication and division.

If the above expression is changed to (10+2)*3, the operation result will be 36. If operators with the same priority are encountered, the operations are performed from left to right. Let's take a look at the application of the simple four operations with an example program.

This sample program allows users to input Celsius temperature and convert it to Fahrenheit temperature through program operation.

The formula for converting Celsius temperature to Fahrenheit temperature is

F=(9/5)*C+32.

[sample procedure: sampletemp.py]

Celsius temperature is converted to Fahrenheit temperature

-*- coding: utf-8 -*-

#converts the input Celsius temperature into Fahrenheit temperature

Tip: F = (9/5) * C+32

Celsius = float( input ("Give the Celsius temperature"))

Fahren = (9 / 5) * Celsius + 32

The execution results of the 08 print ("Celsius temperature {0} is converted to Fahrenheit temperature {1}."format(C,F)) .

**Program Code Resolution:**

Line 02: Let the user input Celsius temperature and call float () function to convert the input into a floating-point data type.

Line 03: Converts the input Celsius temperature to Fahrenheit.

Line 04: Output the conversion between Celsius and Fahrenheit according to the specified format string. Incidentally, the "+" sign can be used to connect two strings.

sample="mno"+"pqrs"

# result sample = "mnopqrs"

**Assignment operator**

The assignment operator "=" consists of at least two operands. Its function is to assign the value to the right of "=" to the variable to the left of the equal sign. Most beginners of many programming languages cannot understand the meaning of the equal sign "=" in programming languages.

It is easy to confuse it with the mathematical equivalent function. In programming languages, the "=" sign is mainly used for assignment, but we understand it from a mathematical point of view, and "=" used to be considered as the concept of "equal."

**For example, the following program statement:**

addition = 0;

addition= addition + 1;

The meaning of addition=0 in the above program statement is also easy to understand, but for the statement addition=addition+1, many beginners often cannot understand the meaning of this statement. In fact, the "=" in Python programming language is mainly used for "assignment."

We can imagine that when a variable is declared, the memory will be allocated, and the memory address will be arranged. Only when the specific value is set to the variable by using the assignment operator "=" will the memory space corresponding to the memory address be allowed to store the specific value.

In other words, addition= addition+1 can be seen as the result of adding 1 to the original data value stored in the sum memory address, and then re-assigning to the memory space corresponding to the sum memory address. The right side of the assignment operator "=" can be a constant, variable or expression, and will eventually assign the value to the variable on the left.

On the left side of the operator can only be variables, not numeric values, functions, expressions, etc. For example, the expression first-second=Third is an illegal program statement.

Python assignment operators have two types of assignment: single assignment and compound assignment.

**1. Single assignment** assigns the value on the right side of the assignment operator "=" to the variable on the left.

For example, the sample1 = 10 assignment operator can assign the same value to multiple variables at the same time, in addition to assigning one value to the variable at a time. If we want multiple variables to have the same variable value at the same time, we can assign variable values together. For example, if you want variables first, second, and third to have values of 100, the assignment statement can be written as follows:

first= second = third = 100 when you want to assign values to multiple variables in the same line of program statements, you can separate variables with ,"." For example, if you want the variable first to have a value of 10, the variable second to have a value of 20, and the variable third to have a value of 30, write the assignment statement as follows: first, second, third = 10, 20, and 30 python also allows ";."

To continuously write several different program statements to separate different expressions.

**For example, the following two lines of program code:**

result= 10

Index = 12 ";"can be used. Write the above two lines on the same line.

Please look at the following demonstration:

result= 10;

Index = 12 # concatenates two program statements or expressions with semicolons in one line

## 2. The compound assignment

The compound assignment operator is formed by combining the assignment operator "=" with other operators. The prerequisite is that the source operand on the right side of "=" must have the same operand as the one receiving the assignment on the left side. If an expression contains multiple compound assignment operators, the operation process must start from the right side and proceed to the left side step by step,

**For example:**

first+= 1 # is equivalent to first = first+1

first-= 1 # is equivalent to first = first-1 with "A+=B;"

For example, a compound assignment statement is an assignment statement "first=first+second;" The simplified writing of is to perform the calculation of first+second first, and then assign the calculation result to the variable first.

In Python, first single equal sign "=" indicates assignment, and two consecutive equal signs "= =" are the "equality" of relational comparison operators and cannot be mixed. Note that when using the assignment operator, if you want to assign one variable to another, the first variable must first set the initial value; otherwise, an error will occur.

For example, result =result*10 because no initial value has been assigned to num variable, if the assignment operator is directly used, an error will occur because result variable has not been set to any initial value.

The following is a sample program for the comprehensive application of assignment operators.

[example program: assigning.py]

# comprehensive application of assignment operator

01 # -*- coding: utf-8 -*-

02 """

03 Assignment application in python

331

```
04 """

05

06 black = 1

07 white = 2

08 red = 3

09

10 green = black+ white * red

11 print("{}."format(black))

12 black += red

13 print("black={0}."format (black, white)) #black=1+3=4

14 black -= white

15 print("black={0}."format(black, white)) #black=4-2=2

16 black *= white

17 print("black={0}."format(black,white)) #black=2*2=4

18 black **= white

19 print("black={0}."format(black,white)) #black=4**2=16

20 black /= white

21 print("black={0}."format(black,white)) #black=16/2=8
```

22 black //= white

23 print("black={0}.”format(black,white)) #black=8//2=4

24 black %= red

25 print("black={0}.”format(black,white)) #black=4%3=1

26 red = "Python"+"fun"

The execution result of the 27 print(s) program will appear.

**Program code analysis:**

Lines 12 and 13: assign the result of adding black and red to variable white, and then output the result value of black.

Lines 14 and 15: assign the result of subtraction between black and white to variable black, and then output the result value of black.

Lines 16 and 17: assign the result of multiplying black and white to variable black, and then output the result value of black.

Lines 18 and 19: assign the result of black and white power to variable black, and then output the result of black.

Lines 20 and 21: assign the result of dividing black and white to variable black, and then output the result value of black.

Lines 22 and 23: assign the result of dividing black and white integers to variable black, and then output the result value of black.

Lines 24 and 25: assign the remainder of black and white to variable black, and then output the result of black.

**Comparison operator**

The comparison operator is also called a relational operator and is used to determine whether the operands on the left and right sides of a conditional expression are equal, greater than or less than. When using relational operators, the results of the operations are either True or False, corresponding to Boolean values of true or false.

If the expression is True, it will get "true"; otherwise, it will get "False." The comparison operator can also be used in series, for example, black<white<=red equals black<red, and white<=red. Note that two consecutive equal signs "= =" are used to indicate the equality relationship, while a single equal sign "=" indicates the assignment operator.

As has been repeatedly stressed above, this gap is easy to cause negligence in writing program code. This is a very popular small "Bug" when debugging programs in the future.

[example program: comparisionsample.py]

# Comprehensive application of comparison operator

```
01 # -*- coding: utf-8 -*-
02 """
03 Comparative Operator Practice
04 """
05 first = 56
06 second = 24
07 third = 38
08 primary = (first == second) # judge whether first equals second
09 secondary = (second! = third) # Judge whether second is not equal to third.
10 tertiary= (first >= third) # judge whether first is greater than or equal to third
11 print('is first equal to second: ',primary) # displays primary
12 print('second is not equal to third: ',secondary) # displays secondary
```

13 print ('whether first is greater than or equal to tertiary: ',tertiary) # displays tertiary.

**Program Code Analysis:**

Line 11:

first=56, second=24, which are not equal, so output False.

Line 12:

second=24, third=38, which are not equal, so the output is True.

Line 13:

first =56, third =38, first>third, so output True.

## Logical operator

Logical Operator (LOGICAL OPERATOR) is used to judge basic logical operations and can control the process of program operation. Logical operators are often used in conjunction with relational operators, and the results of operations are only True and False. Logical operators include and, or, not, etc.

Beginners of programming use a truth table to observe logical operations more clearly. Truth table lists all combinations of operands true (T) and false (F) and the results of logical operations. As long as you understand the working principles of AND, or, and not, plus the aid of truth table, you can be familiar with logical operations quickly without memorizing it.

# 1. Logical and (And)

Logical AND must hold both left and right operands before the operation result is true. When either side is False, the execution result is false. For example, the logical result of the following instruction is true:

first= 10

second= 20

first < second and first ! = second #True Logical and Truth Table

# 2. Logical or (Or)

Logical OR As long as either of the left and right operands holds, the result of the operation is true. For example, the following logical operation is true:

sample = 10

result = 20

sample< result or sample == result #True if the expression sample < result on the left holds, the result of the operation is true, and there is no need to judge the relation comparison expression on the right.

# 3. Logical not (Not)

Logical not is a logical negation with slightly different usage. Only one operand can be operated. It is added to the left of the operand. When the operand is true, the NOT operation result is false. When the operand is false, the not result is true.

For example, the following logic operation result is true:

first= 10

second= 20

Not first<5 #True originally first<5 does not hold (the result is false), adding a not in front of it negates it, so the result is true.

**Next, we use two simple statements to illustrate the use of logical operators:**

value= 24

Result = (value% 6 == 0) and (value% 4 == 0) when using the and operator, result returns True because 24 is divisible by 6 and 4 at the same time.

**Let's look at another example:**

sum= 31

Value = Total% 3 = = or Total% 7 = = 0

When using the or operator, Value returns False because 31 cannot be divided exactly by 3 and 7. In addition, in Python programming language, when logical operations are performed using and or operators, the so-called "Short-Circuit" operation is used.

Let's take the and operator as an example to illustrate that the judging principle of short-circuit operation is that if the first operand returns True, the judgment of the second operation will continue, that is, if the first operand returns False, there is no need to judge further, which can speed up the execution of the program,

**For example:**

print (67>11) and (73>71)

# The first operation result returns True.

In addition, if the short-circuit operation is applied to the or operator, the judgment of the second operand will only proceed when the first operand returns False. However, if the first operand returns True, there is no need to judge further, which can also speed up the execution of the program.

The following example program inputs the results of the two monthly exams and the final exam. As long as one of the monthly exams passes (more than 60 points), the final exam must pass so that the semester's results are considered as passing. Pass is output, otherwise FAIL is output.

[Example Procedure: coursePassOrFail.py]

Progress card python code

```
01 # -*- coding: utf-8 -*-

02 """

03 Enter the results of the two monthly exams and the final exam

04 Only one of the April exams passes, and the final exam passes

The result of the 2005 semester is considered as a PASS. Pass is output 05 PASS; otherwise, output FAIL

06 """

07 firstclass = int(input ("Give your primary monthly test score:"))

08 secondclass = int(input ("Give the result of the secondary monthly exam:"))

09 thirdclass = int(input ("Give the final exam result:"))

11 if (firstclass>=60 or secondclass>=60) and thirdclass>=60:

12- print("PASS")

13 else:
```

14 print("FAIL ")

## Program Code Analysis:

The passing criteria for the title are the following two.

(1) "Only one passes the monthly exam": use logical or to judge.

(2) "Must pass the final exam": use logical and to judge. When an expression uses more than one logical operator, the priority of logical operators must be considered. Logical not will be evaluated first, followed by logical and, and finally logical or.

Two logical operators are used in the sample program: and and or. If the following formula is written directly, the logical AND will be executed first, and the semantics will become that the scores of the second monthly examination and the final examination must be greater than 60 points, and the result of execution will be incorrect. Primary> = 60 or secondclass > = 60 and thirdclass > = 60, so parentheses must be added to force the conditional expression to perform logical or judgment first.

For example, when the sample program is running, the first monthly test score is 90 points, the second monthly test score is 59 points, and the final test score is 80 points. You will get True, so the result will show PASS.

The data actually processed by the bit operator computer at the bottom layer are only 0 and 1, i.e., in binary form. Each bit of binary is also called a bit. Therefore, we can use a bitwise operator to perform logical operations between bits. Bit logic operators are especially used to calculate bit values in integers.

Four-bit logic operators are provided in Python language, namely &, |, and ~. 1.&(AND, bit logic AND operator). When performing AND operation, the corresponding two binary bits are both 1, so the operation result is 1; otherwise, it is 0. For example, if a=12 AND b=38, then a&b will get a result of 4 because the binary representation of 12 is 0000 1100 and the binary representation of 38 is 0010 0110. After performing and operation, the result will be 4 in decimal, as shown

## (XOR, bit logic xor operator)

When performing xor operation, either of the corresponding two binary bits is 1(true), and the operation result is 1(true), but when both are 1(true) or 0(false), the result is 0(false).

For example, if first=12 and second=38, the result obtained by the first second is 42. As shown, when the or operation is performed by 3.| (OR), either of the corresponding two binary bits is 1, and the operation result is 1, that is, the result is 0 only when both bits are 0. For example, if first=12 and second=38, the result obtained by first | second is 46,

## ~ (not)

Not takes the complement of 1, i.e., all binary bits are inverted, i.e., 0 and 1 of all bits are exchanged. For example, first=12, the binary representation is 0000 1100, after the compliment is taken, since all bits of 0 and 1 will be exchanged, the calculated result is -13.

The so-called "compliment" means that when two numbers add up to a certain number (e.g., the decimal is 10), they are said to be complements of the certain number. For example, the 10's complement of 3 is 7, and the 10's complement of 7 is 3. For the binary system, there are two kinds of "1's complement system" and "2's complement system." 1's complement system "refers to the complement of two numbers that are 1 each other if the sum of the two numbers is 1, i.e., the complement of 0 and 1 that are 1 each other.

In other words, in order to obtain the complement of the binary number, one need only change 0 to 1 and 1 to 0. For example, $(111110100101)2$ is complemented by $(10101010101)2$. "2's complement system" must calculate the 1's complement of the number in advance and add 1.

The following example program is an example of the application of bit operators.

[example program: bitwiseapplication.py]

Comprehensive application of bit operators

01 # -*- coding: utf-8 -*-

02 """

Comprehensive Application of 03-bit Operator

04 """

05 first = 12; second = 38

06 bin(first); Bin(second) # Call the bin () function to convert first and second into binary

07 print(first & second) # & operation result is 00000100, and then converted to decimal value

08 print (first second) operation is 10101010, which is then converted into a decimal value.

09 print(first | second) # | the result of the operation is 0101001010, which is then converted into a decimal value.

10 print(~first) # ~ operation is the execution result of the complement program taking

**Program code analysis:**

Line 07:

The binary representation of first=12 is first=00001100, the binary representation of second=38 is second=00100110, and the result of the &bit logic operation is 00000100, which is then converted into a decimal value of 4.

Line 08:

The binary representation of first=12 is first=00001100, the binary representation of second=38 is first = first=00100110, the result of bit logic operation is 00101010, and then the decimal value is 42.

Line 09:

The binary representation of first=12 is first =00001100, the binary representation of second=38 is first = 00100100110, and the result of | bit logic operation is 00101110, which is then converted to a decimal value of 46.

Line 10:

The binary representation of first=12 is first =00001100, and the result of its complement of 2 is 11110011, which is then converted to a decimal value of -13.

**The bit shift operator**

The bit shift operator shifts the binary bits of an integer value left or right by a specified number of bits. Python provides two-bit shift operators, as shown.

345

## 1) < < (left shift operator)

The left shift operator (< <) can shift the operand to the left by n bits. After the left shift, the bits beyond the storage range are discarded, and the bits left blank are supplemented by 0.

The syntax format is as follows: a<<n for example, the expression "12<<2," the binary value of the value 12 is 00001100, and after moving 2 bits to the left, it becomes 00110000, which is 48 decimal.

## 2) > > (right shift operator)

The right shift operator (> >) is the opposite of the left-shift operator, which can shift the operand content right by n bits and truncate the bits beyond the storage range after the right shift. Note the empty bit on the right at this moment. If the value is positive, fill 0 and negative, fill 1.

The syntax format is as follows: a>>n for example, the expression "12>>2," the binary value of the value 12 is 00001100, and after moving 2 bits to the right, it becomes 00000011, that is, 3 in decimal.

a=12 is declared in the program, allowing A and 38 to perform four kinds of bit logic operations and output the operation results. Finally, A is subjected to bit shift operations of left shift and right shift by two bits respectively and output the results.

[example program: bit shift.py]

Comprehensive application of bit operators

```
01 # -*- coding: utf-8 -*-

02 """

Comprehensive Application of 03-bit Operator

04 """

05

06 first=12

07 print ("%f&22.3 =% d"% (first, first&38)) # and operation

08 print ("%f | 22.3 =% d"% (first, first | 22.3)) # or operation

09 print ("%f 22.3 =% d"% (first, first 22.3)) # xor operation

10 print("~%f=%d"%(first,~first)) #NOT operation

11 print("%f<<2=%d" %(first,first<<2)) # shift left

12 print("%f>>2=%d" %(first,first>>2)) # the execution result of
the right shift operation program
```

## Operator Precedence

An expression often contains many operators. Operator precedence determines the sequence of program execution, which has a significant impact on the execution result and should not be taken lightly.

## How to arrange the sequence of operators' execution?

At this time, the operation rules need to be established according to the priority. When an expression uses more than one operator, such as third=first+3*second, the priority of the operator must be considered. This expression will perform 3*second operation first, then add the operation result to first, and finally assign the added result to third. I remember when we were young in math class, the first formula we recited was "multiply and divide first, then add and subtract."

This is the basic concept of priority. When we encounter a Python expression, we first distinguish between operators and operands and then sort them out according to the priority of operators. For example, when there is more than one operator in an expression, the arithmetic operator is executed first, followed by the comparison operator, and finally, the logical operator.

The comparison operators have the same priority and are executed sequentially from left to right, while different arithmetic operators and logical operators have different priorities. The following are the priorities when calculating various operators in Python language.

Finally, consider the combination of operators from left to right, that is, operators with the same priority level will be processed from the leftmost operand. The parenthesis operator has the highest priority. The operation that needs to be executed first is added with the parenthesis "(). The expression in the parenthesis" () "will be executed first.

**For example:**

first = 100 * (90-30+45).

There are 5 operators in the expression above: =, *,-and+, and according to the operator priority rule, the operation in the parenthesis will be executed first with the priority of-,+,*, =.

[Example Program: operatorprecedence.py]

Comprehensive Application of Operator Priority

01 # -*- coding: utf-8 -*-

02 """

 Comprehensive Application of 03 Operator Priority

04 """

05 first = 2; second = 3

06 third = 9*(21/first + (9+first)/second)

07

08 print("first=," first)

09 print("second=," second)

The execution results of the print("9*(4/first +(9+first)/second)=," zthird) will be displayed.

**Hands-on Practice Exercise**

The report card statistics assistant is again time to practice. The theme is to make a report card statistics program. Enter the names of 10 students and their scores in mathematics, English, and Chinese. Calculate the total score and average score and judge which grade belongs to A, B, C, and D according to the average score. 3.8.1 The sample program shows that this time, the students' scores are not inputted one by one, which is too time-consuming.

The author has established the scores.csv file in advance. The file contains the names of 10 students and their scores in mathematics, English, and Chinese. The topic requirements for this exercise are as follows:

(1) Read in a CSV file with the file name scores.csv

(2) Calculate the total score, average score, and grade (A, B, C, D). A: an average of 80 to 100 points b: an average of 60 to 79 points c: an average of 50 to 59 points d: an average of fewer than 50 points

(3) Output the student's name, total score, average score (reserved to one decimal place) and grade. CSV file.

The so-called open data refers to data that can be freely used and distributed. Although some open data require users to identify the data source and the owner, most open platforms for government data can obtain the data free of charge. These open data will be published on the network in common open formats.

If different applications want to exchange data, they must use a common data format. CSV format is one of them. The full name is Comma-Separated Values. Fields are separated by commas and are all plain text files like TXT files. They can be edited by text editors such as Notepad. CSV format is commonly used in spreadsheets and databases.

For example, Excel files can export data to CSV format or import CSV files for editing. Much Open Data on the network will also provide users with directly downloaded CSV format data. When you learn how to process CSV files, you can use these data for more analysis and application.

Python Built-in CSV module can process CSV files very easily. CSV module is a standard library module, which must be imported with import instruction before use. Let's look at the usage of the CSV module. Usage of the CSV module can read CSV file or write to CSV file. Before reading, you must first open the CSV file and then use CSV.reader method to read the contents of the CSV file.

The code is as follows:

[get the module] csv # to load csv.py

With open ("furst.csv," encoding = "utf-8") ascsvfile:

# open file specified as cssvfile

Reader = csv.reader (cssvfile)

# returns reader object

For row in reader:

#for loop reads data row by row

**Tips**

If CSV files and. py files are placed in different folders, the full path of the files must be added. The open () command will open the csvfile and return the file object. The sample program assigns the file object to the CSV file variable. The default file uses unicode encoding.

If the file uses a different encoding, the encoding parameter must be used to set the encoding. The CSV file used in this sample program is in an utf-8 format without BOM, so encoding="utf-8." The csv.reader () function reads the CSV file, converts it into a reader object, and returns it to the caller. The reader object is a string List object that can be an iterator.

In the above program, the reader variable is used to receive the reader object, and then the data is read line by line through the

For loop: getit = csv.reader(csvfile)

 # returns the reader object

For row in reader:

#for loop reads data row by row into row variable list object is Python's Container Type.

Each element can be accessed by using the subscript (index, or index) of the bracketed "[]" collocation element. The subscript starts from 0 and is row[0] and ROW [1] from left to right, respectively. For example, to obtain the value of the 4th element, it can be expressed as follows: name = row[3] trick to open a file using with the statement before reading or writing the file, the file must be opened using the open () function.

When reading or writing is complete, the file must be closed using the close () function to ensure that the data has been correctly read or written to the file. If an exception occurs before calling the close () method, then the close () method will not be called.

**For example:**

f = open("results.csv") # to open the file

Csvfile = f.read() # read file contents

1 / 0 #error

F.close() # The program statement in line 3 of the close file made an error with denominator 0.

Once executed, the program will stop executing, so close () will not be called, which may risk file corruption or data loss. There are two special methods to avoid this problem: one method is to add try ... exception statements to catch errors, and the other method is to use with statements.

Python's with statement is equipped with a special method. After the file is opened, if the program is abnormal, the close () method will be automatically called, so as to ensure that the opened file is closed correctly and safely.

The program code shows that the scores.csv file used in this sample program contains the names of 10 students and their scores in mathematics, English, and Chinese. We need to sum up the scores in the three subjects, calculate the average score, and then use the average score to evaluate the grades.

The first line of the score CSV file is the title and must be skipped. Therefore, we use a variable x to record the currently read line number. The initial value of x is 0, and x must be greater than 0 before the if condition judgment expression is true. The code is as follows:

With open ("results. CSV," encoding = "utf-8") as CSV file:

first= 0 # sets the initial value of first to 0

For row in csv.reader(csvfile):

If first>0: # if first > 0, the if judgment expression is true

...

first+= 1 # is equivalent to indenting different blocks when writing Python programs with first=first+1. The above statement has three blocks, namely with...as block, for-loop block, and if block. The statement of first=0 must be placed outside the for loop, and the statement of first+= 1 must be placed inside the for loop, so that first will accumulate for each loop.

After entering the if block, the scores of the three subjects should be added up. Since the csv.reader function reads in string format, it must be converted into int format before calculation. Then assign the sum result to the variable score.

The score intervals of the four grades are as follows. firstclass: 80 ~ 100 points on average. secondclass: 60 ~ 79 points on average. thirdclass: average 50 ~ 59 points. fourthclass: below 50 on average. An average of 80 to 100 points is rated as "first" and so on, and 80 points are also in this interval. Therefore, the "> =" (greater than or equal to) relational operator must be used. If only average>80 is used to judge, 80 points will not fall in this interval.

The average score of 60 ~ 79 is rated as "second" and so on. This judgment requires two conditions, average>=60 and average<80, and both conditions must be met. Therefore, and must be used to judge: average > = 60 and average < 80. Since these two conditions are a numerical interval, the following expression can be written to indicate that the average value must be within 60 ~ 79. 60 <= average < 80 full if...else statement is as follows:

If average >= 80:

Grade = "first"

elif 60 <= average < 80:

Grade = "second"

elif 50 <= average < 60:

Grade = "third"

Else:

Grade = "Fail"

At last, you only need to output the scoreTotal, average, and grade with a print statement, and the execution result is displayed.

**The following is the complete program code:**

[sample procedure: Review_scores.py] transcript statistics assistant

01 # -*- coding: utf-8 -*-

02 """

03 Program Name: Report Card Assistant

04 Topic Requirements:

05 import CSV file

06 List the sum, average score and grade (first, second, third, fail)

07 first: average 80~100 points

08 second: average 60-79 points

09 third: average 50-59 points

10 fail: below 50 on average

```
11 """

12 import csv

14 print ("{0: < 3} {1: < 5} {2: < 4} {3: < 5} {4: < 5}." format
(","""name," "total score," "average score," "grade"))

15 with open("results.csv,"encoding="utf-8") as csvfile:

16 first = 0

17 for row in csv.reader(csvfile):

19 if first > 0:

20 scoreTotal = int(row[1]) + int(row[2]) + int(row[3])

21 indent = circle(scoreTotal / 3, 1)

23 if indent >= 80:

24 grade = "first"

25 elif 60 <= indent< 80:

26 grade = "second"

27 elif 50 <= indent < 60:

28 grade = "third"

29 else:

30 grade = "fail"
```

32        print("{0:<3}{1:<5}{2:<5}{3:<6}{4:<5}."format(first, row[0], scoreTotal, average, grade))

34 result += 1

By this, we have completed a brief explanation about operators in detail. Operators are important to master programming languages because they can be used to create complex programs and software. The next chapter deals with various advanced programming concepts like loops and conditionals. We will discuss about these topics in detail. Why are you waiting? Let us explore the next chapters.

# Chapter 4: Conditional and Loops in Python

This chapter describes moderate level topics like conditionals and loops in detail. We will use different examples to explain these topics in detail. Let us dive into knowing more about these concepts.

### What is a sequence in Python?

The sequence of program execution is not a highway linking the north and the south. It can run all the way from the north to the south to the end. In fact, the sequence of program execution may be as complicated as a highway on the busy area, with nine turns and 18 turns, which is easy to make people dizzy.

In order to write a good program, it is very important to control the process of program execution. Therefore, it is necessary to use the process control structure of the program. Without them, it is absolutely impossible to use the program to complete any complicated work. In this chapter, we will discuss Python's various process control structures.

The programming language has been continuously developed for decades. Structured Programming has gradually become the mainstream of program development. Its main idea is to execute the entire program in sequence from top to bottom. Python language is mainly executed from top to bottom according to the sequence of program source code, but sometimes the execution sequence will be changed according to needs.

At this time, the computer can be told which sequence to execute the program preferentially through flow control instructions. The process control of the program is like designing a traffic direction extending in all directions for the highway system.

It is recognized that most program codes for process control are executed in sequence from top to bottom line after line, but for operations with high repeatability, it is not suitable to execute in sequence. Any Python program, no matter how complex its structure is, can be expressed or described using three basic control processes: sequence structure, selection structure, and loop structure.

The first line statement of the sequence structure program is the entry point and is executed from top to bottom to the last line statement of the program. The selection structure allows the program to select the program block to be executed according to whether the test condition is established or not. If the condition is True, some program statements are executed. If the condition is False, other program statements are executed.

In a colloquial way, if you encounter a situation A, perform operation A; if this is case b, operation b is executed. Just like when we drive to the intersection and see the signal lamp, the red light will stop, and the green light will pass. In addition, different destinations also have different directions, and you can choose the route according to different situations. In other words, the selection structure represents that the program will determine the "direction" of the program according to the specified conditions.

The function of loop flow control with loop structure is to repeatedly execute the program statements in a program block until the specific ending conditions are met. Python has a for loop and a while loop.

## Selection Process Control

Selection Process Control is a conditional control statement that contains a conditional judgment expression (also referred to as conditional expression or conditional judgment expression for short). If the result of the conditional judgment expression is True (true), a program block is executed. If the result of the conditional judgment expression is false (True), another program block is executed.

The following describes the statements and their functions related to the selection process control in Python language.

## If...Else Conditional Statement

If...else conditional statement is a fairly common and practical statement. If the conditional judgment expression is True (true, or represented by 1), the program statement in the if program block is executed. If the conditional judgment expression is not true (False, or represented by 0), the program statement in the else program block is executed. If there are multiple judgments, elif instruction can be added.

**The syntax of the if conditional statement is as follows:**

If conditional judgment expression:

# If the conditional judgment expression holds, execute the program statement in this program block

Else :

# If the condition does not hold, execute the program statement in this program block. If we want to judge whether the value of variable a is greater than or equal to the value of variable b, the condition judgment expression can be written as follows:

If a >= b:


# If A is greater than or equal to B, execute the program statement in this program block

Else :

# If a "no" is greater than or equal to b, the program statement if ... if...else conditional statement in this program block is executed.

In the use of the if ... else conditional statement, if the condition is not satisfied, there is no need to execute any program statement, and the else part can be omitted:

If conditional judgment expression:

# If the condition is satisfied, execute the program statements in this program block. In addition, if the if ... if...else conditional statement uses logical operators such as and or, it is suggested to add parentheses to distinguish the execution order so as to improve the readability of the program,

For example: if (a==c) and (a>b):

# If A equals C and A is greater than B, execute the program statement in this program block

Else :

# If the above condition does not hold, the program statement in this program block is executed.

In addition, Python language provides a more concise conditional expression of if...else in the following format: X if C else Y returns one of the two expressions according to the conditional judgment expression. In the above expression, X is returned when C is true; otherwise, Y is returned.

For example, to determine whether the integer x is odd or even, the original program would be written as follows:

If (first % 2)==0:

second= "even number"

Else:

second= "odd number"

If print('{0}'.format(second)) is changed to a concise form, only a single line of program statements is required to achieve the same purpose.

**The statements are as follows:**

print('{0}'.format ("even" if (first% 2)==0 else "odd"))

If the if condition determines that the expression is true, it returns "even"; otherwise, it returns "odd." In the following sample program, we will practice the use of the if … if...else statement. The purpose of the sample program is to make a simple leap year judgment program.

Let the user enter the year (4-digit integer year), and the program will determine whether it is a leap year. One of the following two conditions is a leap year: (1) leap every 4 years (divisible by 4) but not every 100 years (divisible by 100).

(2) leap every 400 years (divisible by 400).

[example procedure: leapYear.py]

judge whether it is a leap year

```
01 # -*- coding: utf-8 -*-

02 """

03 program name: leap year judging program

04 Topic Requirements:

05 Enter the year (4-digit integer year) to determine whether it
is a leap year

06 condition 1. Every 4 leap (divisible by 4) and every 100 leap
(divisible by 100)

07 condition 2. Every 400 leap (divisible by 400)

08 One of the two conditions met is a leap year.

09 """

10 year = int(input ("Give year:"))

12 if (year % 4 == 0 and year % 100 ! = 0) or (year % 400 == 0):
```

13 print("{0} is a leap year ."format(year))

14 Else:

The execution results of the

15 print("{0} is the year of peace ."format(year))

**Program Code Resolution:**

Line 10: Enter a year, but remember to call the int () function to convert it to an integer type.

Line 12-15: Judge whether it is a leap year.

Condition 1: every 4 leaps (divisible by 4) and every 100 leaps (not divisible by 100).

Condition 2: every 400 leaps (divisible by 400). One of the two conditions is a leap year. Readers are asked to inquire whether the following years are leap years: 1900 (flat year), 1996 (leap year), 2004 (leap year), 2017 (flat year), 2400 (leap year).

**Multiple Choices**

If there is more than one conditional judgment expression, elif conditional statement can be added. Elif is like the abbreviation of "else if." Although using multiple if conditional statements can solve the problem of executing different program blocks under various conditions, it is still not simple enough. Then, elif conditional statement can be used, and the readability of the program can be improved.

Note that if the statement is a logical "necessity" in our program. Elif and else do not necessarily follow, so there are three situations: if, if/else, if/elif/else.

**The format is as follows:**

If condition judgment

Expression 1:

# If the conditional judgment expression 1 holds, the program statement in this program block is executed

Elif condition judgment

Expression 2:

# If the conditional judgment expression 2 holds, execute the program statement in this program block

Else :

# If none of the above conditions hold, execute the program statement in this program block,

**For example:**

If first==second:

# If first equals second, execute the program statement in this program block

Elif first>b :

# If first is greater than second, execute the program statement in this program block

Else :

# if first is not equal to second and first is less than second, execute the program statement in this program block. The following example program is used to practice the use of IF multiple selection. The purpose of the sample program is to detect the current time to decide which greeting to use.

[sample procedure: currentTime.py]

Detects the current time to decide which greeting

01 # -*- coding: utf-8 -*-

02 """

03 Program Name: Detect the current time to decide which greeting to use

04 Topic Requirements:

05 Judging from the current time (24-hour system)

06 5~10:59, output "good morning"

369

07 11~17:59, output "good afternoon"

08 18~4:59, output "good night"

09 """

11 import time

13 print ("current time: {}." format (time.strftime ("%h:% m:% s"))

14 h = int( time.strftime("%H") )

16 if h>5 and h < 11:

17 print ("good morning!" )

18 elif h >= 11 and h<18:

19 print ("good afternoon!" )

20 else:

21 print ("good night!")

The execution results of the program will be shown on the screen.

The output shows the current time in the sample program to judge whether it is morning, afternoon, or evening, and then displays the appropriate greeting. Python's time module provides various functions related to time. The Time module is a module in Python's standard module library.

Before using it, you need to use the import instruction to import and then call the strftime function to format the time into the format we want. For example, the following program statement is used to obtain the current time.

Import time

Time.strftime ("%h:% m:% s")

 # 18: 36: 16 (6:36:16 p.m. 24-hour)

Time. strftime ("%i:% m:% s")

# 06:36:16 (6: 36: 16 p.m. 12-hour system) format parameters to be set are enclosed in parentheses.

Pay attention to the case of format symbols. The following program statement is used to display the week, month, day, hour, minute, and second.

Print (time.strftime ("%a,% b% d% h:% m:% s")) execution results are as follows: Monday, sep17 15: 49: 29 4.2.3 nested if sometimes there is another layer of if conditional statement in the if conditional statement. This multi-layer selection structure is called nested if conditional statement.

Usually, when demonstrating the use of nested if conditional statements, it is more common to demonstrate multiple choices with numerical ranges or scores. In other words, different grades of certificates will be issued for different grades of achievements.

If it is more than 60 points, the first certificate of competency will be given, if it is more than 70 points, the second certificate of competency will be given, if it is more than 80 points, the third certificate of competency will be given, if it is more than 90 points, the fourth certificate of competency will be given, if it is more than 100 points, the all-round professional certificate of competency will be given.

**Based on nested if statements, we can write the following program:**

Available= int(input ("Give a score:")

If available >= 60:

Print ('First Certificate of Conformity')

If available >= 70:

Print ('Second Certificate of Conformity')

If available >= 80:

Print ('Third Certificate of Conformity')

If available >= 90:

Print ('Fourth Certificate of Conformity')

If getScore == 100:

Print ('All-round Professional Qualification Certificate') is actually an if statement that is explored layer by layer. We can use the if/elif statement to filter the multiple choices one by one according to conditional expression operation and select the matching condition (True) to execute the program statement in a program block.

**The syntax is as follows:**

If Conditional Expression 1:

The program block to be executed in accordance with conditional expression 1

Elif conditional expression 2:

The program block to be executed in accordance with conditional expression 2

Elif conditional expression n:

The program block to be executed according to the conditional expression n

Else:

If all the conditional expressions do not conform, this program block is executed. When the conditional expression 1 does not conform, the program block searches down to the finally conforming conditional expression.

The elif instruction is an abbreviation of else if. Elif statement can generate multiple statements according to the operation of a conditional expression, and its conditional expression must be followed by a colon, which indicates that the following program blocks meet this conditional expression and need to be indented.

The following example program is a typical example of the combined use of nested if and if/elif statements. This program uses if to determine which grade the query results belong to. In addition, another judgment has been added to the sample program. If the score integer value entered is not between 0 and 100, a prompt message of "input error, the number entered must be between 0 and 100" will be output.

Comprehensive use of nested if statements example:

01 # -*- coding: utf-8 -*-

02 """

03 Examples of Comprehensive Use of Nested if Statements

04 """

05 result = int(input ('Give final grade:')

06

07 # First Level if/else Statement: Judge whether the result entered is between 0 and 100

08 if result >= 0 and result <= 100:

09 # 2nd level if/elif/else statement

10 if result <60:

11 print('{0} below cannot obtain certificate of competency'. format(result))

12 elif result >= 60 and result <70:

13 print('{0} result is d'. format(result))

14 elif result >= 70 and result <80:

15 print('{0} result is c'. format(result))

16 elif result >= 80 and result <90:

17 print('{0} result is level b'. format(result))

18 else:

19 print('{0} result is grade a'. format(result))

20 else:

The execution results of the

21 print ('input error, input number must be between 0-100')

**Program code analysis:**

Lines 7-21: first-level if/else statement, used to judge whether the input result is between 0 and 100.

Lines 10-19: the second-level if/elif/else statement, which is used to judge which grade the inquired result belongs to.

In the next section, we will discuss loops one of the most important concepts.

## The Loop Repeat Structure

This mainly refers to the loop control structure. A certain program statement is repeatedly executed according to the set conditions, and the loop will not jump out until the condition judgment is not established. In short, repetitive structures are used to design program blocks that need to be executed repeatedly, that is, to make program code conform to the spirit of structured design.

For example, if you want the computer to calculate the value of 1+2+3+4+...+10, you don't need us to accumulate from 1 to 10 in the program code, which is originally tedious and repetitive, and you can easily achieve the goal by using the loop control structure. Python contains a while loop and a for loop, and the related usage is described below.

## While loop

If the number of loops to be executed is determined, then using the for loop statement is the best choice. However, the while loop is more suitable for certain cycles that cannot be determined. The while loop statement is similar to the for loop statement and belongs to the pre-test loop. The working mode of the pre-test loop is that the loop condition judgment expression must be checked at the beginning of the loop program block.

When the judgment expression result is true, the program statements in the loop block will be executed. We usually call the program statements in the loop block the loop body. While loop also uses a conditional expression to judge whether it is true or false to control the loop flow. When the conditional expression is true, the program statement in the loop will be executed. When the conditional expression is false, the program flow will jump out of the loop.

**The format of the While loop statement is as follows:**

While conditional expression:

# If the conditional expression holds, the flow chart of executing the while loop statement in this program block.

The while loop must include the initial value of the control variable and the expression for increasing or decreasing. When writing the loop program, it must check whether the condition for leaving the loop exists. If the condition does not exist, the loop body will be continuously executed without stopping, resulting in "infinite loop," also called "dead loop."

**The loop structure usually requires three conditions:**

(1) The initial value of the loop variable.

(2) Cyclic conditional expression.

(3) Adjust the increase or decrease the value of cyclic variables.

**For example, the following procedure:**

first=1

While first < 10: # Loop Condition Expression

print( first)

first += 1 # adjusts the increase or decrease value of the loop variable.

When first is less than 10, the program statement in the while loop will be executed, and then first will be added with 1 until first is equal to 10. If the result of the conditional expression is False, it will jump out of the loop.

**For loop**

For loop, also known as count loop, is a loop form commonly used in programming. It can repeatedly execute a fixed number of loops. If the number of loop executions required is known to be fixed when designing the program, then the for-loop statement is the best choice. The for loop in Python language can be used to traverse elements or table items of any sequence. The sequence can be tuples, lists or strings, which are executed in sequence.

**The syntax is as follows:**

 For element variable in sequence:

# Executed instructions

Else:

The program block of #else can be added or not added, that is, when using the for loop, the else statement can be added or not added. The meaning represented by the above Python syntax is that the for loop traverses all elements in a sequence, such as a string or a list, in the order of the elements in the current sequence (item, or table item).

For example, the following x variable values can all be used as traversal sequence elements of a

For loop:

first= "abcdefghijklmnopqrstuvwxyz "

second= ['january', 'march', 'may', 'july', 'august',

'october', 'december']

result= [a, e, 3, 4, 5, j, 7, 8, 9, 10]

In addition, if you want to calculate the number of times a loop is executed, you must set the initial value of the loop, the ending condition, and the increase or decrease value of the loop variable for each loop executed in the for-loop control statement. For loop every round, if the increase or decrease value is not specifically specified, it will automatically accumulate 1 until the condition is met.

For example, the following statement is a tuple (11 ~ 15) and uses the for loop to print out the numeric elements in the tuple: x = [11, 12, 13, 14, 15]

For first in x:

A more efficient way to write tuples is to call the range () function directly. The format of the range () function is as follows: range([initial value], final value [,increase or decrease value]) tuples start from "initial value" to the previous number of "final value." If no initial value is specified, the default value is 0; if no increase or decrease value is specified, the default increment is 1.

An example of calling the range () function is as follows: range (3) means that starting from the subscript value of 0, 3 elements are output, i.e., 0, 1 and 2 are three elements in total.

Range(1,6) means starting from subscript value 1 and ending before subscript value 6-1, that is, subscript number 6 is not included, i.e., 1, 2, 3, 4 and 5 are five elements. ·range (4,10,2) means starting from subscript value 4 and ending before subscript number 10, that is, subscript number 10 is excluded, and the increment value is 2, i.e., 4, 6 and 8 are three elements. The following program code demonstrates the use of the range () function in a for loop to output even numbers between 2 and 11 for i in range (2, 11, 2).

One more thing to pay special attention to when using the for loop is the print () function. If the print () is indented, it means that the operation to be executed in the for loop will be output according to the number of times the loop is executed. If there is no indentation, it means it is not in the for loop, and only the final result will be output.

We know that calling the range () function with the for loop can not only carry out accumulation operations but also carry out more varied accumulation operations with the parameters of the range () function. For example, add up all multiples of 5 within a certain range. The following sample program will demonstrate how to use the for loop to accumulate multiples of 5 within a range of numbers.

[Example Procedure: addition.py]

Accumulate multiples of 5 in a certain numerical range

```
01 # -*- coding: utf-8 -*-

02 """

03 Accumulate multiples of 5 within a certain numerical range

04 """

05 addition = 0 # stores the accumulated result

06

07 # enters for/in loop

08 for count in range(0, 21, 5):

09 addition += count # adds up the values

11 print('5 times cumulative result =',addition)

# Output cumulative result
```

**Program code analysis:**

Lines 08 and 09: Add up the numbers 5, 10, 15 and 20. In addition, when executing a for loop, if you want to know the subscript value of an element, you can call Python's built-in enumerate function. The syntax format of the call is as follows: for subscript value, element variable in enumerate (sequence element).

For example (refer to sample program enumerate. py):

names = ["ram," "raju," "ravi"]

for index, x in enumerate(names):

The execution result of the above statement in print ("{0}-{1}." format (index, x)) is displayed.

**Nested loop**

Next, we will introduce a for nested loop, that is, multiple for loop structures. In the nested for loop structure, the execution process must wait for the inner loop to complete before continuing to execute the outer loop layer by layer.

The double nested for loop structure format is as follows:

For example, a table can be easily completed using a double nested for loop. Let's take a look at how to use the double nested for loop to make the nine tables through the following sample program.

[Example Procedure: 99Table.py]

99 Table

01 # -*- coding: utf-8 -*-

02 """

03 Program Name: Table

04 """

05

06 for x in range(6,68 ):

07 for y in range(1, 9):

08 print("{0}*{1}={52: ^2}."format(y, x, x * y), end=" ")

99 is a very classic example of nested loops. If readers have learned other programming languages, I believe they will be amazed at the brevity of Python. From this example program, we can clearly understand how nested loops work. Hereinafter, the outer layer for the loop is referred to as the x loop, and the inner layer for loop is referred to as the y loop.

When entering the x loop, x=1. When the y loop is executed from 1 to 9, it will return to the x loop to continue execution. The print statement in the y loop will not wrap. The print () statement in the outer x loop will not wrap until the y loop is executed and leaves the y loop. After the execution is completed, the first row of nine tables will be obtained. When all X cycles are completed, the table is completed.

Note that the common mistake for beginners is that the sentences of the inner and outer loops are staggered. In the structure of multiple nested loops, the inner and outer loops cannot be staggered; otherwise, errors will be caused.

The continue instruction and break instruction are the two loop statements we introduced before. Under normal circumstances, the while loop is to judge the condition of the loop before entering the loop body. If the condition is not satisfied, it will leave the loop, while for loop ends the execution of the loop after all the specified elements are fetched. However, the loop can also be interrupted by continue or break. The main purpose of break instruction is to jump out of the current loop body, just like its English meaning, break means "interrupt."

If you want to leave the current loop body under the specified conditions in the loop body, you need to use the break instruction, whose function is to jump off the current for or while loop body and give the control of program execution to the next line of program statements outside the loop body. In other words, the break instruction is used to interrupt the execution of the current loop and jump directly out of the current loop.

**Break**

If a nested loop is encountered, the break instruction will only jump off the loop body of its own layer, and will be used together with the if statement,

**For example:**

For first in range (1, 10):

If first == 5:

Break

Print( first, end= "")

When first is equal to 5, the break statement will be executed to leave the for loop body, that is, the for loop will not continue to execute.

If we hope that a certain loop program can be executed continuously, and we will not leave the loop until a certain condition is met, we can use the break instruction at this time. If we want to design a game of guessing numbers, we require the user to enter a number between 1 and 100.

If the input is wrong, we will inform the user that the input number is too large or too small, and let the user repeat the input until the input number is exactly the same as the original default answer.

At this time, we can use the break command to jump off the loop and output the correct answer or the information such as the end of the game.

**Look at the following program code:**

number=9

while True:

Guess = int(input ('enter a number between 1 and 100->'))

if guess == number:

Print ('you guessed it, the number is:', number)

Break

## Continue instruction

The function of the continue instruction is to force loop statements such as for or while to end the program currently executing in the loop and transfer control of program execution to the beginning of the next loop. In other words, if the continue instruction is encountered during the execution of the loop, the current round of loop will be immediately interrupted, all the program statements that have not yet been executed in the subsequent round of loop will be abandoned, and the program flow will be returned to the beginning of the while or for loop to start the next round of loop.

In contrast, the break instruction will end and jump off the current loop body, while the continue instruction will only end the current loop and will not jump off the current loop,

## For example:

for first in range(1, 10):

if first == 5:

continue

When first is equal to 5, the continue instruction is executed, and the program will not continue to execute, so 5 is not printed by the print statement, and the for loop will continue to execute.

## Practical Exercises

This section will use a sample program to review the above-mentioned related contents and make a simple password verification program. Example program shows that writing a Python program can allow users to enter passwords and perform simple password verification, but the number of entries is limited to three and login is not allowed if the current password is 5656.

## 1. Input Description

When entering for the first time, we can deliberately enter the wrong password, and the program will output "Wrong password!" and ask the user to enter the password again. We can try to enter the wrong password again, and we will also output "Wrong password!" If you enter the wrong password more than three times in a row, you will no longer be allowed to continue entering the password to log in, and you will be asked to enter "password error for three times, cancel login!" If the password entered in the input process is correct, the "correct password" will be output and ends the execution of the program.

## Program Code Description

The complete program code is listed below. The default password for the password is the number 5656, and the variable I is used to record the total number of inputs. If the number of inputs exceeds three, it will jump out of the loop.

[sample procedure: password.py]

simple password verification procedure

```
01 # -*- coding: utf-8 -*-

02 """

03 let users enter passwords,

04 and perform simple password verification

05 However, the number of entries is limited to three. If the number exceeds three, login is not allowed.

06 If the current password is 5656.

07 """

08

09 password=5656 # uses the password variable to store passwords for verification.

10 first=1

12 while first<=3: # the number of inputs is limited to three
```

```
13 new_pw=int(input ("Give password:"))

14 if new_pw ! = password: # if the password entered is
different from the password

15 print ("wrong password! ! ! ")

16 first=first+1

17 continue # Jumps Back to while Start

18 else:

19 print ("correct password! ! ! ")

20 break

21 if first>3:

22 print ("password error 3 times, cancel login! ! ! \n");
```

# Password Error Handling

With this, we have completed the moderate concepts like conditionals and loops that are very pivotal for the development of programs. In the next chapter, we will discuss modules and functions that are important for the application and software development. Python supports both function-oriented and object-oriented paradigms. We will discuss everything python offers for advanced programmers in detail in the next chapters.

# Chapter 5: Modules and Functions in Python

This chapter will introduce the concepts of modules and functions in Python. Structured programming can decompose complex problems into several components and define and implement modules and functions for the components. This chapter will discuss in detail the features of Python modules and functions. Finally, Python's functional programming will be introduced.

## Python Program Structure

Python's program consists of a package, a module, and functions. A module is a set that deals with a certain class of problems. A module consists of functions and classes. A package is a collection of modules.

A package is a toolbox for specific tasks. Python provides many useful toolkits, such as string processing, graphical user interface, Web application, graphical image processing, etc. Using these toolkits can improve the development efficiency of programmers, reduce the complexity of programming, and achieve the effect of code reuse.

These self-contained toolkits and modules are installed in the Lib subdirectory under Python's installation directory.

For example, for the xml folder in the Lib directory, an xml folder is a package that is used to complete XML application development. There are several sub-packages in the xml package: dom, sax, etree, and parsers. The file __init__.py is the registration file of the xml package, without which Python will not recognize the xml package. The xml package is defined in the system dictionary table available on internet websites.

Note that the package must contain at least one __init__.py file. The contents of the __init__.py file can be empty, which is used to identify the current folder as a package.

Modules are important concepts in Python. Python programs are composed of modules one by one. I've already touched on modules, and a Python file is a module. The following will introduce the concept and characteristics of the module.

**Module Creation**

A module organizes a set of related functions or codes into a file. A file is a module. Modules consist of code, functions, or classes. To create a file named myModule.py, a module named myModule is defined. Define a function func () and a class MyClass in the myModule module. A method myFunc () is defined in the MyClass class.

```
01 # custom module

02 def func():

03 print ("MyModule.func()")

04

05 class example:

06 def examplefun(self):

07 print ("MyModule.example.examplefun()")
```

Then create a file called _ myModule.py in the directory where mymodule.py resides. The functions and classes of the myModule module are called in this file.

```
01 # Calls Classes and Functions of Custom Modules

02 import myexample # import module

03

04 myexample.func()

05 myClass=myexample.MyClass()

06 myClass.myFunc()
```

**[Code Description]**

Line 2

Code Import Module myexample.

Line 4

This calls the examples' function. You need to prefix myexample when calling; otherwise, Python does not know the namespace where function() is located.

**Output results:**

myexample.func()

Line 5

This code creates an instance of the class Myexample. You also need to call the class with the prefix myexample.

Line 6

This calls the method myexample() of the class.

**Output results:**

myexample.Myexampleclass.myexample()

Note that myModule.py and call_myModule.py must be placed in the same directory or in the directory listed in sys.path; otherwise, Python interpreter cannot find the customized module.

When Python imports a module, Python first looks for the current path, then the lib directory, site-packages directory (Python\Lib\site-packages) and the directory set by the environment variable PYTHONPATH. If the imported module is not found, search the above path to see if it contains this module. You can search the module's search path through the sys.path statement.

## Module Import

Before using a module's function or class, you must first import the module. The module import has been used many times before, and the module import uses the import statement.

The format of the module import statement is as follows.

import nameofthemodule

This statement can be directly imported into a module. When calling a function or class of a module, you need to prefix it with the module name in the following format.

nameofthemodule.func()

If you do not want to use prefixes in your program, you can import them using the from...import... statement. The format of the from...import... the statement is as follows.

from nameofthemodule import nameofthefunction

This compares the difference between the import statement and the from ... import ... statement. Importing all classes and functions under the module can use import statements in the following format.

from nameofthemodule import *

In addition, the same module file supports multiple import statements. For example, define a module named myexample. The module defines a global variable count and a function (). Every time the function () is called, the value of the variable count is incremented by 1.

01 number =1

02

03 def function ():

04 global number

05 number=number+1

06 return the number

Import myexample module several times to see the result of variable count.

01 import myexample

02 print("count =," myexample.func())

03 myexample.count=10

04 print ("count =," myexample.count)

05

06 import myexample

07 print ("count =," myexample.func())

## [Code Description]

Line 1

Code Import Module myexample.

The second line of code calls the function () in the module. At this time, the value of the variable count is equal to 2.

Output result:

number=2.

The third line of code assigns a value to the variable count in the module myexample, where the value of the variable count is equal to 10.

The fourth line of code gets the value of the variable count.

Output result:

number=10.

The code in line 6 is imported into module myexample again, and the initial value of variable count is 10.

The seventh line of code calls function(), and the value of variable count is increased by 1.

Output result:

number =11.

Import statements in Python are more flexible than those in Java. Python's import statement can be placed anywhere in the program or even in conditional statements.

**Add the following statement after the above code segment:**

01 # import placed in the conditional statement

02 if myexample.number> 1:

03 myexample.number=1

04 else:

05 import myexample

06 print ("count =," myexample.number)

**[Code Description]**

The second line of code judges whether the value of myexample.number is greater than 1.

Line 3 code, if the value of count is greater than 1, set the value of variable count to 1. Since the value of the variable count in the preceding code segment is 11, the value of the variable count is assigned to 1.

Line 5 code, if the value of count is less than or equal to 1, import statement.

The sixth line of code outputs the value of the variable count. Output Result: count=1

**Properties of Modules**

Modules have some built-in attributes that are used to complete specific tasks, such as ___name___, ___doc___. Each module has a name; for example, ___name___ is used to determine whether the current module is the entry of the program. If the current program is in use, ___name___ has a value of "___main___." Usually, a conditional statement is added to each module to test the function of the module separately.

For example, create a module myexample.

01 if ___name___ =='___main___':

02 print ('myexample runs as main program')

03 else:

04 print ('myexample Called by Another Module')

## [Code Description]

The first line of code determines whether this module is running as the main program. Run the module myexample separately, and the output results are as follows. Myexample runs as the main program.

Create another module myexample. This module is very simple, just import module myexample.

01 import myexample

02 print (__doc__)

## [Code Description]

Run the module myexample and output the result:

Myexample is called by another module. The second line of code calls another module attribute __doc__. Since the module does not define a document string, the output result is None.

## Output Result:

None

## Built-in Functions of Modules

Python provides an inline module build-in. The inline module defines some functions that are often used in development. These functions can be used to realize data type conversion, data calculation, sequence processing, and other functions.

The functions commonly used in inline modules will be described below.

## 1. apply()

The apply function has been removed from Python3, so it is no longer available. The function of calling the variable parameter list can only be realized by adding * before the list.

## 2. filter()

Filter () can filter a sequence to determine whether the result returned by the parameters of the custom function is true or not

Filter and return the processing results at one time.

**The declaration of filter () is as follows.**

class filter(object)

filter(function or None, iterable) --> filter object

The following code demonstrates the function of the filter () filter sequence.

Filters out numbers greater than 0 from a given list.

```
01 def func(x):

02 if first> 0:

03 return first

04

05 print (filter (function, range (-39,10))) # calls the filter
function and returns the filter object

06 print (list (filter (function, range (-94,10))) # converts filter
object to list
```

**[Code Description]**

In line 5, use range () to generate the list to be processed, and then transfer the values of the list to func (). Func returns the result to filter () and finally returns the resulting yield as an iterable object, which can be traversed.

**The output is as follows:**

<filter object at 0x1022b2750>

Note that the parameter of the filter function func () in filter () cannot be empty. Otherwise, there is no variable that can store the sequence element, and func () cannot handle filtering.

## 3. reduce()

Continuous operations on elements in a sequence can be handled through loops. For example, to accumulate elements in a sequence. Python's reduce () can also implement continuous processing. In Python2, reduce () exists in global space and can be called directly. In Python3, it is moved to the functools module, so it needs to be introduced before use. The declaration of reduce () is as follows.

reduce(function, sequence[, initial]) -> result

## [Code Description]

Parameter function is a self-defined function, which implements continuous operation of the parameter sequence in function function().Parameter initial can be omitted. If the initial is not empty, the value of initial will be passed into function() for calculation first. If the sequence is empty, the value of initial is processed.

The return value of reduce () is the calculated result of func ().

The following code implements the accumulation of numbers in a list.

01 def addition(first, second):

02 return first+second

03 form functools import reduce

# Introduce reduce

04 print (reduce(addition, range(0, 10)))

05 print (reduce(addition, range(0, 10), 10))

06 print (reduce(addition, range(0, 0), 10))

## [Code Description]

The first line of code defines an addition () function, which provides two parameters and performs an accumulation operation.

Line 4 code, perform accumulation calculation on 0+1+2+3+4+5+6+7+8+9. The output is 45.

Line 5 code, perform accumulation calculation on 10+0+1+2+3+4+5+6+7+8+9. The output is 55.

In line 6, because range(0, 0) returns an empty list, the return result is 10.

The output is 10.

Reduce () can also perform complex cumulative calculations such as multiplication and factorial on numbers. Note that if you use reduce () for cumulative calculation, two parameters must be defined in sum to correspond to the operands on both sides of the addition operator.

## 4. map()

Map () is used to "unpack" tuple, and the first parameter of map () is set to None when calling. Map () is very powerful and can perform the same operation on each element of multiple sequences and return a map object. The declaration of map () is as follows.

class map(object)

map(func, *iterables) --> map object

## [Code Description]

The parameter function is a custom function that implements the operation on each element of the sequence. The parameter iterables is a sequence to be processed, and the number of parameters iterables can be multiple.

The return value of map () is the processed list of sequence elements.

The following code implements the exponentiation of the numbers in the list.

01 def power(first): return first ** first

02 print (map (power, range (1,5))) # print map object

03 print (list (map (power, range (1,5))) # converted to list output

04 def power2(first, second): return first ** second

05 print (map (power2, range (1,5), range (5,1,-1))) # print map object

06 print (list (map (power2, range (1,5), range (5,1,-1))) # converted to list output

**[Code Description]**

The first line of code defines a power () function, which implements the power operation of numbers.

The second line of code passes the numbers 1, 2, 3 and 4 into the function power, in turn, converts the calculation result yield into an iterable object, and outputs the result:

map object at 0x7675678>

The third line of code converts the map object into a list and prints it out, and outputs the result:

[1, 4, 27, 256]

The fourth line of code defines a power2 () function to calculate the Y power of X.

The fifth line of code provides two list parameters. 1 5, 2 4, 3 3 and 4 2 are calculated in turn, and the calculated results yield into an iterable object. Output results:

<map object at 0x19876543234560>

Line 6 converts the map object into a list output.

**Output results:**

[21, 16, 29, 26]

Note that if multiple sequences are provided in map (), the elements in each sequence are calculated one by one. If the length of each sequence is not the same, then the short sequence is supplemented with None before calculation.

**Custom Packages**

A package is one that contains at least __init__.py files . Folders Python package and Java package have the same function, both of which are to realize the reuse of programs. They combine the code that realizes a common function into a package and call the services provided by the package to realize reuse. For example, define a package parent. Create two sub-packages pack and pack2 in the parent package.

A module myModule is defined in the pack package, and a module myModule2 is defined in the pack2 package. Finally, define a module main in package parent and call sub-packages pack and pack2.

**The __init__.py program for the package pack is as follows:**

01 if __name__ =='__main__':

02 print ('run as first program')

03 else:

04 print ('pack initialization')

This code initializes the pack package and directly outputs a string. When the pack package is called by other modules, "pack initialization" will be output. The myexample module of the package pack is shown below.

01 def function():

02 print ("pack.myexample.func()")

03

04 if __name__ =='__main__':

05 print ('myexample runs as first program')

06 else:

07 print ('myexample Called by Another Module')

When pack2 is called by other modules, the __init__.py file will be executed first. The __init__.py program for pack2 is as follows.

```
01 if __name__ =='__main__':
02 print ('run as first program')
03 else:
04 print ('pack2 initialization')
```

The myModule2 modules of pack2 are as follows.

```
01 def func2():
02 print ("pack2.myexample2.func()")
03
04 if __name__ =='__main__':
05 print ('myexample2 runs as main program')
06 else:
07 print ('myexample2 called by another module')
```

The main module below calls the functions in pack and pack2 packages.

```
01 from pack import myexample
```

02 from pack2 import myexample2

03

04 myexample.func()

05 myexample2.func2()

**[Code Description]**

The first line of code imports the myexample module from the pack package. The myexample module is called by the main module, so the output string "myexample is called by another module."

**The output is as follows:**

Pack initialization

Myexample is called by another module. The second line of code imports the myexample2 module from the pack2 package.

**The output is as follows:**

Pack2 initialization

Myexample2 is called by another module. The fourth line of code calls function() of myexample module.

**The output is as follows:**

pack.myexample.func()

Line 5 calls func2 () of myexample2 module.

**The output is as follows:**

pack2.myexample2.function()

__init__.py can also be used to provide a list of modules for the current package. For example, add a line of code before the __init__.py file of the pack.

__all__=["myexample"]

__all__ is used to record the modules contained in the current pack. The contents in square brackets are the list of module names. If the number of modules exceeds 2, separate them with commas. Similarly, a similar line of code was added to the pack2 package.

__all__=["myexample2"]

In this way, all modules in pack and pack2 can be imported in the main module at one time.

**The modified main module is as follows:**

01 from pack import *

02 from pack2 import *

03 myexample.func()

05 myexample2.func2()

## [Code Description]

Line 1 code, first execute the __init__.py file of the pack and then look for the modules contained in the pack in the __all__ attribute. If the __init__.py file of the pack does not use the __all__ attribute to record the module name, the main module will not recognize the myexample module when it is called.

Python will prompt the following error.

NameError: name 'myexample' is not defined.

Line 2 code has the same function as line 1 code.

## Function

A function is a piece of code that can be called repeatedly and returns the desired result by entering the parameter value. The previous example has used Python's built-in functions many times and has also customized some functions. Python's functions have many new features, which will be described one by one below.

## Definition of function

A function definition is very simple, using the keyword def definition. Functions must be defined before use, and the type of function is the type of return value. Python functions are defined in the following format.

01 def function name (parameter 1, parameter 2 ...):

02 ...

03 return expression

The function name can be a string of letters, numbers, or underscores, but cannot begin with a number. The parameters of the function are placed in a pair of parentheses. The number of parameters can be one or more. The parameters are separated by commas. Such parameters are called formal parameters.

The parenthesis ends with a colon, and the body of the function follows the colon. It uses a dictionary to implement a switch statement. Now wrap this code into a function. It involves three parameters: two operands and an operator.

The modified code is as follows.

01 # Function

02 from __future__ import division

03 def calculation (first, second, operator):

04 result={

05 "+":first+second,

06 "-":first-second,

07 "*":first * second,

08 "/":first / second

09 }

## [Code Description]

The third line of code defines the function calculation(); the first and second are the two operands of the four operations, and the operator is the operator. The values of these three parameters are passed from the actual parameters.

Lines 4 to 9 are the main body of the function, realizing the operation of operands.

## Call of function

01 # Function

02 print (calculation(1, 2, "+"))

## [Code Description]

calculation () is written after the print statement and directly outputs the return value of the function. The output is "3."

Note that the actual parameters must correspond to the formal parameters one by one, otherwise erroneous calculations will occur — exceptions to parameters with default values.

## Parameters of function

In C and C++, there are two ways to pass parameters: value passing and reference passing. Anything in Python is an object, so parameters only support the way references are passed. Python binds the value of the actual parameter to the name of the formal parameter through a name binding mechanism. That is, the formal parameter is passed to the local namespace where the function is located, and the formal parameter and the actual parameter point to the same storage space in memory In between.

The parameters of the function support default values. When a parameter does not pass an actual value, the function uses the default parameter calculation. For example, you can provide a default value for all parameters of calculation ().

Default Parameter for functions

01 # Function

02 def calculation(first=1, second=1, operator="+"):

03 result = {

04 "+" : first+second,

05 "-" : first-second,

06 "*" : first * second,

```
07 "/" : first / second

08 }

09 return result.get(operator)
```

# returns the calculation result

```
11 print (calculation(1, 2))

12 print (calculation(1, 2, "-"))

13 print (calculation(first=3, operator="-"))

14 print (calculation(second=4, operator="-"))

15 print (calculation(second=3, first=4, operator="-"))
```

**[Code Description]**

The code in line 2 defines the default value of the parameter by using an assignment expression.

In line 11, the values of parameters x and y are assigned to 1 and 2 respectively, and the default value "+" is used for parameter operator. The output is "3."

Line 12 provides 3 actual parameters, which will override the default values of formal parameters, respectively. The output result is "-1."

Line 13 code, specify the values of parameters y and operator. The output result is "-2." The parameters must be passed in the form of assignment expressions. Otherwise, the Python interpreter will mistakenly assume x=3, y="- ." Therefore, the following wording is wrong.

print(calculation(3, "-"))

Line 14 code, specify the values of parameters x and operator. The output is "3."

Line 15 code, using assignment expression to pass parameters, can reverse the order of the parameter list. The output is "1."

Parameters can be variables or built-in data structures such as tuples and lists.

01 # list is passed as a parameter

02 def calculation(args=[], operator="+"):

03 first = args[0]

04 second = args[1]

05 result = {

06 "+" : first+second,

07 "-" : first-second,

08 "*" : first * second,

```
09 "/" : first/ second

10 }

12 print(calculation([1, 2]))
```

**[Code Description]**

The second line of code combines the parameters x and y into one parameter and passes the values of x and y through the args list.

Lines 3 and 4 of code, take out parameter values from the list and assign them to variables x and y respectively. Line 12 code, pass the list [1,2] to calculation (). The output is "3."

Because parameters implement the mechanism of name binding, unexpected results may occur when using default parameters.

```
01 def join(args=[]):

02 args.join(0)

03 print (args)

04

05 join()

06 join([1])
```

07 join()

## [Code Description]

The first line of code defines a join () function, and the argument is a default list.

The second line of code joins an element 0 to the list.

Line 5 calls join (), using the default list. The output is' [0]'.

Line 6 code, passed a list [1], join () is joined with an element 0. The output is "[1, 0]."

The seventh line of code calls join () again, and the list used at this time is args called for the first time, so args will add another element 0 on the original basis.

The output is' [0, 0]'.

To avoid this problem, a conditional judgment statement can be added to join (). If there are no elements in the list args, empty the args list before adding elements.

01 def join(args=[]):

02 if len(args) <=0:

03 args=[]

04 args.join(0)

05 print (args)

06

07 join()

08 join([1])

09 join()

## [Code Description]

The second line of code uses len () to determine whether the length of the list args is greater than 0. If less than or equal to 0, args is set to an empty list, i.e., function parameters are unbound.

Line 4 adds an element 0 to the list.

Line 7 calls join (), using the default list. The output is' [0]'.

In line 8, a list [1] is passed, and an element 0 is joined to join (). The output is "[1, 0]."

The 9th line of code calls join (), which cancels the name binding of the parameter through the judgment of len(args). The output is' [0]'. In development, it is often necessary to pass variable-length parameters.

This requirement can be met by using the identifier "*" before the parameter of the function. "*" can refer to tuples and combine multiple parameters into one tuple.

01 # Pass Variable Parameters

02 def function(*args):

03 print args

04 function(1, 2, 3)

**[Code Description]**

Line 2 code, use identifier "*" before argument args.

The code in line 3 outputs the value of the parameter. Because the parameter uses the form of "*args," the actual parameter passed in is "packed" into a tuple, and the output result is "(1, 2, 3)."

The fourth line of code calls the function func (). The parameters "1," "2" and "3" become elements of args tuples.

Python also provides another identifier "* *." Add "* *" before the formal parameter to refer to a dictionary and generate the dictionary according to the assignment expression of the actual parameter. For example, the following code implements matching tuple elements in a dictionary.

When defining a function, two parameters are designed: one is the tuple to be matched, which is denoted as "* t"; the other is a dictionary, which means "*d." When the function is called, the actual parameters are divided into two parts: one part is several numbers or strings, and the other part is assignment expression.

```
01 # Pass Variable Parameters
02 def find(*one, **two):
03 keys = one.keys()
04 values = two.values()
05 print(keys)
06 print (values)
07 for arg in t:
08 for key in keys:
09 if arg == key:
10 print ("find:,"d[key])
12 find("one," "three," one="1,"two="2,"three="3")
```

**[Code Description]**

"*t" in line 2 corresponds to "one" and "three" in line 12. "One" and "three" form a tuple t. "**d" corresponds to "one="1," two="2," three="3"," generating a dictionary {one: "1,"two:"2,"three: "3"}.

**Line 5 code output results:**

['three', 'two', 'one']

**Line 6 code output results:**

['3', '2', '1']

Lines 7 to 10 look up the value in tuple t in dictionary d. If found, output.

find: 1

find: 3

Note that "*" must be written before "* *," which is a grammatical rule.

### Return value of function

The return of a function uses a return statement, which can be followed by a variable or expression. Let's perfect calculation () and add a return statement.

The code is as follows:

01 from __future__ import division

02 def calculation(first, second, operator):

```
03 result={

04 "+":first+second,

05 "-":first-second,

06 "*":first * second,

07 "/":first / second

08 }

09 return result.get(operator)

# returns the calculation result
```

## [Code Description]

Line 9 calls the dictionary's get (), obtains the corresponding expression, and returns the calculated result.

For C and Java, if the function body is not returned by return statement, but the function is called in the assignment statement, the program will have errors after compilation. Python does not have this syntax restriction. Even if a function does not return a value, it can still get the return value.

## For example:

```
01 # function without return statement returns None

02 def function():
```

03 pass

04

05 print (function())

**[Code Description]**

The second line of code defines a function (), the main body of the function does not have any implementation code, and pass keyword is equivalent to a placeholder.

The fifth line of code outputs the return value of function (). Because there is no return statement, the return value is None. The output is "None."

None is an object in Python and does not belong to numbers or strings. When the return statement in the function does not take any parameters, the returned result is also None.

01 def function ():

02 return

03

04 print (function ())

If you need to return multiple values, you can "package" these values into tuples. When calling, unpack the returned tuple. The following code implements the inversion of input variables.

For example, enter 0, 1, and 2 and return 2, 1, and 0.

```
01 # return returns multiple values

02 def function(first, second, third):

03 l=[first, second, third]

04 l.reverse()

05 numbers=tuple(l)

06 return numbers

07

08 first, second, third=func(0, 1, 2)

09 print (first, second, third)
```

**[Code Description]**

The second line of code defines a function (), which returns the 3 values after inverting the 3 parameters passed in. The third line of code "packages" the three parameters into a list. Line 4 code inversion list. The fifth line of code loads the list into a tuple. The sixth line of code returns tuples, that is, 3 numbers.

The 8th line of code calls function () to obtain the returned tuple and "unpack" it into 3 variables. The ninth line of code outputs the values of the three variables.

A slight improvement in the code can also lead to a second solution.

```
01 def function(one, two, three):
02 l=[one, two, three]
03 l.reverse()
04 one, two, three=tuple(l)
05 return one, two, three
06
07 one, two, three =function(0, 1, 2)
08 print (one, two, three)
```

**[Code Description]**

The fourth line of code "unpacks" tuples and assigns the inverted values to variables A, B and C respectively. In line 5, you can return multiple values with comma-separated expressions after the return.

Line 7 calls func (), assigning a, b and c to x, y and z respectively.

You can use more than one return statement in a function. For example, in each branch of the if ... else ... statement, different results are returned.

# Multiple return Statements

```
02 def function(one):
03 if one> 0:
04 return "one> 0"
05 elif one ==0:
06 return "one ==0"
07 else:
08 return "one<0"
09
10 print (function(-2))
```

**[Code Description]**

Return "one> 0" when the passed-in parameter is greater than 0. When the passed-in parameter is equal to 0, "one = = 0" is returned. When the passed-in parameter is less than 0, return "one<0."

Note that multiple return statements are not recommended. Too many return statements often complicate the program, so the code needs to be refactored.

If there is more than one return statement in the program, you can reduce the return statement by adding a variable.

## Reconstruction of function

```
01 # Multiple return Statements

02 def function(one):

03 if one> 0:

04 result="one> 0"

05 elif one ==0:

06 result="one ==0"

07 else:

08 result="one<0"

09 return result

11 print (func(-2))
```

## [Code Description]

In lines 4, 6 and 8, a variable result is added to record the status of program branches through assignment statements. The ninth line of code returns the value of result, so that the result of each branch can be returned by calling the same return statement.

## Nesting of functions

Nesting of functions refers to calling other functions inside a function. C and C++ only allow nesting within function bodies, while Python not only supports nesting within function bodies but also supports nesting of function definitions. For example, calculate the value of expression (one+two)*(first-second). The calculation step can be divided into three steps: first, calculate the expression one+two, then calculate the expression first-second, and finally calculate the product of the results of the first two steps. Therefore, the three functions can be designed. The first function sum () calculates the value of one+two, the second function sub () calculates the value of m+n, and the third function calculates the product of the first two.

The following code demonstrates the calling operation between functions.

```
01 # nested function

02 def sum(add, sub):

03 return add+sub

04 def sub(add, sub):

05 return add-sub

06 def function():

07 ex=1
```

```
08 ey=2

09 em=3

10 en=4

11 return sum(ex, ey) * sub(em, en)

13 print (function())
```

## [Code Description]

The second line of code defines the function sum (), sum () with two parameters a and b. Parameters a and b are used to calculate the value of expression x+y.

The code in line 3 calculates the value of a+b, that is, returns the result of X+Y.

The fourth line of code defines the function sub (), sub () with two parameters a and b.

The code in line 5 calculates the value of a−b, i.e., returns the result of m−n.

The 11th line of code calls sum (), sub (), and performs multiplication in the return statement.

Line 13 code, call function function ().

**The output is shown below:**

-3

Note that the number of nesting levels of functions should not be too high. Otherwise, it is easy to cause problems such as poor readability and difficult maintenance of the code. Nested calls to general functions should be controlled within 3 levels.

The above code can also be implemented in another form, i.e., the functions sum () and sub () are placed inside func ().

The following code implements the definition of sum (), sub () inside function ().

01 # nested function

02 def function():

03 ex=1

04 yov=2

05 men=3

06 nod=4

07 def sum(am, bam): # internal function

08 return am+bam

09 def sub(am, bam): # internal function

10 return am-bam

11 return sum(ex, yov) * sub(am, bn)

13 print (function())

**[Code Description]**

In line 7, sum () is defined inside function ().

Line 9 code defines sub () inside function ().

Line 11 code, call sum () and sub () and then perform multiplication. The output is "-3."

Internal functions sum (), sub () can also directly call variables defined by external function function ().

The following code implements the variables of the internal function sum (), sub () that refer to the external function function ().

01 # nested function, directly using the variable

02 def function () of the outer function:

03 first= 1

04 second = 2

05 third = 3

06 fourth = 4

07 def sum(): # internal function

08 return first + second

09 def sub(): # internal function

10 return third - fourth

11 return sum() * sub()

13 print (function())

**[Code Description]**

In line 7, the function sum () has no parameters.

Line 8 code calls external variables x, y inside sum ().

In line 9, the function sub () also has no arguments.

Line 10 code calls external variables m, n inside sub ().

Line 11 code, calculate the value of sum()*sub (). The output result is "-3"

Be careful not to define functions inside them.

This method is not easy to maintain the program, and it is easy to cause logical confusion. Moreover, the more levels of nested definition functions, the higher the cost of program maintenance.

## Recursive functions

Recursive functions can call themselves directly or indirectly within the function body, that is, the nesting of functions is the function itself. Recursion is a program design method. Recursion can reduce repeated codes and make the program concise. The process of recursion is divided into two stages-recursion and regression. The principle of the recursive function is as follows.

In the first stage, recursive functions call themselves internally. Each function call restarts executing the code of the function until a certain level of the recursive program ends.

In the second stage, recursive functions return from back to forth. Recursive functions return from the last level until they are returned to the function body called for the first time. That is, after the recursion step-by-step call is completed, it returns step-by-step in the reverse order.

Note that recursive functions need to write conditions for recursion to end; otherwise, the recursive program will not end. Generally, the program is ended by judging the statement.

Calculating factorial is a classical recursive implementation. First of all, review the calculation formula of factorial.

For example, calculate 5! As a result when designing a program, one can judge whether n is equal to 1. Each recursive call passes in parameter n-1. Until n=1, returns 1! is equal to 1. Then return to 2!、3!、4!、5!

## Process of calculating factorials using recursion

The following code recursively implements the factorial calculation process.

01 # Calculates factorial

02 def refund(n):

03 one = 1

04 if second > 1: # end judgment of recursion

05 one = n

06 true = true * refund(n-1) # recursion

07 print ("%d! =" %i, n)

08 return n # return

09

10 refund(5)

## [Code Description]

The second line of code defines a recursive function. The definition of a recursive function is no different from that of an

436

ordinary function. The third line of code defines a variable I for the output of the print statement.

Line 4 code is used to judge the passed parameter n. If n is greater than 1, the function can continue recursion. Otherwise, the result of the current calculation is returned.

The fifth line of code assigns the value of n to I and uses I to record the current recursive number.

Line 6 calls function refunc () itself, passing parameter n-1. The seventh line of code outputs the result of the factorial calculation.

The eighth line of code returns the calculation result of factorial of each level.

Line 10 calls the recursive function refund.

**The output of each recursion is as follows:**

1! =1

2! =2

3! =6

4! =24

5! =120

Note that every time a recursive function is called, all variables in the function will be copied before the recursive function is executed. The program needs more storage space, which will affect the performance of the program to some extent. Therefore, it is better to use other methods to improve programs that do not need recursion.

You can use the aforementioned reduce () to quickly implement factorial operations.

01 # Calculates factorial with reduce

02 from func tools import reduce # python3 reduce is no longer in the global, must be manually introduced

03 print ("5! =," reduce(lambda x, y: x * y, range(1, 6)))

Using reduce () requires only one line of code to calculate 5!.

**Lambda function**

Lambda function is used to create an anonymous function whose name is not bound to the identifier. Using lambda function can return some simple operation results.

Lambda functions have the following format:

Lambda variable 1, variable 2 ...: expression

Among them, the variable list is used for expression calculation. Lambda belongs to a function, so a colon is required after the variable list. Lambda is usually assigned to a variable, which can be used as a function.

**For example:**

01 # assignment

02 function=lambda variable 1, variable 2 ...: expression

# Call

04 function()

This binds lambda and variable function, whose name is the function name. Lambda function can eliminate internal functions.

For example, the program for calculating (one+two) * (three−nfour) in subsection can be modified to replace the functions sum (), sub () with lambda functions.

01 # lambda

02 def func():

03 one = 1

04 two = 2

05 three= 3

06 four = 4

07 sum = lambda one, two : one + two

08 print (sum)

09 sub = lambda three, four : three - four

10 print (sub)

11 return sum(one, two) * sub(three, four)

13 print (function())

## [Code description]

Line 7 defines the lambda function, realizes the calculation expression first+second, and assigns the lambda function to the variable sum.

The eighth line of code outputs the value of the variable sum, which holds the address of the lambda function.

## The output is shown below:

<function <lambda> at 0x00B4D3B0>

Lines 9 and 10 have the same function as lines 7 and 8.

Line 11 calculates the product of sum () and sub (). The output is "-3."

Note that lambda is also called an expression. Only expressions can be used in lambda, and multiple statements such as judgment and loop cannot be used. In the previous example, lambda is assigned to a variable and can also be used directly as a function.

Function usage of lambda

01 # lambda

02 print ((lambda first: -first)(-2))

## [Code Description]

The code in line 2 defines the anonymous function lambda x: -x, which is used to return the absolute value of a number. The parameter of the function is -2, and the output result is "2."

By this, we have discussed in detail about functions and modules that are important for software development using python. We will, in the next chapter, discuss about object-oriented concepts in detail.

# Chapter 6: Object-oriented Programming in Python

This chapter will describe object-oriented concepts in python in detail with examples. This is important for a better understanding of the robustness of the python language and the opportunities it gives. We will go through concepts like classes and objects in detail. Let us dive into it in a detailed mode.

**What Is Object-Oriented Programming?**

Object-oriented technology is an important technology in the field of software engineering. This kind of software development idea naturally simulates human's understanding of the objective world and has become the mainstream of computer software engineering at present.

Python, as an object-oriented computer programming language, it is very important to master the idea of object-oriented programming. Therefore, we have arranged two chapters to explain it. We hope that through the study of these two chapters, everyone can establish the idea of object-oriented programming and learn to use this idea to develop programs.

## Overview of Object-Oriented Programming

There are various forms of things in the real world, and there are various connections between these things. In the program, objects are used to map real things, and the relationships between objects are used to describe the relationships between things. This idea is object-oriented.

When we talk about object-oriented, we naturally think of process-oriented. Process-oriented is to analyze the steps to solve the problem, and then use functions to implement these steps one by one, one by one when using.

Object-oriented is to decompose the problem-solving things into multiple objects, and the purpose of establishing objects is not to complete one step by one but to describe the behavior of one thing in the process of solving the whole problem. The following is an example of gobang to illustrate the difference between process-oriented and object-oriented programming.

First, use process-oriented:

1. Start the game.

2. Sunspots go first

3. Draw the picture

4. Judging winning or losing

5. It's Bai Zi's turn

6. Draw the picture

7. Judging winning or losing

8. Return to Step 2

9. Output Final Results

The above steps are implemented by functions, respectively, and the problem is solved.

Object-oriented design is to solve the problem from another way of thinking. When using object-oriented thinking to realize gobang, the whole gobang can be divided into three types of objects, as follows.

1. Black and white parties: the two parties behave the same

2. Chessboard system: responsible for drawing pictures

3. Rule system: responsible for judging such things as foul, winning or losing, etc.

Among the above three-class objects, the first-class object (black and white parties) is responsible for receiving the user's input and notifying the second-class object (chessboard system) to draw pieces on the chessboard, while the third-class object (rule system) judges the chessboard.

Object-oriented ensures the unity of functions, thus making the code easier to maintain. For example, if we want to add the function of regret chess now, then a series of steps of input, judgment, and display needs to be changed, even the loops between steps need to be adjusted on a large scale, which is obviously very troublesome.

If object-oriented development is used, only the chessboard object needs to be changed. The chessboard object saves the chessboard scores of both black and white parties, only needs simple backtracking, and the display and rules do not need to be changed. At the same time, the calling sequence of the whole object function will not change, and its changes are only partial. Thus, compared with process-oriented, object-oriented programming is more convenient for later code maintenance and function expansion.

## Categories and Objects

In object-oriented programming, the two most important core concepts are class and object. Objects are concrete things in real life. They can be seen and touched. For example, the book you are holding is an object.

Compared with objects, classes are abstract, which is a general designation for a group of things with the same characteristics and behaviors. For example, when I was a child, my mother said to you, "Son, you should take that kind of person as an example!" The type of people here refers to a group of people who have excellent academic results and are polite. They have the same characteristics, so they are called "type" people.

## Relationship between class and object

As the saying goes, "people are grouped by category, and things are grouped by group," we collectively refer to the collection of things with similar characteristics and behaviors as categories, such as animals, airplanes, etc. Class is an abstract description of a certain kind of thing, while the object is an individual of this kind of thing in reality.

## Relationship between classes and objects

The toy model can be regarded as a class and each toy as an object. Thus, the relationship between the toy model and the toy can be regarded as the relationship between the class and the object. Class is used to describe the common features of multiple objects and is a template for objects. The object is used to describe individuals in reality. It is an instance of a class. As can be seen from the examples, objects are created according to classes, and one class can correspond to multiple objects.

## Definition of category

In daily life, to describe a kind of thing, it is necessary to explain its characteristics as well as its uses. For example, when describing such things as human beings, it is usually necessary to give a definition or name to such things. Human characteristics include height, weight, sex, occupation, etc. Human behaviors include running, speaking, etc.

The combination of human characteristics and behaviors can completely describe human beings. The design idea of an object-oriented program is based on this design, which includes the features and behaviors of things in classes. Among them, the characteristics of things are taken as the attributes of classes, the behaviors of things are taken as the methods of classes, and objects are an instance of classes.

So, to create an object, you need to define a class first. Class is composed of 3 parts.

(1) Class Name: The name of the class, whose initial letter must be uppercase, such as Person.

(2) Attributes: used to describe the characteristics of things, such as people's names, ages, etc.

(3) Method: Used to describe the behavior of things; for example, people have behaviors such as talking and smiling.

In Python, you can use the class keyword to declare a class with the following basic syntax format:

Class classname:

The property of the class

Method of class

**The following is a sample code:**

class Ox:

# attribute

# Method

```
    def eat(grass):
```

Print ("-eating grass--")

In the above example, the class is used to define a class named Ox, in which there is an eat method. As can be seen from the example, the format of the method is the same as that of the function. The main difference is that the method must explicitly declare a self-parameter and be located at the beginning of the parameter list. Self represents the instance of the class (object) itself, which can be used to refer to the attributes and methods of the object. The specific usage of self will be introduced later with practical application.

## Creating objects from classes

If a program wants to complete specific functions, classes alone are not enough, and instance objects need to be created according to classes. In Python programs, you can use the following syntax to create an object:

Object Name = ClassName ()

For example, create an object Ox of Ox class with the following sample code:

Ox= Ox()

In the above code, Ox is actually a variable that can be used to access the properties and methods of the class. To add attributes to an object, you can:

Object Name. New Attribute Name = Value. For example, use cat to add the color attribute to an object of Cat class.

**The sample code is as follows:**

Ox.color = "white"

Next, a complete case is used to demonstrate how to create objects, add attributes, and call methods.

Example helicopter.py

```
1 # Define Class

2   class Helicopter:

3 # move

4     def fly(autom):

5         print (" Helicopter Running ..."
```

```
6 # honking

7     def toot(autom):

8         print ("the plane is honking ... beeping ...")
```

9 # creates an object and saves its reference with the variable JB23

```
10 Jb23 = Flight()
```

11 # Add Attribute Representing Color

```
12 JB23.color = "black"
```

13 # Call Method

```
14 JB23.move()
```

```
15 JB23.toot()
```

16 # Access Attributes

```
17 print(JB23.color)
```

In the example, a Plane class is defined, two methods move, and toot are defined in the class, then an object JB23 of Plane class is created, color attribute is dynamically added and assigned to "black," then move () and toot () methods are called in turn, and the value of color attribute is printed out.

Structural Methods and Destructural Methods

In Python programs, two special methods are provided: __init__ () and __del__ (), which are respectively used to initialize the properties of the object and release the resources occupied by the class. This section mainly introduces these two methods in detail.

## Construction method

In the case of a section, we dynamically added the color attribute to the objects referenced by JB23. Just imagine, if you create another Plane class object, you need to add attributes in the form of "object name.attribute name." For each object you create, you need to add attributes once, which is obviously very troublesome.

To solve this problem, attributes can be set when creating an object. Python provides a construction method with a fixed name of __init__ (two underscores begin and two underscores end). When creating an instance of a class, the system will automatically call the constructor to initialize the class.

In order to make everyone better understand, the following is a case to demonstrate how to use the construction method for initialization.

# to define the class

2　class Plane:

3 # construction method

4     def __init__(autom):

Color = "black"

6 # honking

7     def toot(autom):

8 print ("%s plane is honking ..." (autom.color))

9 # creates an object and saves its reference with the variable plane

10 plane = Plane()

No.11 plane honked

12 plane.toot()

These lines re-implemented the __init__ () method, adding the color attribute to the Plane class and assigning it a value of "black," and accessing the value of the color attribute in the toot method.

## Operation results

No matter how many Plane objects are created, the initial value of the color attribute is "black" by default. If you want to modify the default value of the property after the object is created, you can set the value of the property by passing parameters in the construction method. The following is a case to demonstrate how to use the construction method with parameters, as shown.

Example uses the parametric construction method. py

1 # Define Class

2   class Plane:

3 # belt parameter construction method

4     def __init__(autom, color):

Color = color6 # honking

7     def toot(autom):

8 print ("%s color plane honking ..." %autom.color)

9 # creates an object and saves its reference with the variable JB23

10 JB23 = Plane ("Snow White")

11 # creates an object and saves its reference with variable ferrari

12 ferrari = Plane ("red")

No.13 plane honked

14 JB23.toot()

15 ferrari.toot()

In examples, lines 4 to 5 customize the construction method with parameters and assign the value of the parameters to the color attribute to ensure that the value of the color attribute changes with the value received by the parameters, and then it is still accessed in the toot method.

## Destructural methods

Earlier, we introduced the __init__ () method. When an object is created, the Python interpreter will call the __init__ () method by default. When deleting an object to release the resources occupied by the class, the Python interpreter calls another method by default, which is the __del__ () method.

Next, a case is used to demonstrate how to use destructor to release the occupied resources, as shown.

Example uses the destructor. py

```python
# Define Class

class Person:

    def __init__(autom, name, age):

        autom.name = name

        autom.love = love

    def __del__(autom):
```

Print ("-del----") laowang = person ("Lao Wang," 30)

In the example, a class named Person is defined, the initial values of name and age are set in the __init__ () method, a print statement is added in the __del__ () method, and then an object of the Person class is created using a custom construction method.

Thus we have given a brief introduction to object-oriented programming in this chapter. In the next chapter, we will discuss Files in python in detail. Come along with us to enjoy the final chapter of this book.

# Chapter 7: Files in Python

This chapter will give a brief introduction to files in python. We will have various examples that will help us understand the files, their structure, and implementation.

## What are Files in Python?

The data can be stored using either a database or a file. The database maintains the integrity and relevance of the data and makes the data safer and more reliable. Using files to store data is very simple and easy to use, and there is no need to install database management systems and other operating environments.

Files are usually used to store application software parameters or temporary data. Python's file operation is very similar to Java's file operation. Python provides modules such as os and os.path to process files.

### Files and streams

### Common Operation of Files

Files are usually used to store data or application system parameters. Python provides os, os.path, shutil, and other modules to process files, including functions such as opening files, reading and writing files, copying and deleting files.

## Creation of Files

In Python3, the global file () function has been removed, and the open () function has been retained. The function open () can be used to open or create files. This function can specify the processing mode and set the open file to read-only, write-only, or read-write status.

The declaration of open () is as follows:

open(file, mode='r', buffering=-1, encoding=None,

errors=None, newline=None, closefd=Trueopener=None) -> file object

## [Code Description]

The parameter file is the name of the opened file. If the file does not exist, open () creates a file named name and then opens the file. The parameter mode refers to the open mode of the file. Parameter buffering sets the cache mode. 0 means no cache; 1 indicates line buffering. If it is greater than 1, it indicates the size of the buffer, in bytes.

Here, open () returns a file object, which can perform various operations on the file.

Opening Mode of Files notes that "B" mode must be used for reading and writing files such as pictures and videos.

The file class is used for file management. It can create, open, read and write, close files, etc.

**File processing is generally divided into the following 3 steps:**

1) Create and open a file and use the file () function to return a file object.

2) Call read (), write () and other methods of the file object to process the file.

3) Call close () to close the file and release the resources occupied by the file object.

Note that the close () method is necessary. Although Python provides a garbage collection mechanism to clean up objects that are no longer used, it is a good habit to manually release resources that are no longer needed. It also explicitly tells Python's garbage collector that the object needs to be cleaned.

The following code demonstrates the creation, writing, and closing of files.

01 # Create File

02 context='''This is countryside'''

03 f=open('rod.txt', 'w') # open file

04 f.write(context) # write string to file

Close () # close file

**[Code Description]**

The third line of code calls open () to create the file hello.txt and sets the access mode of the file to "W." Open () returns file object f.

The fourth line of code writes the value of the variable context into the file hello.txt

Line 5 calls the close () method of object f to release the resources occupied by object f.

These three steps will also be followed in the operations of reading, writing, deleting, and copying files explained later.

## Reading of files

There are many ways to read a file. You can use readline (), readlines (), or Read () functions to read a file. The implementation method of reading files by these functions will be introduced one by one.

## 1. readline ()

Readline () reads one line of the file at a time, and the file needs to be read cyclically using a permanent true expression. However, when the file pointer moves to the end of the file, there will be an error reading the file using readline (). Therefore, a judgment statement needs to be added to the program to judge whether the file pointer moves to the end of the file, and the loop is interrupted by the statement. The following code demonstrates the use of readline ().

01 # Use readline () to Read Files

02 f=open("rod.txt")

03 while True:

04 line=f.readline()

05 if line:

06 print (line)

07 else:

08 break

09 f.close()

**[Code Description]**

The code in line 3 uses "True" as the loop condition to form a permanent true loop.

Line 4 calls readline () to read every line of the hello.txt file. Each cycle outputs the following results in turn.

This is countryside

Line 5 code, judge whether the variable LINE is true. If true, the content of the current line is output; otherwise, exit the loop. If the fourth line of code is changed to the following statement, the reading method is slightly different, but the reading content is exactly the same.

line=f.readline(2)

This line of code does not mean that only 2 bytes are read per line, but that each line reads 2 bytes at a time until the end of the line.

## 2. Multi-line reading method readlines ()

To read a file using readlines (), you need to return the elements in the list by looping through readlines (). The readlines () function reads multiple lines of data in a file at once.

The following code demonstrates how readlines () reads a file.

01 # use readlines () to read files

02 f=file('rod.txt')

03 lines=f.readlines()

04 for line in lines: # read multiple lines at once

05 print (line)

06 f.close()

**[Code Description]**

The third line of code calls readlines () to store all the contents of the file rod.txt in the list lines.

The fourth line of code loops through the contents of the list lines.

Line 5 code output list lines for each element

```
01 f=open("rod.txt")

02 context=f.read(5) # reads the first 5 bytes of the file

03 print (context)

04 print (f.tell()) # returns the current pointer position of the
file object

05 context=f.read(5) # continue reading 5 bytes of content

06 print (context)

07 print (f.tell()) # output file current pointer position

08 f.close()
```

**[Code Description]**

The second line of code calls read(5) to read the contents of the first 5 bytes in the hello.txt file and store it in the variable context. At this point, the pointer of the file moves to the 5th byte.

The third line of code outputs the result of the variable context and the output is "hello."

Line 4 calls tell () to output the current file

Line 5 code calls read(5) again to read the contents of bytes 6 to 10.

The output of line 6 is "world."

Line 7 code outputs the current file pointer position: 10.

Note that the location of the file pointer will be recorded inside the file object for the next operation. As long as the file object does not execute the close () method, the file pointer will not be released.

## Writing of files

The implementation of file writing also has many methods. You can use the write (), writelines () methods to write files. It uses the write () method to write strings to files, while the writelines () method can write the contents stored in the list to files.

The following code demonstrates how to write elements in the list to a file.

01 # use writelines () to write files

```
02 f=file("rod.txt," "w+")

03 li=["hello country side\n," "hello city\n"]

04 f.writelines(li)

05 f.close()
```

**[Code Description]**

The second line of code uses the "w+" mode to create and open the file hello.txt

Line 3 defines a list Li. Li stores 2 elements, each representing 1 line in the file, and "\n" is used for line feed.

The fourth line of code calls writelines () to write the contents of list li into the file.

The contents of the document are as follows.

hello countryside

hello City

The above two methods will erase the original contents of the file before writing and rewrite the new contents, which is equivalent to "overwriting." If you need to keep the original contents of the file and just add new contents, you can open the file using mode "a+."

The following code demonstrates the join operation of the file.

```
01 # Joins New Content to File

02 f=file("rod.txt," "first+") # is written by joining a+

03 new_context="It is over"

04 f.write(getdetails)

05 f.close()
```

**[Code Description]**

The second line of code uses the mode "first+" to open the file hello.txt

The fourth line of code calls the write () method, the original contents of the hello.txt file remain unchanged, and the contents of the variable getdetails are written to the end of the rod.txt file. Txt is as follows.

hello countryside

hello City

goodbye

Writing files using writelines () is faster. If there are too many strings to write to a file, you can use writelines () to improve efficiency. If only a small number of strings need to be written, write () can be used directly.

## Deletion of documents

The deletion of files requires the use of os modules and os.path modules. Os module provides operating system-level interface functions for system environment, files, directories, etc. File Handling Functions Commonly Used in os Modules Note that the use of the OS module's open () function is different from that of the built-in open () function.

The removal of the file needs to be implemented by calling the remove () function. Before deleting a file, it is necessary to determine whether the file exists or not, if so, delete the file; otherwise, nothing will be done.

The following code demonstrates the deletion of the file:

01 import os

03 file("rod.txt," "w")

04 if os.path.exists("rod.txt"):

05 os.remove("rod.txt")

## [Code Description]

Line 3 code creates the file hello.txt

The fourth line of code calls the existing () of os.path module to determine whether the file hello.txt exists.

Line 5 calls remove () to delete the file hello.txt

466

## Reproduction of documents

The file class does not provide a method for directly copying files, but the read () and write () methods can be used to copy files. The following code copies the contents of hello.txt to hello2.txt.

```
01 # uses read (), write () to copy

Txt

03 src=file("rod.txt," "w")

04 li=["hello world\n," "hello US\n"]

05 src.writelines(li)

06 src.close()

07 # copy rod.txt to rod2.txt

08 src=open("rod.txt," "r")

09 dst=open("rod2.txt," "w")

10 dst.write(src.read())

11 src.close()

12 dst.close()
```

## [Code Description]

Line 8 code opens the file hello.txt as read-only.

Line 9 code opens the file hello2.txt in a write-only manner.

In line 10, read () the contents of hello.txt, and then write these contents into rod2.txt. Shutil module is another file and directory management interface, providing some functions for copying files and directories. Copyfile () function can copy files.

The declaration of copyfile () function is as follows:

copyfile(src, dst)

**[Code Description]**

The parameter src represents the path of the source file and src is a string type.

The parameter dst represents the path of the target file, and dst is a string type.

This function copies the file pointed to by src to the file pointed to by dst.

The file can be cut using the move () function, which is declared as follows.


copyfile(src, dst, *, follow_symlinks=True)

The parameter of move () is the same as copyfile (), move A file or directory is moved to a specified location, and the moved file can be renamed according to the parameter dst. The following code uses shutil module to copy files.

01 # shutil Module Implements File Replication

02 import shutil

03

04 shutil.copyfile("rod.txt,""rod2.txt")

05 shutil.move("rod.txt,"."./")

06 shutil.move("rod2.txt,""rod3.txt")

## [Code Description]

The fourth line of code calls copyfile (), copying the contents of hello.txt to hello2.txt.

Line 5 calls move (), copies hello.txt to the parent directory of the current directory, and then deletes hello.txt. Txt and paste it into the parent directory.

Line 6 calls move () to move hello2.txt to the current directory and name it hello3.txt. Txt will be deleted.

## Renaming of files

The function rename () of the os module can rename files or directories. The following code demonstrates the file renaming operation. If there is a file named hello.txt in the current directory, rename it hi.txt; if there is a hi.txt file, rename it hello.txt.

01 # Modify File Name

02 import os

03 li=os.listdir(.")

04 print (li)

05 if "hello.txt" in li:

06 os.rename("hello.txt," "hi.txt")

07 elif "hi.txt" in li:

08 os.rename("hi.txt," "hello.txt")

**[Code Description]**

The third line of code calls listdir () to return the file list of the current directory, where ."" indicates the current directory.

Thus, we have ended this book that explained a lot of python topics in detail with the help of various examples. This is enough to start a small-medium-level project which can help you implement all these concepts. Use GitHub to find different python projects and start reading them. All the best for your Coding Career. Cheers!

# Conclusion

Thank you for making it through to the end of *Python for beginners*. Let's hope it was informative and able to provide you with all of the tools you need to achieve your goals whatever they may be.

The next step is to implement these concepts to build coding projects and software applications. We have discussed a lot of concepts from basics to advanced stuff in detail.

Finally, if you found this book useful in any way, a review on Amazon is always appreciated!

# Python Machine Learning

*The Ultimate and Complete Guide for Beginners on Data Science and Machine Learning with Python (Learning Technology, Principles, and Applications)*

By

Kevin Cooper

# Introduction

Congratulations for purchasing *Python Machine Learning: The Ultimate and Complete Guide for Beginners on Data Science and Machine Learning with Python (Learning Technology, Principles, and Applications)* and thank you for doing so.

With the world going global, data science is the ultimate secret sauce of technology, and it is on it that Artificial Intelligence lies. From predictive analysis like weather forecast to pattern discovery, data science can produce data from huge elements.

If you want to know more about data science, Python, and some of the fields attached to it, this book will take you through the journey of technology. It will discuss the importance as well as the benefits of data science to the world. And as a fuel of any industry, you will read about how data science impacts virtually all angles of the enterprise.

Away from data science and its applications, this book will discuss linear algebra and why it is vital to prepare you to make an entrance into the universe of machine learning. It will discuss in details every aspect of machine learning, leading to the types of machine learning and their algorithms as well as their use cases. The book will break the ground with the discussion of Python, its benefits, learning Python with machine learning, and ultimately, neural networks.

If you want to learn everything about Python, the details about its language, the basic needs of machine learning, Python for data science, and so much more, this book discuss some of these topics and many more.

In conclusion, thank you for picking up this book even when there are several topics like this on the market. We went extra miles to package it with as much information on Python for the beginner as much. And we believe that you will have a good time reading it.

# Chapter 1: What are Data Science and Deep Learning?

There is an increasing need for storage of big data with the world going global. Until 2010, this need has become the primary concern and challenges of the enterprises. Building solutions and frameworks for data storage was a critical focus. However, to process this data becomes the next focus since the problem of building solutions and structures has been solved through frameworks, particularly Hadoop, among others. Here, the secret sauce is data science. Through data science, the science-fiction movies in Hollywood can become an actual reality. And the imminent hope of Artificial Intelligent is data science. As a result, understanding of data science and its benefits to businesses is quite vital. As you read on, you will have an accurate knowledge of the functions of data, its meaning in obtaining significant insights from large and complex data sets in our environments and surroundings.

## Why Data Science Is Important

By convention, through the use of simple BI tools, we can also analyze the data we had since they are small and structured in size. Unlike the traditional structured data, the majority of the data in recent times are semi-structured or unstructured.

The capacity to produce data from huge elements is through some sources like instruments, multimedia forms, sensors, financial logs, and text files. The variety and volume of the data are so massive that regular tools of BI have no capacity of processing it. Consequently, to analyze and prepare valuable insights out it, there is a need for advanced and more sophisticated algorithms and analytical tools.

Data science becomes famous not only through this reason and to know how different domains make use of it, but we also need to dig deeper.

As the owner of a business, through the available data such as purchase history of your customers' income, history of their past browsing, and age, you will have a clear grasp of the exact needs of your customers. It is likely you have this entire data in advance, but will gain more precision with the recommendation of the product by training models through the variety and vast amount of data now in your possession. More business would come your way with this technique, and it would be amazing.

Let's take a look at another example to have more understanding of the role of decision making in data science. If your car can drive you around through its intelligence, how would life be for you? For its environment, automatic cars generate a plan by collecting live data with the aid of cameras, lasers, and radars. Using machine learning algorithms, it decides when to overtake, at what time to make a turn with the use of this data, and the time or moment to speed up and down.

In predictive analyzes, data science is useful as well – for example, weather forecast. Building models will be achievable through the analysis and collection of data from radars, aircraft, satellites, and ships. Not only will these models help in the prediction of any disasters when they occur, but will also help to forecast the weather. The process will save several precious lives and help people take necessary measures beforehand.

It is now time to understand the meaning of data science since we have had a clear grasp of the need for it.

## What is Data Science?

It is becoming increasing to use the word data science; however, what is the meaning of this term? Do people need specific skills befitting of data scientists? Can we make any distinction between BI and data science? How do they make predictions and decisions in data science? You will have answers to some of these questions down the line.

But first, let's define data science. In a layman term, it is a combination of different algorithms, principles of machine learning, and tools to identify raw data from hidden patterns. But, from the decades of research by the statisticians, how is this process different?

Prediction and explanation are where we can find the thin line.

Through the processing of data history, it is usual for data analysts to explain the situation. Alternatively, while data analysts utilize different advanced algorithms of machine learning to discover the occasion of a specific future event, they also do critical analysis to have insight from it. Part of the process also is for the data analyst to examine the data around various angles, which may not be part of the earlier discovery.

Therefore, data analysts use data science in the process of making predictions and decisions through machine learning, predictive analytics (decision and predictive science), and casual analytics.

## *Predictive casual analytics:*

With the application of predictive causal analytics, you will soon be on your way to having a model that can predict the likelihood of a specific future event. It will be a matter of concern for you if the customer will be making prompt credit payments in the future when you offer money on credit. In this process, to have a prediction of whether future payments will be punctual or not, you will have to carry out predictive analytics on the history of payment of the customer by developing a model.

## *Prescription analytics:*

There will be a requirement for prescriptive analytics when you are set to get a model that, through dynamic parameters, has the intellectual capacity of modifying the decision it takes itself. Though it provides advice, it is a comparatively recent discipline. In other words, apart from prediction, it makes suggestions on a variety of given associated outcomes and actions. For example, Google's self-driving cars. To guide a self-driving vehicle, they make use of the data they gather. And to bring intelligence to it, you can process algorithms on this data. To this end, taking decisions is part of the capacities of the car, including the path they must take, speed up or slow down, and when to turn.

## *Making predictions through machine learning:*

Machine learning algorithms are the best bet when there is a need for creating a model for establishing the trend in the future as the owner of transactional data of a finance company. The supervised learning is the necessary sum of this dynamic. Since the data are in your possession that a data scientist can then train the machine, it becomes supervised. For example, through the use of past evidence of fraudulent acquisition, you can direct a model of fraud recognition.

## *Machine learning for the discovery of the pattern:*

To have the capacity of making meaningful predictions, there may be a need to identify the concealed trends when you have no parameters based on which you can make predictions. Because your grouping of the label is not defined already, this process is unsupervised. And for the discovery of pattern, clustering is the most common algorithm they use. As a telephone company staff, some regions will need towers when you need to establish a network. To make sure that there's optimum signal strength for the entire users, identify those tower locations, and here, you can use clustering method.

# Data Science vs. Business Intelligence (BI)

- For the description of trends, business intelligence finds insight and hindsight by analyzing the data used before. You will have the ability to obtain data from sources in internal and external, create dashboards to run queries as you prepare it through business intelligence and get solutions to the problems such issues with business or analysis of quarterly revenue. To evaluate the effect of specific events shortly is another feature of business intelligence.

- As an investigative method with the focal point on evaluating the current or past data, data science has an approach of forward-looking to predict the outcomes of the future to make informed decisions. Data science is a go-to when it comes to getting precise answers to queries that are undefined as to "how" and "what" events happen.

# Data Science Lifecycle

The situation of charging into analysis and collection of data without proper framing of the business or perhaps not having enough understanding of the requirement is a common mistake people make in data science. As a result, to look out for the smooth operation of the project, following the entire segments of the lifecycle of data science is quire essential.

## *Phase 1 – Discovery:*

Having a clear grasp of the variety of requirements, specifications, required budget, and priorities of the project are vital. The capability to probe uncertainties is a must. Next is the stage of assessment where you know whether you possess the necessary resources, including supporting the project with technology, people, data, and time. Also, formulating IH, that is, initial hypotheses for analyzing and framing the problem of the business is required in this stage.

## *Phase 2 – Preparation of data:*

The analytical sandbox to execute diagnostics for the whole period of the development is what you need in this stage. Also, before modeling, you must preprocess, condition, and explore data. Also, to ensure the sandbox has the data you have obtained, it is essential you complete the process of extract, transform, load, and convert, that is, ETLT. For data transformation, visualization, and cleaning make use of R. Then, you will have to carry out analytics of exploratory on the data after preparing and cleaning it.

## *Phase 3 – model planning:*

This phase is to describe the connection between variables by determining the techniques and methods. These connections will initiate the source so that the algorithms will apply in the stage that will follow. You will make use of different visualization tools and statistical formulas to apply EDA, Exploratory Data Analytics.

Here are model planning tools;

- R
- ACCESS/SAS
- SQL Analysis Services
1. By utilizing basic predictive models and conventional data mining, **SQL Analysis services** know how to execute analytics that are in-database.
2. To create reusable and repeatable model flow diagrams, when people want to use Hadoop to get into data, they use **SAS/ACCESS**.
3. Apart from offering a suitable environment for building interpretive models, **R** has a complete set of modeling capabilities.

By getting insights into your data's characteristics, now is the time to build a model after applying the algorithms when you have decided on which to use.

## Phase 4 – Building the model:

To test and train purposes, it is now time to develop datasets. Also, it is time for consideration on if all the accessible tools you have need new robust environments such as parallel or fast processing, or if they are going to be sufficient for models' processing. At this point, for model building, it is essential to evaluate different learning procedures such as association, clustering, and classification.

Here are tools for building a model;

- WEKA
- SAS Enterprise Miner
- Alpine Miner
- Statistica
- Matlab
- SPCS Modeler

## Phase 5 – Operationalize:

Now is the moment of delivering final code, technical documents, briefing, and reports. Also, in some situations, in an immediate production setting, people implement a guide task. They do this to have a clear understanding of not only the performance but also other connected restraints on a lesser degree far ahead of the entire operation.

## *Phase 6 – Communicate results:*

To know if you could accomplish your purpose that you set out to for initially now is the time to evaluate it. This evaluation is quite crucial. Therefore, based on the criteria you developed in Phase 1, you will discover all the vital outcomes and stakeholders must be in the loop to determine whether the consequences of the plan are successful in the last phase.

# Secret Sauces of Data Scientists

Data scientists need to acquire the skills of written and verbal communication, especially strong soft skills. While being conscious of their audience by using appropriate language and jargon, data scientists need to have the magic to deliver the results in a compelling, insightful, and understandable way in the point of communicating and providing the results. Also, there must be a connection between the business goal and the results where the project spawns in the first place.

Furthermore, knowledge about probabilities, mathematics, and statistics as well as strong computer programming are some of the skills data scientists need to draw upon to select the correct solution approach, have a grasp of the data, improve on it, and also implement the solution.

APIs and data science are essential off-the-shelf factors to discuss. Anyone can consider that they can use them relative ease and as a result, they don't need any crucial expertise in some fields or a well-rounded, influential data scientist. Indeed, anyone can likely achieve a decent result after using some of these products with no effort depending on the problem they desire to solve. However, they might have omitted many parts of data science where chops and experience are significantly critical.

Part of the skills needed necessarily is to;

- Maximize results through the approach customization and with the skills to significantly modify the existing ones as required or the skills to write new algorithms, identify the solution to some of these issues.
- Integrate the various data sources and databases sources including NoSQL, RDBMS, NewSQL, after querying and accessing them into analytics-driven data sources such as data lake, OLAP, warehouse.
- Choose and discover the optimal data features (variables) and data sources, as well as creating needed new ones.
- Work effectively, cross-functionally, and in collaboration with entire company groups and departments.

Even with education, becoming a data scientist has no single path. Among some of the universities' curriculum are analytic-specific programs and data science, particularly at the master's level. Also, there are certification programs by other organizations and some universities. Irrespective of means to learn data science, it is essential for data scientists to have acquired highly technical skills and advanced quantitative knowledge, mainly in mathematics, statistics, and computer science.

## An In-depth Look into Deep Learning

To classify and predict information, a technique that trains a computer to filter observations or inputs like sound, text, or image, is what can be considered as deep learning. Deep learning gets its inspiration through the manner of how our brains filter information. Instead of task-related algorithms, deep learning is a part of machine learning family that is principally derived from learning data representations. In the early 90s, cognitive neuroscientists proposed a class of theories about brain development, and deep learning has a close relationship to this proposition. The model and methods these researchers put together correlate with the development of the human neocortex. Similar to the brain, neural networks make use of layered filters' chain of command whereby each layer leans from the previous layer and then passes its output to the next layer. Consequently, in its effort, deep learning imitates the actions of neurons' layers in the neocortex.

With almost 100 billion neurons in the human brain, these neurons have a connection with about 100,000 of its neighbors.

Indeed, though at the degree that aligns with machines, this same model is what we are attempting at creating.

To impersonate the manner at which the human brain functions to produce real magic is the purpose of deep learning. Therefore, what is the meaning of this in relations to axons, neurons, dendrites, and so many others? An axon transfers to the dendrites of the next neuron with the signal from one neuron. Even though it is far from being a physical connection, a synapse is where that signal is passed in such process.

Though the neurons function together to produce some severe charms, you have plenty of them and are useless. Well, deep learning gets its idea from this process! By putting an input you get from an observation into one layer, it turns to an output that invariably becomes the input for the next layer, and so on. Till the final output signal, this process occurs over and over.

Through input values, node, which is the neuron, gets a signal which passes through the neuron to convey the output signal. The input layer is similar to the human senses; some things that we smell, see, feel, and so on. For a single observation, these are independent variables. Then, a computer can make use of the bits of binary data when the information is broken down into numbers. For these variables to be in the same range, you may have to normalize or standardize them.

It is likely for the value of our input to be continuous as in the case of price. Also, it can be yes or no as in the case of binary, or it can be dog, cat, sloth, hedgehog, and so on, in case of categorical. There will be a situation of various out variables with categorical and not just one variable.

It also helps to keep in mind that there will be a connection with the same single observation of your output value from the input values. For example, when your inspection of the vehicle, salary, and age are your input values, you will also find a correlation to the similar view of the same person in the value of your output. It is essential to pay attention to this analysis, even though it appears so necessary.

And also vital to Artificial Neural Networks, ANNs are the weights that each the synapses get assigned. AAN decides the extent that the signal can pass along through the adjustment of the weights. The decision of the change in the masses as well as training the network happens all at the same time.

If you want to know what occurs inside the neuron, there is the analysis of the weighted sum as well as the process of adding up all of the values. Subsequently, a function that is applied to this specific neuron is the application of an activation function. Whether it has any requirement of passing along a signal or not is what the neuron understands from that. The repletion of this process happens for thousands or even hundreds of thousands of times! In the place where our input values come from the nodes, that is, the things we want to predict or things we know already, and our predictions, which is the output values, and in between those, we have a hidden layer, or layers, where the information travels before it hits the output is where we have created an artificial neural net. Instead of the manner the information going straight into your brain, you have the understanding of the information you see through your eyes.

# Chapter 2: Data Science and Applications

To some extents, data science is recently becoming the most popular field. Nearly all of the world businesses today use data science. Consequently, the fuel of any industry is data science. Industries that use data science include transport, banking, education, e-commerce, manufacturing, finance, and so on. To this end, related to the convention of data science are various applications. Multiple disciplines stem from this single career line. With massive numbers of applications, data science has become quite essential for all industries. It has shaped and kept so many businesses in any trends around the world.

It is not overnight that the function of data science applications develops. Cheaper storage and computing have made tremendous contributions to shorten tasks people do in a day within a few hours. To see how these applications have shaped today's industries, it will be essential to discuss some of these critical applications. Also, the way they transform the world and revolutionize people's perceptions of data. Ultimately, it is vital to address various situations industries use data to make them better.

# Banking and Finance

Finance takes the leading position when it comes to data science applications. Every year, losses and bad debts were on the rise, and businesses were going down. Grief was the order of the day for those surviving. However, since they sanctioned loans while they have paperwork that provided them with various data, they needed rescue, and that is where data scientists came in to help.

As a vital element to match their competition, it is now more than a trend for the banking industries to engage in the applications of data science. Right now, making smarter decisions, enhancing performance, and focusing their resources have been possible for banks because of those big data technologies. Some of the cases of data science applications include;

## *Fraud detection*

For fraud involving credit cards prevention and detection, insurance, accounting, and so many more, data science application becomes crucial. Banks are being proactive with the security of their employees and customers. It is now faster for banks to resist activity on an account to minimize losses since they detect fraud quickly. As a result, they have been able to avoid significant loses and achieve necessary protection when they implement a series of fraud detection schemes.

The fraud detection vital steps include:

- Estimation of model
- Getting data samplings for preliminary testing and model estimation
- Deployment and testing stage

Data scientists need to fine-tune and train individual data set since they are different. There are demands for expertise in techniques of data-mining, including forecasting, classification, association, and clustering, to transform the in-depth theoretical knowledge into practical applications. For example, the bank's fraud protection system can put unusual high transactions on hold pending the confirmation from the account holder. Algorithms of fraud detection can also investigate multiple accounts opened in a short period with the same data, or unusual high purchases of popular items of new accounts.

## Customer data management

It is part of the obligations of the banks to analyze, store, or collect vast numbers of data. With these data, data science applications are transforming them into a possibility for banks to learn more about their customers. Doing this will drive new revenue opportunities instead of seeing those data as a mere compliance exercise. People widely use digital banking, and it is more popular these days. The result of this influx produces terabytes of data by customers; therefore, isolating genuinely relevant data is the first line of action for data scientists. With the customers' preferences, interactions, and behaviors, then, data science applications will isolate the information of the most relevant clients and process them to enhance the decision-making of the business.

## Investment banks risk modeling

While it serves the most critical purposes during the pricing of financial investments, investment banks have a high priority for risk modeling since it helps regulate commercial activities. For investment goals and to conduct corporate reorganizations or restructuring, investment banking evaluates values of businesses to facilitate acquisitions and mergers as well as create capital in corporate financing. For banks, as a result, risk modeling seems exceedingly substantial, and with more data science tools in reserve and information at hand, they can assess it to their benefit. Now, for efficient risk modeling and better data-driven decisions, with data science applications, innovators in the industry are leveraging these new technologies.

## Personalized marketing

Providing a customized offer that fits the preferences and needs of particular customers is crucial to success in marketing. Now it is possible to make the right offer on the correct device to the right customer at the right time. For a new product, people target selection to identify the potential customers with the use of data science application. With the aid of apps, scientists create a model that predicts the probability of a customer's response to an offer or promotion through their demographics, historical purchase, and behavioral data. Thus, banks have improved their customer relations, personalize outreach, and efficient marketing through data science applications.

# Health and Medicine

An innovative potential industry to implement the solutions of data science in health and medicine. From the exploration of genetic disease to the discovery of drug and computerizing medical records, data analytics is taking medical science to an entirely new level. It is perhaps astonishing that this dynamic is just the beginning. Through finances, data science and healthcare are most times connected as the industry makes efforts to cut down on its expenses with the help of a large amount of data. There is quite a significant development between medicine and data science, and their advancement is crucial. Here are some of the impacts data science applications have on medicine and health.

## *Analysis of medical image*

Medical imaging is one of the most significant benefits the healthcare sectors get from data science application. As significant research, Big Data Analytics in healthcare indicates that some of the imaging techniques in medicine and health are X-ray, magnetic resonance imaging (MRI), mammography, computed tomography, and so many others. More applications in development will effectively extract data from images, present an accurate interpretation, and enhance the quality of the image. As these data science applications suggest better treatment solutions, they also boost the accuracy of diagnoses.

## *Genomics and genetics*

Sophisticated therapy individualization is made possible through studies in genomics and genetics. Finding the individual biological correlation between disease, genetics, and drug response and also understand the effect of the DNA on our health is the primary purpose of this study. In the research of the disease, with an in-depth understanding of genetic issues in reaction to specific conditions and drugs, the integration of various kinds of data with genomic data comes through data science techniques. It may be useful to look into some of these frameworks and technologies. For a short time of processing efficient data, MapReduce allows reading genetic sequences mapping, retrieving genomic data is accessible through SQL, BAM file computation, and manipulation. Also, principally to DNA interpretation to predict the molecular effects of genetic variation, The Deep Genomics makes a substantial impact. Scientists have the ability to understand the manner at which genetic variations impact a genetic code with their database.

## *Drugs creation*

Involving various disciplines, the process of drug discovery is highly complicated. Most times, the most excellent ideas pass through billions of enormous time and financial expenditure and testing. Typically, getting a drug submitted officially can take up to twelve years. With an addition of a perspective to the individual stage of drug compound screening to the prediction of success rate derived from the biological factors, the process is now shortened and simplified with the aid of data science applications. Using simulations rather than the "lab experiments," and advanced mathematical modeling, these applications can forecast how the compound will act in the body. With computational drug discovery, it produces simulations of computer model as a biologically relevant network simplifying the prediction of future results with high accuracy.

## *Virtual assistance for customer and patients support*

The idea that some patients don't necessarily have to visit doctors in person is the concept behind the clinical process optimization. Also, doctors don't necessarily have to visit too when the patients can get more effective solutions with the use of a mobile application. Commonly as chatbots, the AI-powered mobile apps can provide vital healthcare support. Derived from a massive network connecting symptoms to causes, it is as simple as receiving vital information about your medical condition after you describe your symptoms. When necessary, applications can assign an appointment with a doctor and also remind you to take your medicine on time. Allowing doctors to have their focus on more critical cases, these applications save patients' time on waiting in line for an appointment as well as promote a healthy lifestyle.

## Industry knowledge

To offer the best possible treatment and improve the services, knowledge management in healthcare is vital. It brings together externally generated information and internal expertise. With the creation of new technologies and the rapid changes in the industry every day, effective distribution, storing, and gathering of different facts is essential. For healthcare organizations to achieve progressive results, the integration of various sources of knowledge and their combined use in the treatment process is secure through data science applications.

# Oil and Gas

The primary force behind various trends in industries like marketing, finance, internet, among others, is machine learning and data science. And there appears to be no exception for oil and gas industry through the extracting of important observations with some applications in the sectors in upstream, midstream, and downstream. As a result, within the industry, a valuable asset to companies is refined data. Data science applications are quite useful in some of these sectors of oil and gas.

## Immediate drag calculation and torque using neural networks

There is a need to analyze, in drilling, the structured visual data, which operators get through logging. Also, they can capture the electronic drilling recorder and contextual data, which takes the pattern of daily report of drilling log. It is essential to make an instant decision because of the time-bound disposition of drilling operations. As a result, companies predict drilling key performance indicators; analyze rig states for real-time data visualization with the use of neural networks. Using the AI, they can estimate the coefficient of regular and friction contact forces between the wellbore and the string. Also, in any given well, they can calculate on the drill strings real-time the drag and torque. Historical data of pump washouts is what operators can utilize, and through the alerts on their phone, they will be able to know when and if there will be a washout.

### Predicting well production profile through feature extraction models

The recurring neural networks and time series forecasting is part of the optimization of oil and gas production. Rates of gas-to-oil ratios and oil rates prediction is a significant KPIs. Operators can calculate bottom-hole pressure, choke, wellhead temperature, and daily oil rate prediction of data of nearby well with the use of feature extraction models. In the event of predicting production decline, they make use of fractured parameters. Also, for pattern recognition on sucker rod dynamometer cards, they utilize neural networks and deep learning.

### Downstream optimization

To process gas and crude oil, oil refineries use a massive volume of water. Now, there is a system that tackles water solution management in the oil and gas industry. Also, with the aid of distribution by analyzing data effectively, there is an increase in modeling speed for forecasting revenues through cloud-based services.

# The Internet

Anytime anyone thinks about data science, the first idea that comes to mind is the internet. It is typical of thinking of Google when we talk about searching for something on the internet. However, Bing, Yahoo, AOL, Ask, and some others also search engines. For these search engines to give back to you in a fraction of second when you put a search on them, data science algorithms are all that they all have in common. Every day, Google process more than 20 petabytes, and these search engines are known today with the help of data science.

### Targeted advertising

Of all the data science applications, the whole digital marketing spectrum is a significant challenge against the search engines. The data science algorithms decide the distribution of digital billboards and banner displays on different websites. And against the traditional advertisements, data science algorithms have helped marketers get a higher click-through-rates. Using the behavior of a user, they can target them with specific adverts. And at the same time and in the same place online, one user might see ads on anger management while another user sees another ad on a keto diet.

## Website recommendations

This case is something familiar to everyone as you see suggestions of the same products even on eBay and Amazon. Doing this add so much to the user experience while it helps to discover appropriate products from several products available with them. Leaning on the relevant information and interest of the users, so many businesses have promoted their products and services with this engine. To improve user experience, some giants on the internet, including Google Play, Amazon, Netflix, and others have used this system. They derived these recommendations on the results of a user's previous search.

## Advanced image recognition

The face recognition algorithm makes use of automatic tag suggestion feature when a user uploads their picture on social media like Facebook and start getting tag suggestions. For some time now, Facebook has made significant capacity and accuracy with its image recognition. Also, by uploading an image to the internet, you have the option of searching for them on Google, providing the results of related search with the use of image recognition.

## Speech recognition

Siri, Google Voice, Cortana, and so many others are some of the best speech recognition products. It makes it easy for those who are not in the position of typing a message to use speech recognition tools. Their speech will be converted to text when they speak out their words. Though the accuracy of speech recognition is not certain.

# Travel and Tourism

There are several constant challenges and changes, even with the exceptional opportunities data science has brought to many industries. And there is no exception when it comes to travel and tourism. Today, there is a rise in travel culture since a broader audience has been able to afford it. Therefore, by getting more extensive than ever before, there is a dramatic change in the target market. As a worldwide trend, travel, and tourism is no more a privilege of the noble and the rich.

The data science algorithms have become essential in this industry to process massive data and also delight the requirements of the rising numbers of consumers. To enhance their services every day, the hotels, airlines, booking and reservation websites, and several others now see big data are a vital tool. The travel industry uses some of these tools to make it more efficient;

## Customer segmentation and personalized marketing

To appreciate travel experience, personalization has become a preferred trend for some people. The customer segmentation is the general stack of services to please the needs of every group through the adaptation and segmenting of the customers according to their preferences. Hence, finding a solution that will align with all situations is crucial. Collecting users' social media data to unify, behavioral, and metadata, geolocation is what customer segmentation and personalized marketing all about. For the future, it assumes and processes the preferences of the user.

## Analysis of customer sentiment

Recognizing emotional elements in the text and analyzing textual data is what sentiment analysis does. The service provider, as well as the owner of a business, can learn about the customers' real attitude towards their brands through sentiment analysis. The reviews of customers have a huge role when it comes to the travel industry. This analysis is because to make decisions, travelers read reviews customers posted on various websites and platforms and then act upon these recommendations. As a result, providing sentiment analysis is one of the service packages of some modern booking websites for those travel hotels and agencies that are willing to cooperate with them.

## Recommendation engine

This concept is one of the most promising and efficient, according to some experts. In their everyday work, some central booking and travel web platforms use recommendation engines. Mainly, through the available offers, they match the needs and wishes of customers with these recommendations. Based on preferences and previous search, the travel and tourism companies have the ability to provide alternative travel dates, rental deals, new routes, attractions, and destination when they apply the data-powered recommendation engine solutions. Offering suitable provisions to all these customers, booking service providers, and travel agencies achieve this with the use of recommendation engines.

## Travel support bots

With the provisions of exceptional assistance in travel arrangements and support for the customers, travel bots are indeed changing the travel industry nowadays. Saving user's money and time, answering questions, suggesting new places to visit and organizing the trips have the influence of an AI-powered travel bot. It is the best possible solution for customers support due to its support of multiple languages and 24/7 accessibility mode. It is significant to add that these bots are always learning and as such, are becoming more helpful and smarter every day. Therefore, solving the major tasks of travel and tourism is what chatbot can do. Both customers and business owners benefit from these chatbots.

## *Route optimization*

In the travel and tourism industry, route optimization plays a significant role. It can be quite challenging to account for several destinations, plan trips, schedules, and working distances and hours. With route optimization, it becomes easy to do some of the following:

- Time management
- Minimization of the travel costs
- Minimization of distance

For sure, data science improves lives and also continues to change the faces of several industries, giving them the opportunity of providing unique experiences for their customers with high satisfaction rates. Apart from shifting our attitudes, data science has become one of the promising technologies that bring changes to different businesses. With several solutions the data science applications provide, it is no doubt that its benefits cannot be over-emphasized.

# Chapter 3: Probability – Fundamental – Statistics – Data Types

Things are quite straightforward in Knowledge Representation and Reasoning; KR&R. Exclusive of doubt, formulating and representing propositions is easy. The thing is, when uncertainty makes itself known, problems begin to arise – for example, an expert system designed to replace a doctor. For diagnosing patients, a doctor possesses no formal knowledge of treating the patient and no official rules based off of symptoms. In this situation, to determine if the patient has a specific condition and also the cure for it, it is the probability the expert system will use to formulate the highest probability chance.

## Real-Life Probability Examples

As a mathematical term, probability has to do with the possibility that an event may occur like taking out from a bag of assorted colors a piece of green or drawing an ace from a deck of cards. In all daily decision-making process, you use probability even without having a clue of the consequences. While you may determine the best course of action is to make judgment calls using subjective probability, you may not perform actual probability problems sometimes.

## Organize around the weather

You can make plans with the weather in mind since you use probability almost every day. Predicting the weather condition is not possible for meteorologists and as a result, to establish the possibility that there will be snow, hail, or rain, they utilize instruments and tools. For example, it has rained with the conditions of the weather that is 60 out of 100 days amid the same conditions when there is a 60 percent chance of rain. Intuitively, rather than going to work with an umbrella or putting on sandals, closed-toed shoes, maybe preferred outfit to wear. Also, not only do meteorologists analyze probable weather patterns for that week or day but with the historical databases that they also examine to calculate approximately low and high temperatures.

## Strategies in sports

For competitions and games, the probability is what coaches and athletes utilize to influence the best strategies for sports. When putting any player in the lineup, a coach of baseball evaluates the batting average of such a player. For example, out of every ten at-bats, an athlete may get a base hit two if the player's batting average is 200. The odd is even higher for a player to even have, out of every ten at-bats, four hits when such a player has a 400-batting average. Another example is when; field goal attempts from over 40 yards out of 15, a high-school football kicker makes nine in a season, his next goal effort from the same space may be about 60 percent chance. We can have an equation like this:

9/15 = 0.60 or 60 percent

## Insurance option

To conclude on the plans that are best for your family and even for you and the required deductible amounts, probability plays a vital role in analyzing insurance policies. For example, you make use of probability to know how possible it can be that you will need to make a declaration when you choose a car insurance policy. You may likely make consideration for not only liability but comprehensive insurance on your car when 12 percent or of every 100 drivers over the past year, 12 out of them in your community have crashed into a deer. Also, if following a deer-connected event run $2,8000, not to be in a situation where you cannot afford to cover certain expenses, you might consider a lower deductible on car repairs.

## Recreational and games activities

Probability is what you use when you engage in video or card games or play board games that has the involvement of chance or luck. A required video game covert missile or the chances of getting the cards you need in poker is what you must weigh. Also, the determination of the extent of the risk you will be eager to take rests on the possibility of getting those tokens or cards. For example, as Wolfram Math World suggests, getting three of a class in a poker hand is the odds of 46.3-to-1, about a chance of 2 percent. However, you will have about 42 percent or 1.4-to-1 odds that you will catch one pair. It is through the help of probability that you settle on the manner with which you intend to play the game when you assess what is at stake.

## Statistics

The basis of modern science is on the statements of probability and statistical significance. In one example, according to studies, cigarette smokers have a 20 times greater likelihood of developing lung cancer than those that don't smoke. In another research, the next 200,000 years will have the possibility of a catastrophic meteorite impact on Earth. Also, against the second male children, the first-born male children exhibit IQ test scores of 2.82 points. But, why do scientists talk in ambiguous expressions? Why don't they say it that lung cancer is as a result of cigarette smoking? And they could have informed people if there needs to be an establishment of a colony on the moon to escape the disaster of the extraterrestrial.

The rationale behind these recent analyses is an accurate reflection of the data. It is not common to have absolute conclusions in scientific data. Some smokers can reduce the risk of lung cancer if they quit, while some smokers never contract the disease, other than lung cancer; it was cardiovascular diseases that kill some smokers prematurely. As a form of allowing scientists to make more accurate statements about their data, it is the statistic function to quantify variability since there is an exhibition of variability in all data.

Those statistics offer evidence that something is incorrect may be a common misconception. However, statistics have no such features. Instead, to observe a specific result, they provide a measure of the probability. Scientists can put numbers to probability through statistic techniques, taking a step away from the statement that someone is more likely to develop lung cancer if they smoke cigarettes to a report that says it is nearly 20 times greater in cigarette smokers compared to nonsmokers for the probability of developing lung cancer. It is a powerful tool the quantification of probability statistics offers and scientists use it thoroughly, yet they frequently misunderstand it.

## Statistics in data analysis

Developed for data analysis is a large number of procedures for statistics they are in two parts of inferential and descriptive:

## Descriptive statistics:

With the use of measures for deviation like mean, median, and standard, scientists have the capability of quickly summing up significant attributes of a dataset through descriptive statistics. They allow scientists to put the research within a broad context while offering a general sense of the group they study. For example, initiated in 1959, potential research on mortality was

Cancer Prevention Study 1 (CPS-1). Among other variables, investigators gave reports of demographics and ages of the participants to let them compare, at the time, the United States' broader population and also the study group. The age of the volunteers was from ages 30 to 108 with age in the middle as 52 years. The research had 57 percent female as subjects, 2 percent black, and 97 percent white. Also, in 1960, the total population of female in the US was 51 percent, black was about 11 percent, and white was 89 percent. The statistics of descriptive easily identified CPS-1's recognized shortcoming by suggesting that the research made no effort to sufficiently consider illness profiles in the US marginal groups when 97 percent of participants were white.

## Inferential statistics:

When scientists want to make a considered opinion about data, making suppositions about bigger populaces with the use of smaller samples of data, discover connection between variables in datasets, and model patterns in data, they make use of inferential statistics. From the perspective of statistics, the term "population" may differ from the ordinary meaning that it belongs to a collection of people. The larger group is a geometric population used by a dataset for making suppositions about a society, locations of an oil field, meteor impacts, corn plants, or some various set of measurements accordingly.

With regards to scientific studies, the process of shifting results to larger populations from small sample sizes is quite essential. For example, though there was conscription of about 1 million and 1.2 million individuals in that order for the Cancer Prevention Studies I and II, their representation is for a tiny portion of the 1960 and 1980 United States people that totaled about 179 and 226 million. Correlation, testing/point estimation, and regression are some of the standard inferential techniques. For example, Tor Bjerkedal and Peter Kristensen analyzed 250,000 male's test scores in IQ for personnel of the Norwegian military in 2007. According to their examination, the IQ test scores of the first-born male children scored higher points of 2.82 +/- 0.07 than second-born male children, 95 percent confidence level of a statistical difference.

The vital concept in the analysis of data is the phrase "statistically significant," and most times, people misunderstand it. Similar to the frequent application of the term *significant*, most people assume that a result is momentous or essential when they call it significant. However, the case is different. Instead, an estimate of the probability is statistical significance that the difference or observed association is because of chance instead of any actual connection. In other words, when there is no valid existing difference or link, statistical significance tests describe the probability that the difference or a temporary link would take place. Because it has a similar implication in statistics typical of regular verbal communication, though people can measure it, the measure of significance is most times expressed in terms of confidence.

# Data Types

To do Exploratory Data Analysis, EDA, you need to have a clear grasp of measurement scales, which are also the different data types because specific data types have correlated with the use of individual statistical measurements. To select the precise visualization process, there is also the requirement of identifying data types with which you are handling. The manner with which you can categorize various types of variables is data types. Now, let's take an in-depth look at the main types of variables and their examples, and we may refer to them as measurement scales sometimes.

## *Categorical data*

Characteristics are the representation of categorical data. As a result, it stands for things such as someone's language, gender, and so on. Also, numerical values have a connection with categorical data like 0 for female and 1 for male. Be aware that those numbers have no mathematical meaning.

## *Nominal data*

The discrete units are the representation of nominal values, and they use them to label variables without any quantitative value. They are nothing but "labels." It is important to note that nominal data has no order. Hence, nothing would change about the meaning even if you improve the order of its values. For example, the value may not change when a question is asking you for your gender, and you need to choose between female and male. The order has no value.

## *Ordinal data*

Ordered and discrete units are what ordinal values represent. Except for the importance of its ordering, ordinal data is therefore almost similar to nominal data. For example, when a question asks you about your educational background and has the order of elementary, high school, undergraduate, and graduate. If you observe, there is a difference between college and high school and also between high school and elementary. Here is where the major limitation of ordinal data suffices; it is hard to know the differences between the values. Due to this limitation, they use ordinal scales to measure non-numerical features such as customer satisfaction, happiness, etc.

## *Numerical Data*

### **Discrete data**

When its values are separate and distinct, then we refer to discrete data. In other words, when the data can take on specific benefits, then we speak of discrete data. It is possible to count this type of data, but we cannot measure it. Classification is the category that its information represents. A perfect instance is the number of heads in 100-coin flips. To know if you are dealing with discrete data or not, try to ask the following two questions: can you divide it into smaller and smaller parts, or can you count it?

## Continuous data

Measurements are what continuous data represents, and as such, you can only measure them, but you can't count their values. For example, with the use of intervals on the real number lines, you can describe someone's height.

## Interval data

The representation of ordered units with similar differences is interval values. Consequently, in the course of a variable that contains ordered numeric values and where we know the actual differences between the values is interval data. For example, a feature that includes a temperature of a given place may have the temperature in -10, -5, 0, +5, +10, and +15. Interval values have a setback since they have no "true zero." It implies that there is no such thing as the temperature in regards to the example. Subtracting and adding is possible with interval data. However, they don't give room for division, calculation, or multiplication of ratios. Ultimately, it is hard to apply plenty of inferential and descriptive statistics because there is no true zero.

## Ratio data

Also, with a similar difference, ratio values are ordered units. The contrast of an absolute zero is what ratio values have, the same as the interval values. For example, weight, length, height, and so on.

# The Importance of Data Types

Since scientists can only use statistical techniques with specific data types, then data types are an essential concept. You may have a wrong analysis if you continue to analyze data differently than categorical data. As a result, you will have the ability to choose the correct technique of study when you have a clear understanding of the data with which you are dealing. It is essential to go over every data once more. However, in regards to what statistic techniques one can apply. There is a need to understand the basics of descriptive statistics before you can comprehend what we have to discuss right now. Note: you can read all about descriptive statistics down the line in this chapter.

# Statistical Methods

## *Nominal data*

The sense behind dealing with nominal data is to accumulate information with the aid of:

**Frequencies:**

The degree upon which an occasion takes place concerning a dataset or over a period is the frequency.

**Proportion:**

When you divide the frequency by the total number of events, you can easily calculate the proportion. For example, how often an event occurs divided by how often the event could occur.

**Percentage:**

Here, the technique required is visualization, and a bar chart or a pie chat is all that you need to visualize nominal data. To transform nominal data into a numeric feature, you can make use of one-hot encoding in data science.

## *Ordinal data*

The same technique you use in nominal data can be applied with ordinal data. However, some additional tools here there for you to access. Consequently, proportions, percentages, and frequencies are the data you can use for your summary. Bar charts and pie charts can be used to visualize them. Also, for the review of your data, you can use median, interquartile range, mode, and percentiles.

## *Continuous data*

You can use most techniques for your data description when you are dealing with constant data. For the summary of your data, you can use range, median, percentiles, standard deviation, interquartile range, and mean.

**Visualization techniques:**

A box-plot or a histogram, checking the variability, central tendency, kurtosis of a distribution, and modality all come to mind when you are attempting to visualize continuous data. You need to be aware that when you have any outliers, a histogram may not reveal that. That is the reason for the use of box-plots.

# Descriptive Statistics

As an essential aspect of machine learning, to have an understanding of your data, you need descriptive statistical analysis since making predictions is what machine is all about. On the other hand, as a necessary initial step, you conclude from data through statistics. Your dataset needs to go through descriptive statistical analysis. Most people often get to wrong conclusions by losing a considerable amount of beneficial understandings regarding their data since they skip this part. It is better to be careful when running your descriptive statistics, take your time, and for further analysis, ensure your data complements all prerequisites.

## *Normal Distribution*

Since almost all statistical tests require normally distributed data, the most critical concept of statistics is the normal distribution. When scientists plot it, it is essentially the depiction of the patterns of large samples of data. Sometimes, they refer to it as the "Gaussian curve," or the "bell curve."

There is a requirement that a normal distribution is given for calculation and inferential statistics of probabilities. The implication of this is that you must be careful of what statistical test you apply to your data if it not normally distributed since they could lead to wrong conclusions.

If your data is symmetrical, unimodal, centered, and bell-shaped, a normal distribution is given. Each side is an exact mirror of the other in a perfectly normal distribution.

## *Central tendency*

Mean, mode, and the median is what we need to tackle in statistics. Also, these three are referred to as the "Central Tendency." Apart from being the most popular, these three are distinctive "averages."

With regards to its consideration as a measure that is most consistent of the central propensity for formulating a hypothesis about a population from a particular model, the mean is the average. For the clustering of your data value around its mean, mode, or median, central tendency determines the tendency. When the values' number is divided, the mean is computed by the sum of all values.

The category or value that frequently happens contained by the data is the mode. When there is no repletion of number or similarity in the class, there is no mode in a dataset. Also, it is likely for a dataset to have more than one mode. For categorical variables, the single central tendency measure is the mode since you can compute such as the variable "gender" average. Percentages and numbers are the only categorical variables you can report.

Also known as the "50th percentile," the midpoint or "middle" value in your data is the median. More than the mean, the median is much less affected by skewed data and outliers. For example, when a housing prizes dataset is from $100,000 to £300,000 yet has more than $3million worth of houses. Divided by the number of values and the sum of all values, the expensive homes will profoundly impact the mean. As all data points "middle" value, these outliers will not profoundly affect the median. Consequently, for your data description, the median is a much more suited statistic.

# Chapter 4: Linear Algebra

A field of mathematics that scientists all over the world confirm to be a prerequisite to an in-depth understanding of machine learning is linear algebra. Though with various notations and tools, difficult findings and theories, linear algebra is a broad discipline, and the bolts and nuts taken from the field are practical for practitioners of machine learning. That is why it is possible to focus on the relevant or the right parts with a solid foundation of the concept of linear algebra. And from a machine learning perspective, it is vital to know the exact meaning of linear algebra. Also, it is critical to know whether linear algebra is the mathematics of data, or if it has any remarkable impact on the field of statistics, and how linear algebra is the cause of several practical mathematical tools including computer graphics and Fourier series.

As the mathematics of data, linear algebra is a branch of mathematics and the language of data as vectors and matrices. A linear combination is the total of linear algebra. It is the utilization of arithmetic on vectors which are columns of numbers and matrices which arrays of numbers. As a study of vector mappings and spaces, linear algebra is about planes and lines that are needed for linear transforms.

To start on this journey, you need to know the basic inferential and descriptive statistics. However, knowing more mathematics is required once you have covered the basic concepts in machine learning. There is a need for more mathematics in a situation where they make any underlying assumption and their limitations to understand how these algorithms work.

## The Importance of Linear Algebra

If you are on a journey of learning machine learning and data science, it is vital to know the importance of the reason linear algebra is essential with these four examples:

### *Example 1:*

Imagine the perception you have when you attempt to take in the picture of a flower. Well, it is easy since you can make out leaves and flower. However, it can be such a challenging task when, for the computer to engage in the same job, you are asked to mark that logic. Since the brain of human has passed through evolution for millions of years, you can identify the flower. To have the power of telling if the color of an image is black or red, we have no clue of the things that go on in the background. To perform the task is the only our brains have been trained to do.

However, it is a difficult task to make a computer engage in a similar mission, and it is a dynamic feature of study in computer science and machine learning in general. We may need to reflect on a specific question ahead of making identification of image attributes; so, what is the process of storing this image by a machine?

To prepare the single 0 and 1 is how they design computers nowadays. Therefore, how can they store such an image inside a network with various attributes like the color? The accomplishment of this storage is through the construct containing the intensities of pixel known as Matrix. As a result, it is in the capacity of how they process this matrix to make out colors and some other things. At the back end will all the operation anyone wants to carry out on this stage will happen using matrices and linear algebra.

## Example 2:

Have you heard the term "XGBOOST?" Any domain of data science domain household knows that data science competitions winners employ quite often an algorithm. To give predictions, it takes the Matrix form to store the numeric data. Not only does it offer more precise results, but XGBOOST is also capable of faster data process. Furthermore, apart from XGBOOST, other numerous algorithms make use of Matrices for data processing and storage.

## Example 3:

As the latest catchword around now, deep learning uses matrices for storing inputs, including giving topnotch answers to these questions using text or speech or image. Also stockpiled in the matrices are weights that a neural network trained.

## Example 4:

Dealing with text is one more dynamic field of machine learning research, and term-document matrix, words' bag, and so on are some of the techniques they frequently use. In the same manner, to perform tasks such as language translation, language generation, semantic analysis, and so many others, all these methods store counts of words within documents and to perform tasks, accumulate this occurrence count in a matrix form.

Thus, let's hope that, to some extents, you have had some understanding of machine learning and its connection with linear algebra. To employ matrices for data processing and storage, we know the text, image, or any general data. It is now time to experience the linear algebra from the top.

# Linear Algebra Problems Representation

It is with an uncomplicated problem that we may want to begin. Let's consider that the cost of 1 bat and 2 balls or 100 units is 2 bats and 1 ball. Finding the value of a bat and a ball is what we are required to do now. Let's assume Rs 'x' is the value of a ball while Rs 'y' is that of a bat. Depending on the circumstance, anything can be the values of Rs 'x,' and 'y,' i.e., variables is 'y' and 'x.' to interpret this form in mathematics, we will go like this;

*(1) .................... 2x + y = 100*

Likewise, the subsequent condition may have a similarity like this;

*(2) ........................... . X + 2y = 100*

Right now, to satisfy both the equations, 'y' and 'x' value is what we need and to find the prices of ball and bat. The solution to a set of linear equations is finding 'x,' and 'y' values are the basic problem of linear algebra. The big picture is data has a representation in the linear equations form in linear algebra. And in turn, the vectors and matrices forms are the representation of these linear equations. Depending on the condition, there may be variation in the equations and those of variables, yet their form is in vectors and matrices representations.

## Visualize the Problem

Usually, visualizing the data problems can be quite helpful, and doing that will help a case such as this. The linear equations are the representation of flat objects. To have a clear understanding of the line, it may be a good idea, to begin with, the simplest one. A collection of the entire points that gratify the given equation is a line corresponding to an equation. For example;

Our equation (1) gets satisfied with (30, 40), (50, 0), and (0,100/3, 100/3) points. As a result, it is on our equation's corresponding line (1) that these lines should lay. Similarly, our equation (2) enjoys some of these points (100/3, 100/3), (100, 0), and (0, 50).

At present, the dot that sits on the two lines is quite paramount to seek satisfaction on both conditions. By instinct, the connection point is what we need to find on the two lines. We can use the operations of elementary algebraic such as subtraction, addition, and substitution to solve the problem.

(1)............................ $2x + y = 100$

(2)........................ . . $X + 2y = 100$

(1) Equation is:

$y = (100 - x)/2$

In equation (2), y value will be:

(3)........................ $x + 2* (100 - x)/2 = 100$

You can solve equation (3) for **x** as well as **y** afterward since a single variable x equation is in equation (3).

Right now, explore as we take a step further even though the equation looks simple.

# Complicating the Problem

With three variables, let's assume an array of three conditions is given to you and put to identify the value of the entire variables, each as given below. We can make out what ensue by solving the problem.

(4) ........................ $x+y+z=1$

(5) ............................. $2x+y=1$

(6) ............................. $5x+3y+2z=4$

We get the result below in equation (4);

(7) ............................. $z=1-x-y$

Then, in equation (6), while we replace merit of z with, we have;

$5x+3y+2(1-x-y) = 4$

(8) ........................ $3x+y=2$

At this time, in the above problem of bar and ball, and as the two variables instance, let's solve equations (8) and (5) to find 'x' and 'y' values. When we know 'x' and 'y,' to find 'z' value, we can use (7).

In this case, it will increase our efforts of problem-solving with the addition of more variable. In 10 equations, let us visualize that we get 10 variables. It can be time-consuming and tedious when we attempt to solve 10 equations at once. Now, let's take a plunge into the ocean of data science. How do we now proffer a solution when data points we have are in millions?

In the original data set, data points are in millions. Utilizing the approach mentioned above, it might be quite challenging to reach solutions. Then, imagine if it is mandatory for us to repeat it several times and to tender a solution, can take so many years. Besides, the war has never ended with just this one. As a result, what do we do? Quit and run away? Certainly, NO!

For us to give a solution to a massive group of linear equations, the matrix is what we need. However, let's turn to matrices and visualize our problem in physical importance before we go further. Directly related to how to use matrices is the next step.

## Planes

The three variables in a linear equation, whose coordinates satisfy the equation, represent the set of all points. By such an equation, can you decipher its physical representation? Attempt to image 2 variables, while adding the third one, in the same instance in any comparison. As you should know, it is a three-dimensional analog of line and that it represents. Indeed, the representation of a plane is three variables of a linear equation. Three variables represent a plane in a linear equation. More precisely, extending up to infinity, a plane is a flat geometric object.

It indicates that we desire to unearth the connection of those planes on the instance of a line by finding solutions to 3 variables linear equation. If you look deeply, in which ways can a group of three planes intersect? Let's see if things are possible in these four cases;

1. The intersection is not present
2. The intersection of the three planes at a point
3. In a line, the intersection of planes
4. Intersection happens with a plane

Most of the super mathematicians and regular individuals like us can only visualize things in 3-Dimensions, and it is ~~complicated~~ unachievable for humans to visualize things in 4 (or 10000) dimension. Therefore, how is it possible for mathematicians to effectively tackle data of higher proportion? In their heads are tricks and one such ploy mathematicians utilize to take care of data of larger size is matrices.

Right away, it's time to move on to the main focus, which is the matrix.

## Matrix

Matrix is the process of writing the same items collectively for our necessity to manipulate and handle them. In data science, while training several algorithms, the matrix is what they use to accumulate information such as how an artificial neural network stores weights. Technically, as far as data science is concerned, a 2-D collection of numbers is a matrix.

$$\begin{array}{ccc} 1 & 2 & 3 \\ \hline 4 & 5 & 6 \\ \hline 7 & 8 & 9 \end{array}$$

Usually, '*i*' denotes rows and '*j*' denotes column. The *i'th* row indexes the elements and the *j*th column. Through some alphabet like elements of A by A (ij), we mean the matrix.

In the matrix above;

A12 = 2

Reach the second column after getting along the first row to get the result.

## Matrix's related words

**Order of matrix** – row*column, i.e., 3*4 is the matrix's order if a matrix has 3 rows and 4 columns.

**Square matrix** – when the number of columns is the same as that of rows.

**Diagonal matrix** – diagonal matrix has elements of non-diagonal that is the same as 0.

**Upper triangular matrix** – the elements under diagonal is the same as 0 in the square matrix.

**Lower triangular matrix** – the elements over the diagonal is the same as 0 in the square matrix.

**Scalar matrix** – the diagonal elements is the same as some constant k in the square matrix.

**Identity matrix** – the complete non-diagonal elements are the same as 0, and all diagonal elements are the same as 1 in the square matrix.

**Column matrix** – sometimes a representation of a vector, there is only one column in the matrix.

**Row matrix** – there is the only row in a matrix.

**Trace** – a square matrix total diagonal elements.

# Chapter 5: Understanding the Fundamentals of Machine Learning

Artificial intelligence is the karma of the human race.

In this century, more than any other innovation, the significant power of artificial intelligence will shape our future. AI acceleration rate is more than astonishing. Over the past four decades after two AI winters, the game is now changing with a variety of available data and rapidly growing volumes, affordable data storage, and more powerful and cheaper computational processing.

A great buzzword is machine learning, and it makes it easier when you learn the programming angle along with the theoretical side together. Together, we will walk around all the technology that powers virtually our daily lives, which are the core algorithms and concepts of machine learning. As you read on, you will know how to start building the same applications and models as well as identifying its functionality at the conceptual level.

## *Prerequisites to start with machine learning*

You need to meet the following requirements if you attempt to have a clear understanding of the concepts presented:

- Comprehensive knowledge of intro-level algebra. You need to have an understanding of graphs and also be at ease when it comes to linear equations, coefficients and variables, and calculus.
- Programming basics proficiency with in-depth expertise of coding in Python. It is not required for you to have any prior experience with machine learning. However, you have to be able to write and read the underlying programming construct of Python code, including lists, function invocations/definitions, conditional expression, loops, and dictionaries.

Basic knowledge of the following Python libraries:

1. Pandas
2. NumPy
3. SciPy
4. SciKit-Learn
5. Matplotlib (and Seaborn)

## The semantic tree

Artificial intelligence is the study of agents with the perception of the world around them; formulate plans to accomplish their goals with decision making. Artificial intelligence encompasses machine learning. To empower computers with learning on their own is its goal. The learning algorithm of a machine facilitates the prediction of things with no explicit pre-programmed models and rules, the building of models that explain the world, and the discovery of patterns in observed data.

# Six Jars of Machine Learning

The following components encompass the process of getting input and offering output, and they are;

- Learning
- Loss
- Task
- Data
- Evaluation
- Model

## *Learning*

The responsibility of minimizing the error is the function of this algorithm. The algorithm defines the manner the variables in the equation are given value, so the output computed is close to actual production. For example:

In $y = mx+c$, the learning algorithm finds the values of m and c so that y) computed) is close to y (actual).

## *Loss*

The difference between the actual output value and the output value that our model predicts or the rate of the error is the function of the loss. Minimizing the function of loss is quite vital for us to solve a problem.

## Task

The thing we must do with the given data is what the task specifies for us. Task depends on the questions one has to solve with the available information. For example, based on the data, you can design a task to measure the happiness level of the employee or the performance of the employee.

## Data

The fuel of machine learning is data, and you must learn to provide a proper history of data on the output and input. For example, an HR needs to give provision of all the employee information to have a prediction on whether or not an employee stayed or left or will leave the company.

## Evaluation

We need to see the accuracy of the model to resolve the problem that we aim it to solve by identifying how well our model performs.

*Accuracy = number of correct predictions/total number of predictions*

When you test with some parts data, you can identify the precision that we gathered initially but make no use of it to train the model.

## Model

The machine generates a formula that maps output and input or a model based on the data and input we provide. Where (x) is input and (y) is the output, a model can be like anyone of these equations;

$$\hat{y} = \hat{f}(x) \text{ [our approximation]}$$

$$\hat{y} = mx + c$$
$$\hat{y} = ax^2 + bx + c$$
$$\hat{y} = ax^3 + bx^2 + cx + d$$
$$\hat{y} = ax^4 + bx^3 + cx + d$$
$$\vdots$$

There are three types of machine learning algorithms

1. Supervised learning
2. Unsupervised learning
3. Reinforcement learning

## Supervised learning

For us to have an in-depth understanding of a supervised learning algorithm, we may first need to be familiar with the term "learning," since, as humans, we learn from our experiences. Therefore, when we tend to know the manner with which machine experience something, we will discover the extraordinary thing that machine data is the experience for them. Thus, as well as learning from the data which we learn from training data, learning from the data is the role of the algorithm of machine learning or any learning model. The things a supervised machine learning algorithm is attempting to do will be much more precise in mathematical terms.

For example, also known as one dimensional function, one variable, (that is, the x here) is $f(x) = x$. Likewise, two dimensional function example (two variables are x and y) is $f(x,y) = x + y$, and n-dimensional function example is $f(x_1, x_2........., x_N)$.

Types of functions are as follows:

## Linear function:

When the graph of the function graph is a straight line, then we have linear function. We have linear function when any $x_1$, $x_2..............., x_N$, the exponent of variables is comes to be 0 or 1. $f(x,y) = x+y+1$, $f(x) = x+1$, $f(x) = 2$ are a few examples of the linear functions.

As you will see, the function of the graph below is linear since it has a straight line and it is the graph for $f(x) = x+1$.

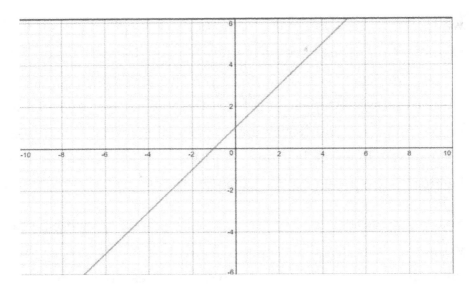

*f(x)=x+1 graph*

## Non-Linear function:

When the function graph is not a straight line, then we have the non-linear function. Also known as non-linear function, the exponents of the variables in the function are older than 0 or 1. Some examples of the non-linear function are $f(x) = x^3$, $f(x) = x^2$. The graph below is not a straight line and therefore, is for $f(x) = x^2$, showing the non-linear function.

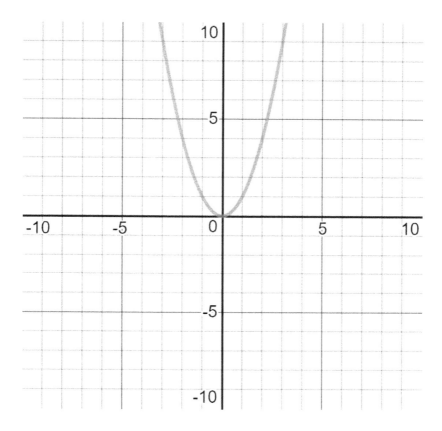

Graph for f(x)=x²

The attempt to identify this function f(x1, x2........, xN) is what we are trying to do in supervised machine learning, where the features are x1, x2........, xN. Based on the data we are dealing with, this function could be anything linear or non-linear. To predict the output for us, when we obtain this function, then, we feed on the features. There are two types of supervised machine learning, depending on the output type.

## Regression:

There is a regression problem when the output value is continuous. For example, we may call it regression since weight is a constant value when we are attempting to predict the weight of a person based on features like height.

## Classification:

The classification problem is the process of the output value being discrete. For example, when a bank establishes the prediction of whether an individual is a fraud or not on specific features, then, the classification problem is this type of problem. Also, classifying the breed a dog belongs to is another excellent example of a classification problem.

# Machine Learning Roadmap

Learning and revising the linear algebra is the right place to start. You will have a basic introduction to the entire core concepts of linear algebra. And take notice of matrix multiplication, vectors, Eigenvector decomposition, and determinants, as the whole lot of them contributes as the cogs that make machine learning algorithms work.

Your next focus should be calculus. Here, understanding and learning how to utilize derivatives for optimization and also their meaning must be your focal point. Make an effort to go through at least sections 1 and 2 of Multivariable Calculus and Single Variable Calculus.

Then, as we discussed earlier, go through the Python libraries used in machine learning, including Numpy, Matplotlib, SKLearn, and Pandas. These are tools of machine learning, and without them, you cannot get anywhere with machine learning.

Then, the next step is coding. Before utilizing the premade models in SciKit, you must learn to implement all algorithms from scratch in Python. Not only would you know how it works, but it would also give you an in-depth and better knowledge. While you may start anywhere you want, here are the following orders to follow for your algorithms:

- Linear Regression
- Logistic Regression
- Naive Bayes Classifier
- K – Nearest Neighbors (KNN)
- K – Means
- Support Vector Machine (SVM)
- Decision Trees
- Random Forests
- Gradient Boosting

## *Linear Regression*

By fitting the observed data to a linear equation, linear regression is all about the effort to develop the correlation connecting two variables. To be an explanatory variable is the consideration for individual variable while a dependent variable is a consideration for the other. For example, you can use a model of linear regression to relate people's heights against their weights. In the initial stage, you must establish if at all, there is a connection between the interested variables before you try to fit in the linear model to observed data. It doesn't mean that single variable produces the other, that is, higher college grades don't cause higher SAT scores, except that the two variables have no significant connection. For determining the relationship strength between two variables, a helpful tool is a scatterplot. There may likely be any provision of a useful model while fitting a linear regression model to the data when there is no connection between the dependent variable and the projected descriptive, that is, there is no indication of any decreasing or increasing trends the scatterplot. The correlation coefficient is an indispensable numerical degree of connection between two variables, such that the correlation strength of the experimental data for both variables is a value connection -1 and 1. Where $Y$ is, the dependent variable and $X$ is the explanatory variables, an equation of the line of linear regression has the form $Y = a + bX$. As the intercept (the value of $y$ when $x = o$), the slope of the line is $b$ and $a$.

## *Logistic Regression*

As an extension of the linear regression model for classification problems and with two likely results, logistic regression models the probabilities for classification problems. Logistic regression is the solution for classification. To press a linear equation output between 0 and 1, it is the function of logistic rather than fitting a hyper-plane or straight line that the logistic regression model uses. The definition of the logistic function is as follows:

$$\text{logistic}(\eta) = \frac{1}{1 + \exp(-\eta)}$$

As such, it comes across in this form;

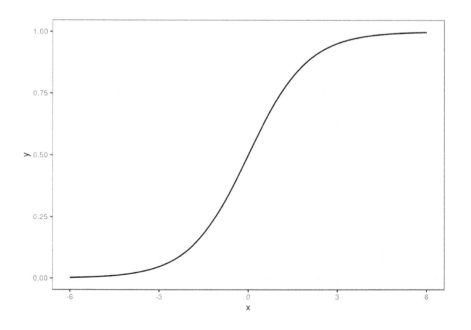

To logistic regression from linear regression is a straightforward step. Between the features and outcome, and in the linear regression model, we have modeled them with a linear equation.

$$\hat{y}^{(i)} = \beta_0 + \beta_1 x^{(i)}_1 + \ldots + \beta_p x^{(i)}_p$$

We have a preference for probabilities connecting 0 and 1 for classification, and into the logistic function do we wrap the right side of the equation. Doing this will force the output to guess just values connecting 0 and 1.

## *Naïve Bayes Classifier*

Naïve Bayes is a straightforward machine learning classifier that is commonly-used yet effective. With the use of the Maximum A Posteriori decision rule in a Bayesian setting, Naïve Bayes is a probabilistic classifier that makes classifications. Also, it has its representation with the use of an elementary Bayesian network. The classifiers of Naïve Bayes are a traditional solution for problems like spam decision and have been particularly famous for text classification.

## The model

With the features, x_o through x_n and classes c_o through c_k, the goal of any probabilistic classifier is not only to return the most likely type, but also to determine the probability of the features happening in each category. Consequently, we may wish to have the capacity to calculate P(c_i / x_o, ........, x_n for each group. The Bayes rule is what we use to do this. Bayes rule has this feature;

$$P(A|B) = \frac{P(B|A)P(A)}{P(B)}$$

It is likely to have a class c_i replacing A and B x_o as our combination of features utilizing the framework of classification in x_n. P9x_o,......., x_n) may be normally hard for us to calculate with P(B) as nomination, we can merely maintain the term P(c_i / x_o,.....,x_n) $\propto$ P(x_o,......., x_n / c_i) * P(c_i) instead of ignoring it, where calculating it can be quite easy when $\propto$ means "is propositional to" .P(c_i); it may be more difficult to compute i.P(x_o,......., x_n / c_i) a class of the proportion of the data set. For computation simplification, we make the assumption that x_o through x_n are conditionally independent given c_i, which gives us the power to say that P(x_o,...., x_n / c_i) = P(x_o / c_i) * P(x_1 / c_i). Though the classifier nonetheless functions well in nearly all conditions, it acquires the term naïve Bayes classifier as the postulation is most liable not true. As a result, our final representation of class probability is the following;

$$P(c_i|x_0, \ldots, x_n) \propto P(x_0, \ldots, x_n|c_i)P(c_i)$$
$$\propto P(c_i) \prod_{j=1}^{n} P(x_j|c_i)$$

When you calculate the individual P(x_j / c_i) terms will depend on what distribution your features follow. Where the elements may be word counts, in the text of word classification, features may follow a multinomial distribution. In other cases, they may develop a Gaussian distribution where features are continuous.

## K – Nearest Neighbors (KNN)

A simple algorithm that classifies the new case or data, based on the same measure, and stores all the available instances is K Nearest Neighbor. Based on how its neighbors are classified, it is mostly used to classify a data point. For example, wine with Myricetin and Rutime as the chemical components. Let's take the consideration of measurement of Myricetin vs. Rutime level with two data points, White and Red wines. Founded on how much Myricetin and how much Rutime chemical substance presents in the wines, the two of them have been analyzed and then fall on that graph.

Integrated into the mainstream of the process of voting, 'k' is a stricture that submits to the nearest neighbors' number in KNN. Also, it is wise to know whether the new wince is white or red if we assume to add a fresh glass of wine in the dataset.

In this situation, we are required to find out what the neighbors are. We can assume that k = 5 to achieve that. Then, the manner of the classification of the new data and with the greater part of votes from its five neighbors, red is the neighbor four out of five neighbors, red would be the classification of the new point.

## *K – Means*

Without any target labels, K-means is an unsupervised learning algorithm that gives the ability to identify the same groups or clusters of data points within your data. Where assignment to the clusters is based on some distance or similarity measure to a centroid by grouping the data into K clusters is the issue with K means. Now, how do we solve this issue? It is okay if we could outline the steps involved.

1.  To its nearest centroid is where each data point is assigned when we initiate the K starting centroids, and this process is what we can do randomly.

2. Attached to the respective cluster, we compute the centroids as the mean of the data points.

3. Pending the moment we can induce our stopping criteria, steps 1 and 2 is what we will do.

To be more precise, it is for squared Euclidean distance or Euclidean distance that we are attempting to optimize for in case you are wondering what is happening. To the cluster that minimizes this squared distance or groups closest to them is where they assign the data points. As it is written formally like this:

$$J = \sum_{n=1}^{N} \sum_{k=1}^{K} r_{nk} \left\| x_n - \mu_k \right\|^2$$

For each data point to its assigned cluster, $J$ is simply the sum of squared distances. Where $(x\_n)$, the data point, is attached to the $(k)$ cluster, and 0 otherwise, an indicator function, $r$ is equal to 1.

## Support Vector Machine (SVM)

As an algorithm of a supervised machine learning algorithm, they use support vector machine for regression or challenges in classification. But it is in classification problems that they mostly use it. We design an item of each data in this algorithm as a tip in the space of n-dimension, where the features number you have is n, with the value of an individual coordinate as the

548

same as the value of each feature. Then, through obtaining the hyper-plane which differentiates both classes quite well enough, we perform classification.

## How Support Vector Machine works

Once we have the understating of segregating both classes with a hyper-plane, we need to know how we can categorize the exact hyper-plane. The rule-of-thumb to identify the accurate hyper-plane is to select the hyper-plane that segregates both classes better. And between these classes of two, having a linear hyper-plane is possible in support vector machine. However, to have a hyper-plane, do we have to attach this feature by hand is another burning question? The answer is no. Because the kernel trick is the feature support vector machine has. By transforming the input of low dimensional space to a space of higher dimensional, these technique converts not a separate problem to separate problem. In the issue of non-linear separation is where this is most useful. Based on defined outputs or labels, as it finds out the procedure to separate that data, it also does some extremely complex data transformations.

## *Decision Trees*

For prediction and classification, decision trees are the most popular and powerful tools. Similar to the structure of the tree, a decision tree is like a flowchart, where a test result is the representation of each branch, where terminal node, i.e., each leaf node contains a set label, and each internal node denotes a test on an attribute. Decision trees have some strengths which include understandable rules generation, requiring little computation to execute classification, provision of a comprehensible clue of which domains are a primarily significant classification or prediction, and ability to handle both continuous and categorical variables. Where the purpose is to predict a constant characteristic value, weaknesses of decision trees include the fact that they are less appropriate for estimation tasks, and with reasonably insignificant quantity and many classes of training samples, are prone to errors in classification problems.

## *Random Forest*

The random forest grows several classification trees. All you need to do is to place the input vector down each of the trees in the forest to classify a new object from an input vector. When we say that the tree "votes" for that class, we are saying that each tree gives a classification. Overall the trees in the forest, the forest decide the categorization that has the most votes. The random forest grows each tree as follows:

- The sample of N cases at random – however *with replacement*, from the original data if the training set is N for the number of cases. For growing the tree, this model will be the collection of training.
- With the best split on these M is used to split the node, a number m<<M, which is M input variables, is specified

such that at each node, m variables are randomly picked out of the M. In the course of the forest growing, the M value is assumed.

- Since no pruning is likely; each tree can grow to the most extensive degree on the cards.

## Gradient Boosting

By attempting to understand what boosting is, we can correctly define gradient boosting. The technique of converting weak learners into active learners, we are talking of boosting. In boosting, a modified version of the unique data set is a fit on each new tree. Hence, several models get their training from gradient boosting in a sequential, additive, and gradual approach. Utilizing the two algorithms distinguishing the weak learners' shortcoming, such as decision trees are the main distinction between gradient boosting algorithm and AdaBoost. Whereas the gradient boosting runs similar operation with the use loss function gradients ($y = ax + b + e$, *because it is the term of error, e needs a special mention*), the AdaBoost model identifies the shortcomings by high weight data points.

# Chapter 6: Types of Machine Learning

Even though this chapter will be talking about types of machine learning, you may come across some parts that we have discussed earlier in the last chapter. But this chapter goes more in-depth into this same excellent subject called machine learning.

You see, machine learning has made huge impacts by amplifying multiple elements of the business operation, becoming a diverse and reliable business tool from a science fiction fancy. With the implementation of its algorithms essential for the maintenance of competitiveness in several industries and fields, the influence of machine learning on the performance of companies is quite significant. Requiring a lot of resources, machine learning implementation into the operations of the business is a tactical measure. As a result, understanding various perks different machine learning algorithms bring to the table and your desired work for the machine learning.

As you read on, not only will you know the great purpose of the algorithms of machine learning, but you will also have an in-depth insight into the machine learning algorithms' significant types.

# Types of Machine Learning Algorithms

## *Algorithms of supervised machine learning*

For the involvement of an operation's unswerving management, supervised learning algorithms come to play here. In this situation, while the developer place firm restrictions on the process of each algorithm, it is also the developer's work to label sample data corpus. A favored form of this algorithm is machine learning:

- For you to feed the algorithm, you only select the type of output and samples of information.
- Including false/true or yes/no, the desire of this type of results.

It is more or less like connecting the missing links with this process from the perspective of the machine. Making predictions of unseen, unavailable, and future data based on data of labeled sample and scaling the scope of data is the primary purpose of supervised learning. Regression and classification are the two main procedures of supervised machine learning.

## Classification:

In a case where the algorithm obtains a manual training when you label incoming data based on the samples of the past data, not only categorize specific types of objects accordingly but to also recognize particular kinds of objects is the process of classification. Whether to perform a binary recognition, an optional image, and character, in a situation where there is compliant or non-compliant of a bit of data to individual requirements in a true or false approach, it is in the power of the system to know how to differentiate types of information.

## Regression:

For you to calculate and identify continuous outcomes is the process of regression. Not only the groupings such as widths, heights, and so on but also their values are what the system is supposed to understand, as well as the numbers and their significance.

Some of the algorithms that are widely used include:

- Support vector machines
- Linear regression
- Nearest neighbors
- Logistical regression
- Random forest
- Decision trees
- Gradient boosted trees
- Neural networks
- Naive Bayes

## *Use cares of supervised learning algorithms*

Trend forecasting in retail commerce, stock trading, and sales, as well as price prediction, is supervised learning's mainly universal fields of use. For the two situations, to calculate possible outcomes and assess the possibility, the algorithm utilizes incoming data. Highspot and Seismic are the platforms of sales enablement that make use of this type of an algorithm by looking for consideration while presenting scenarios from several angles.

As the sequence of ad content delivery component, ad tech operation is part of business cases for supervised learning. The algorithm of supervised learning has the role of keeping the spending of the budget under particular margins such as overall budget for a specific period or a single purchase price scope, and also assessing possible prices of ad spaces and its value in the course of the real-time bidding process.

## *Algorithms of unsupervised machine learning*

The process whereby the builder has no involvement in undeviating power is unsupervised learning. The desired results have not been defined and are not known in case of the unsupervised machine learning algorithms, unlike the primary position of supervised learning where the role of the developers is to classify the data since they know the results. More distinction between them is that it is on unlabeled data that unsupervised learning nourishes, while the exclusive use of data is what supervised learning purposes.

Some of the things developers use the algorithm of unsupervised machine for include

- Extraction of valuable insights
- Exploration of the information structure
- Increasing efficiency of operation through implementation
- Detection of patterns

In other words, by sifting through it, unsupervised machine learning describes information and makes sense of it. Here are some of the methods unsupervised learning algorithm applies for data description:

## Clustering:

Based on their internal patterns devoid of prior knowledge of group credentials and used to segment it into meaningful groups, that is, clusters, the process of clustering is simply data exploration. The individual data objects similarity defines the credentials and the test as well as used for anomalies detection features of its dissimilarity.

## Dimensionality reduction:

With the incoming data, the noise is so overwhelming. Even while distilling the pertinent information and for the removal of this noise, the algorithm of machine learning makes use of dimensionality reduction.

Hence, the algorithms that developers use widely include:

- K – means clustering
- t – Distributed Stochastic Neighbor Embedding, T - SNE
- Association rule
- Principal Component Analysis, PCA

## *Unsupervised learning machine used cases*

For a maximum impact, the domains where they use unsupervised learning are ad-tech and digital marketing. Also, in most cases, for them to make befitting adjustment of the service while exploring the customer information, they apply the use of this algorithm. Indeed, in the incoming data, the fact is plenty of self-styled "known unknowns." exist. Having the power for the extraction of appropriate foreknowledge out of unlabeled data while they make sense of it is the actual effectiveness of the business operation.

The data management of the recent gets itself ready through the unsupervised algorithms. This algorithm of machine learning has its implementation among the most cutting-edge platforms of data management like Salesforce and Lotame at the moment. Thus, with the use of specific credentials, including the setting of particular software, personal data elements, behavioral data, and so on, they can use unsupervised learning to identify target audience groups. Also, for the campaign performance patterns identification, as well as ad content, they can use this algorithm to develop more efficient targeting.

## *Algorithms of semi-supervised machine learning*

Between supervised and unsupervised algorithms, it is the middle ground that the algorithms of semi-supervised learning represent. Mainly, the semi-supervised model absorbs a thing of its own through a combination of some aspects of both.

Algorithms of semi-supervised work in some of these ways:

1. For shaping of the requirements of the operation, that is, train itself, the algorithm of semi-supervised machine learning makes use of a restricted labeled set sample data.

2. The results of the limitation in a model with incomplete training that label data that is not marked in a sequential task. They consider pseudo-labeled data for the results because of the sample data set boundaries.

3. Ultimately, for the combination of predictive and descriptive features of unsupervised and supervised learning, there is a development of a distinct algorithm with the combination of pseudo-labeled and labeled data collections.

For clustering to group data into different elements, while identifying data assets, semi-supervised learning makes use of the process of classification.

## Use cases of semi-supervised machine learning

Through the support of semi-supervised learning, healthcare, and legal industries as well as others, manage speech and image analysis and classification of the content of the web. They apply semi-supervised learning for the systems of the content aggregation and crawling engines in the case of classification of web content. It arranges collections of labels in specific configurations and uses them for content analysis in both cases. However, for further sorting, this process usually requires the input of a human. uClassify is the perfect example of this procedure. General Architecture for Text Engineering, GATE is another popular tool of this category.

Based on a sample corpus and labeling performance, an algorithm provides viable speech and image analytic model and in the case of expression and image analysis, coherent transcription. For example, this can be a CT or MRI scan. There is a possibility of identifying anomalies in the image by providing a model with a small set of exemplary scans.

# Algorithms of Reinforcement Machine Learning

Machine learning artificial intelligence has its representation in reinforcement learning. Essentially, reinforcement learning is all about a system that is self-sustained and improves itself with the use of the combination of the interactions with the incoming data and the combination of labeled data throughout the contiguous sequences of tries and fails.

Exploitation or exploration is the technique of reinforcement machine learning uses. They are simple mechanics, that is, a situation happed, they observe the consequences, and subsequent action takes consideration for the first action's outcomes.

Occurring upon particular tasks performance, they are the reward signals in the center of reinforcement learning algorithms. Indeed, the reinforcement algorithms navigation tool is the reward signals, giving it an understating of the action course, whether wrong or right.

Here are the main types of reward signals:

- Encouraging the performance of particular sequences of action is the positive reward signal

- Pressing to stop the algorithm by correcting it from getting is the signal, and it also penalizes for performing specific activities is the negative reward signal

However, based on the information quality, the role of the reward signal may vary. Therefore, further classification of the reward signals may be found on the operation prerequisites. Generally, the concept of the system is to minimize negatives and maximize the positive.

The standard reinforcement learning algorithms are:

- Monte-Carlo Tree Search (MCTS)
- Q-Learning
- Asynchronous Actor-Critic Agents (A3C)
- Temporal Difference (TD)

## *Reinforcement machine learning algorithms use cases*

For inconsistent and limited information available, reinforcement machine learning matches these instances. As a result of interactions with data and relevant processes, the operating procedures of an algorithm can form. This type of machine learning is what video games like contemporary NPCs mostly use. As it provides viable challenges, flexibility to the reactions of AI is what reinforcement learning offers to the player's action. For example, in the Grand Theft Auto series, for moving people and vehicles, a feature of collision detection uses this type of machine learning algorithm.

Also, relying on reinforcement learning algorithms are self-driving vehicles. For example, it is likely for the car that self-drives to activate the 'turn left' scenario and so on with 'turn left' road detection. AlphaGo is the most popular model of this reinforcement learning variation which, by calculating the sequences of actions out of the current board position, outplayed him when diving at loggerhead with the second-best Go player in the world.

Also, also using reinforcement learning are the Ad Tech and Marketing operations. Making use of the retargeting process much more efficient and flexible is possible through this algorithm of machine learning to deliver conversion through close adaptation of the user's surrounding context and behavior. Also, to adjust and amplify chatbots' dialogue generation and natural language process, NLP is part of functions for which people use reinforcement learning:

- Advance more informative, engaging responses
- Impersonate a message style input
- According to the reaction of the user, identifying relevant answers

More than a technical feat, it is typical of a UX challenge for some bot with the emergence of Google DialogFlow.

As it is, solving various problems are possible for multiple algorithms of machine learning algorithms. A dominant pattern capable of valuable insights extraction process out of the entire information classes and handling a wide variety of tasks is the combination of different algorithms.

# Pattern Recognition and why it Matters

Due to the emergence of machine learning and big data, several previously speculated or deduced data became available. Based on more credible sources and for businesses to gain value-added benefits, this data provided the means to use more sophisticated techniques of data analysis. In other words, since we are equipped with more information, it is now time to further our goal from simply obtaining information to understanding and analyzing the data that was already coming to us.

Rooted in the middle of all the tools used in Big Data is pattern recognition. Pattern recognition involves the analytics of big data, uncovers the hidden meanings behind the data while getting the juice out of it. The company receives its strategic advantage through pattern recognition, and that makes it capable of continuous evolution and improvement in the market that is ever-changing.

## *What is pattern recognition?*

The process of segmenting and distinguishing data following common elements or with the set criteria which unique algorithms perform is pattern recognition. Because pattern recognition gives room for further improvement and enables learning per se, it is one of the integral elements of machine learning technology.

Through its features, pattern recognition identifies things. Through flat lines and spikes, flows, and ebbs, these patterns tell stories to the data. Some of what data can include:

- Image
- Text
- Sounds
- Sentiments, and so on

Pattern recognition algorithms can process any information of the sequential nature, enabling the practical use of the sequence and also making it understandable.

## *Pattern recognition models*

Pattern recognition has three main models, and they are:

- Statistical: for the identification of the place a piece belongs. For example, to identify whether it is a football or not. The supervised machine learning is what this model uses.
- Structural/Syntactic: for the definition of a more complicated correlation between elements. For example,

parts of speech. Semi-supervised machine learning is the technique this model uses.

- Template matching: for complementing the features of the object with the predefined template and identifying of the object by proxy. Plagiarism checking is one of the uses of such a model.

## *How pattern recognition works*

A lot is going on underneath even though self-descriptive is the most significant part of the pattern recognition operation. Mostly, algorithms of pattern recognition have two main parts, and they are:

- Explorative – data commonalities recognition
- Descriptive – specific manner commonalities categorization

Including the use in the big data analytics and for the extraction of insights out of the data, they make use of the combination of these two elements. To uncover a critical understanding of details in the subject matter, it is with the correlation of the common factors analysis.

Here is the picture of the pattern recognition process:

1. Through input or tracking, and from its sources, you gather data
2. Then, you clean up the data from noise

3. Then, you examine the information for common elements or relevant features
4. Subsequently, you group these elements in specific sections
5. For data sets insights, you analyze the segments
6. Then, you implement the extracts insights into the operation of the business

## Pattern recognition use cases

### Audience research, stock market – data analytics

The interconnection between data analytics and the technology of pattern recognition is so profound that it is easy to confuse the two of them. For example, an analytic tool which is the software of stock market pattern recognition. While placing it into a broader perspective on the data analytics context and reveals its distinct features, i.e., the patterns itself, the use of pattern recognition is for data description.

Here are the exceptional use cases of pattern recognition:

- Forecast for the stock market – for the prediction of the possible results, they use pattern recognition for stock exchange comparative analysis. Businesses that engage in the study of pattern recognition include YardCharts.
- Audience research – through selected features, segmenting, and analyzing available data of the user is

what pattern recognition refers. Among the companies that provide these features is Google Analytics.

## Natural language processing – text translation, text analysis, chatbots, text generation

A machine learning field that has its focus on comprehensive training of the machines on communication and message generation is natural language processing (NLP). Though it seems like hard science-fiction, it has not dealt with "reading between the lines" with the essence of community in reality, and also with the direct expression of the message. By constructing its variation while finding the connections, natural language processing deciphers the text in explicit forms. To differentiate the sentences is where the process begins; while ultimately classifying the manner people can use these words in a sentence, then, that is the process of sorting out speech parts and the point the words integrate well.

To achieve this and to handle the proceedings, natural language processing combines specific techniques like segmentation, tagging, and parsing to create a model. At various stages, there is involvement of the algorithms of unsupervised and supervised machine learning in the process.

Some of the fields that use natural language process include:

- Detection of plagiarism – with the assistance of web crawler focused on a comparative study of the text, this field is a variation of text analysis. To check for matches elsewhere, tokens are the forms the words then get. Copyscape is an excellent tool that does this.

- Text analysis – for topic modeling and discovery, categorization, Buzzsumo, content marketing tools, uses this technique.

- Text generation – automated generation of content or for AI Assistants and chatbots. For example, Twitterbot updates, email auto-generation, and so on.

- Contextual extraction and text summarization – finding the meaning of the text. An example of some of these online tools for this task is Text Summarizer.

- Text translation – for recreating a near similar matching of the message in other languages, and in addition to word substitution and text analysis, the engine also combines sentiment and context analysis. Google Translate is mainly a well-known example.

- Text adaptation and correction – for simplification of the text, people use this method in addition to correcting formal mistakes and grammar, – from the words' choice to the structure. One of such prominent examples is Grammarly.

Other use cases include recognition of optical character which they use for verification of signature and classification of the document. Prominent for analysis and conversion of images into text that is machine-encoded, its common uses include text translation, handwriting recognition, and document classification.

There is also image recognition, which is all about the identification of face and visual search. The simple concept behind image recognition is to understand what is in the picture, and the two main use cases of image recognition include face detection and visual search. Voice recognition is another use case, and it deals with the importance of sound as a source of information.

Ultimately, the key to further evolution of computational technology is pattern recognition. With the aid of pattern recognition, big data analytics can progress further, and everyone can benefit from the machine learning algorithms as they get smarter and smarter every day.

# Chapter 7: What is Python? Setting Up the Environment in Python

Python, in technical terms, is a high-level, object-oriented programming language that has the integration of vibrant semantics mainly for the development of web and app. Since Python provides dynamic binding and typing options, in the subject of Rapid Application Development, it is exceptionally fascinating. Relatively, Python is straightforward. Because it has the requirement of a distinctive syntax with focus on readability, Python is so simple to learn. Much more comfortable than any other languages, Python code translation and reading is convenient for developers. As a result, with this simplicity, there is a reduction in the program's expenses for development and maintenance since it gives room for collaborative work by the teams without the significant barriers of experience or language.

Also, because it is easy to assign programs in a style of modules and across various projects, it has the potential of reusing code, Python maintains the use of packages and modules. Apart from the fact that you can easily export or import your modules, you can also scale your package or module to apply them in other projects when you have developed them. In both source and binary form, the two standard interpreters and the library are available for free, which is one of the most promising benefits of

Python. Along with the complete tools that are necessary, Python is available on several leading platforms, and there is no exclusivity either. Therefore, for those developers who want to save themselves again the hassles of paying high costs of development, it is an exciting opportunity.

Don't get overwhelmed in this point as you will soon have a clear grasp of so many things about Python soon enough. The essential point is for you to know that the programming language developers use to create software in the form of an app or on the web is Python.

## The Use of Python

As a language of general-purpose, developers use Python for almost anything. Most fundamentally, the written code is not translated into a format that is computer-readable at runtime, meaning, the language is in interpretational form. Whereas, before the developers even run the program, the conversion of most programming languages is taking place. Because the main intention for using it was initially on small projects, they call this language a "scripting language."

Since its inception, rather than just common ones, the "scripting language" concept has evolved significantly since they now use Python to write commercial, large applications. With the popularity gained by the internet, there has been significant growth on this dependence on Python. This reliance is on a substantial mainstream of web platforms and applications such as YouTube, Google search engine, and also the New York Stock Exchange, NYSE's web-related transaction system. For such a language to power a system of stock exchange means, it must be quite powerful. And while their space machinery and equipment are getting extensive programming, NASA also uses Python. Also, they use Python to display images and numbers, process text, save data, and scientific equations solution. Primarily, to process a variety of elements people encounter on their devices, they use it behind the scene.

## Benefits of learning Python

Mainly, as your first language, there are several benefits when you set your mind to learning Python, and we will take time to talk about them.

As instrumentation for other programming frameworks and languages, as a language, it is incredibly straightforward to learn Python. If you are working as a beginner with some form of coding style as a complete beginner, it is absolute you want to read on.

People widely use Python, include prominent companies such as Pinterest, Google, Yahoo!, Disney, IBM, Nokia, and so much more. Also, having their reliance on Python as their most crucial programming language is the Raspberry Pi and lover's dream of DIY. By now, the importance of all these and why they matter may have been creeping into your mind, and that is because you will always have a way of utilizing the skill when you learn Python. It is possible to be profitable for you as a Python developer regardless to say that because several businesses rely on the language.

Here are some other benefits of Python:

1. Because it is for general purpose and it is the ideal language, platforms with big data, automation, and data mining bank on Python.
2. Since it is so easy to read and work with, you can use Python to develop prototypes.
3. Unlike massive languages like Java and C#, a setting with additional dynamic coding is some of the things Python allows. Also, it gives room to be quite productive and organized when experienced coders work with Python.
4. Even if you have no experience in programming, reading Python can be quite uncomplicated. For anyone, they can start running with the language is what anyone can start doing, and it only requires plenty of practice and a bit of patience. Also, its simplicity earns it a perfect choice to use for larger development teams and even multi-programmers.
5. What powers Django, an open and complete source of framework for the web application, is Python. Also,

simplifying the procedure is through frameworks like Rails and Ruby.

6. As a community-developed and an open-source, the support it has is massive. Every day, as they continue to improve core functionality, developers of like-minded in their millions work with the language. In the latest variant of Python, with the progression of time and as an excellent way of networking with other developers, there are continuous updates and improvements.

## Python Environment Setup

Because it gives allows you to execute the code you write, as you work with the programming language of any level, setting up an environment for development is one of the most essential things you will do. If you don't do this, it may be challenging enough for you to confirm the progress of things if there are no syntax errors in your applications or website.

Also, to convert your code and for what the computer can peruse and implement, you will need an interpreter that makes up your entire application. It may not be possible for you to run your code without this interpreter. For the conversion of your system, the first thing to do is to make use of a Python shell. And that will call upon a "bang" line when you use it the interpreter.

Two ways of doing this are when you attempt to create a file or an application. With the use of Notepad++ or WordPad, which is a simple text editor, it is easy for you to execute a program.

Also, with the use of a Python shell, you can create an application. For each method, here are some of the disadvantages as well as advantages.

## Text File vs. Python Shell

For system interaction, you can use a shell, which is a tool or program. For example, to submit arguments and commands, with the use of a "terminal" or power line, you can tap into the Windows operating system. More than an operating system shell, things are a little distinctively when you work with Python. In an understandable form, not only does the Python shell feed the code to the system, but you can also use it to interact with an interpreter. It is the interpreter that converts the code after it has examined it into usable commands if you've written a program in Python and you intend to execute it. It is essential to note that it is after the application has been implemented that all of this process is done.

As you type the code into the system or computer, both the conversion and interpretation take place in a shell in real-time. This means that there is actual execution of the program as you type. You will have some impression of how your final code will perform, and the things you program will likely do when you do this. You may notice that nothing happens until you feed the document into an interpreter when a text file is what you use to write code. If you have the Python installed on your computer, and with the use of a command line, you can call upon the interpreter, however, after you have already written the code, you can do the step. If the interpreter runs into issues since they can be as ambiguous as using a shell, not only can this method be frustrating, you will have a hard time spotting errors in your code. However, since it is easy and straightforward to do, most developers have a preference for using an editing tool like a text editor. With increased functionality such as Notepad++, text editors are developed explicitly with programming in mind.

## The Best Place to Start

It is essential to configure the development environment ahead of doing anything with a programming language. Now, for the execution of your custom programs, it is time to discuss how you will set up Python and the interpreter.

For a majority of Linux distributions or Mac, Python is already pre-installed. Nonetheless, based on how old your system is, an updated version is what you may need to download. Note that you can run the following command after you have opened the terminal to check your version of Python:

```
Python -V
```

From the Python Software Foundation, you may need to download Python if you are running Windows.

### How to get Python

The appropriate place to go is the Python official site if you wish to download Python. Specific to your operating processor or system, there are versions like 32 or 64 bit. So, the particular version is all that is required of you when downloading.

If you are on Mac, it is perfectly fine for you to use since it is probably you will have Python installed already on your computer. And to activate and manage them, installing the latest version is ideal through Homebrew. For you to get more details, you can go to the Homebrew homepage. Also, if you prefer, you can use the PSF for your direct Python download. As for the Linux users, the designer of Linux has most Linux distributions already included Python. If necessary, you can use the package manager if you want to upgrade as you confirm the current version on your system. From the PSF, you can download Python if you are using Windows.

Note that during installation, if you are using Windows, the option that adds Python.exe to your system path is what you must be sure to select. In the option "Add Python.exe to the path, select the option next to it and for the install location, choose your local hard drive.

### The version of Python to use

With the two core versions of Python, novice and beginners coders can get tangled in confusion as to which one of them to choose. Python 2.x and 3.x are the two versions of Python. Talking about Python, these two versions of Python are suitable to develop, and the good news is they are both quite identical.

Currently in active development is Python 3.x version. What this implies is that, with the continuous development of the open-source community, it is continually receiving new functionalities and features. Python 3.5.x version may be the perfect option if you have a preference for bleeding-edge such as supports and elements. Still actively maintained by the community are Python 2.7.x and 3.4.x versions, including Python 3.2.x version. This maintenance is essential when you encounter problems and need help. And for the fact that you will get the most support from the libraries of third-party since version 2.7.x has been around for so long. You may also want to stick with the older version in the event where you discover that to the newer version of Python; they have not been ported while looking at libraries.

Most fundamentally, once you have some knowledge about one version of Python, it is easy to make the jump to another version. You may still need to learn the new functions and features if you are jumping to a current version. You may not have any issues if you are moving backward, although it is necessary that if you are moving to the older version to get a grip of what utilities are not congruent with it. In due course, the Python version you like to use is up to you. There is no right or wrong approach to it if you are making a jump from one version to another or also to use the newer or older version even if it comes to your realization to do so later on.

## *Features of Python*

Most times, as a language that is object-oriented and incredibly powerful, Python is comparable to PHP, Ruby, Perl, Java, and Scheme. For developers, it is quite an exciting working with this language with some of the several notable features of Python including:

1. It is much easier to read the programs any developers write because Python makes use of an elegant syntax. They quite come close to the manner with which we write our words which is closer to the language of the humans, rather than code interpretation, a style that computers use to study. For example, at runtime, and while in quotes, the command of "print" will display anything preceding it.

2. Getting your program up and running is more comfortable with Python since it is easy and straightforward to use. Similar to ad-hoc programming skills, the consideration for Python is that it is ideal for the development of the prototype. Also, it has no compromise maintainability.

3. With the provision of incorporated maintenance for various general programming undertakings such as files

modification, searching through text, and syncing with the web browser, Python has Standard Python Library. Your content may have to be developed from scratch for a majority of other languages.

4. For the simplification of testing for short snippets of code, there is an inclusion of an interactive mode. You will also have IDLE, a development setting, and it is faster and easier with the help of the development environment.

5. Even if you have already compiled them in C or C++, there is an opportunity of extending the language by adding new modules. Even better, once you have created them in future projects, you can use the modules as shortcuts.

6. Through the provision of a programmable users' interface of an app, you can also embed Python into an application. If you are developing an app in a terminal that has the requirement of running with Python or that will teach coding, this dynamic is a great feature.

7. Python has compatibility with several operating systems and computers such as MacOs, Linux, Windows, OS/2, several Unix brands, and so on. Also, if necessary, you can quickly jump between them since the interface of Python is the same as each of those platforms.

8. As there is no licensing fee and to download and use it will not cost you any penny and use, Python is genuinely

free. Also, even though it is copyrighted, and since it is under an open-source license that the language is available, you can freely redistribute or modify it.

# What is Django?

Written in Python, Django is an open-source and free web application framework. A collection of modules is a framework that makes development easier. Instead of creating from scratch, since they are in a group, they allow you to create websites and applications from an existing source. Websites, no matter if one person designs them, can have functionality such as management and admin panels, authentication support, comment boxes, file upload support, contact forms, and so many more. In other words, you may need to develop these components yourself if you were creating a website from scratch. Rather than using a framework, you only need to configure them properly to match your site since these components are already built.

You can use a big collection of the modules Django provides in your projects. Significantly, developers can save a lot of time and headaches by using frameworks, and Django is also part of them. Also, it might interest you that they create Django with front-end developer in mind. For those that are familiar with working with HTML, such as front-end developers and designers, they will feel comfortable with Django's template language, which is easy to learn. However, developers can as well augment the template language as they want with its highly extensible and flexible features.

You will want to remember the framework of Django if you are going to be working with Python, particularly for web design or web applications. Indeed, it will come in handy. Though they designed it with the complete minimalist in mind, another framework that is great to work with is Python-based is CherryPy. When you have some experience working with Python, CherryPy is a framework you will want to explore.

# The Difference between Python and Other Languages

Since it is easy to learn and understand, Python stands out among the rest. Similar to Python, some people consider Ruby as a great place to start; however, Ruby has a four-year head start. Apart from the fact that it is much more popular with C developers, it has a significant foothold in the enterprise. The fact that it is easy to cross over between the two languages makes it so.

In the labor market, both Python and Ruby have their significant share of development. As a result, in terms of a career, it is beneficial to choose either language. Also, another application people use most times is PHP though the application is different. Ultimately, since each style has its niche, everything boils down to the things that you will be developing.

## The use of the languages

A server scripting language they use mainly to create interactive and dynamic websites is PHP. Apart from the fact that they use it to build anything from a single blog to a substantial corporate style website, PHP is the best language for creating HTML.

An object-oriented, general-purpose, and high-level language is Python. As versatile as it is, you can use Python for virtually anything. Developers use Python to develop indexers, desktop GUI apps, daemons, website crawlers, and mobile and web applications.

Used in combination with data entities and web application, Ruby is an object-oriented, high-level language. Its existence is mainly to take away the focus from query tasks. Its dynamic type system is where Ruby becomes most famous as it performs type checking during runtime. Part of its features is automatic memory management.

Note that when the commands and syntax a language recognizes are closer to human language rather than that of a computer, they refer to such word as "high-level." High-level as a term is a description of a word that is not locked down to a specific type of computer.

Python is the best language among the three styles for a complete beginner and programmers mostly recommend it because of its use of syntax that emphasizes ease of use and simplicity. Whereas, experienced programmers with other languages will have a better use for with Ruby. As for developers who are familiar with C languages, PHP is the best for them.

# Chapter 8: Guide to Machine Learning With Python

The *age of data* that we live in can only be enriched with more storage resources and better power of computation. As there is a rise in the information or data every day, making sense of all the data is the real challenge. By developing intelligent systems that use the methodologies and concepts from machine learning and data mining, organizations and businesses are attempting to tackle the situation. Among them, the most exceptional field of computer science is machine learning. We will be on the right path if our defining factor for machine learning as the science and application of algorithms that offer a sense of the data.

## The basic need for machine learning

At present, the most advanced and intelligent species on earth are human beings since we solve and evaluate complicated problems. AI, on the other side, is yet to surpass the intelligence levels of humans in a variety of aspects even as it is still in its initial stage. We may have to consider then the need to make a machine learn. Based on data, with scale and efficiency, the most suitable reason for doing this is to make decisions.

Recently, to obtain vital information from data to solve problems as well as performing various real-world tasks, businesses are making a massive investment in newer technologies such as deep learning, artificial intelligence, and machine learning. It is precisely decisions that are data-driven taken by machines, especially for the automation of the process. Rather than utilizing programming, they can make use of these data-driven decisions in the problems that cannot be programmed inherently. While we require solving real-world problems through high-scale efficiency, human intelligence is still quite critical. And that brings about the rise in machine learning.

## *When and why making machines learn?*

Even though we have to move ahead of the need for machine learning, we still need to tackle the situations that must propel us to make the machine learn. We have various circumstances that require the need for computers to make data-driven decisions at a vast scale and with efficiency. Machine learning would be more productive with some of the following situations.

### Lack of expertise in human

Where human skill is deficient can be the domain that we need the machine to make data-driven decisions in the first place. For example, navigating spatial planets or unknown territories.

### Dynamic circumstances

We have the nature of dynamic in some situations, i.e., over time; they are changing. We may require the machine to take a data-driven decision as it learns in behaviors or conditions such as this. For example, the availability of infrastructure in a company and network connectivity.

## Translation challenges from expertise to computational tasks

Human knowledge is in several domains; however, translating this expertise into computational tasks can be quite hard. Machine learning is needed in such situations. Cognitive tasks and area of speech recognition can be some perfect examples.

# Machine Learning with Python – Ecosystem

With the capabilities of high-level programming language, Python is a popular object-oriented programming language. Python is popular these days because of its portability capability and syntax that is easy to learn. As it is, they write Python as the successor of programming language names "ABC." In 1991, they released the first version of Python. From a TV show called Monty Python's Flying Circus, Guido van Rossum picked the name Python.

## *Python's strengths and weaknesses*

Since there are strength and weakness sides to every programming language, Python has its own as well.

## Strengths

As some surveys and research indicate, the most popular language, as well as the fifth most significant language for data science and machine learning, is Python. Some of the strengths that give Python these fair shares include:

**Easy to understand and learn** – Python's syntax is more straightforward. As a result, learning and understanding the language is relatively easy, even for beginners.

**Multi-purpose language** – since it has excellent support for structured programming, Python is a multi-purpose programming language, with added support for functional programming and object-oriented programming.

**A considerable number of modules** – for developers to cover all features of programming, Python gives them a massive amount of modules. And it makes Python an extensive language since these modules are available easily for use.

**Open-source community support** – Python has the broad support of a large developer community since it is an open-source programming language. Because of this good advantage, the Python community quickly fixes the bugs. Python is adaptive and robust because of this characteristic.

**Scalability** – since it makes provision of an improved structure for supporting large programs than shell-scripts, Python is a scalable programming language.

**Weakness**

While it may be a powerful and popular programming language, slow execution speed is the weakness of Python. With comparison to compiled languages since Python is an interpreted language, the execution speed of Python is slow. For the Python community, this situation can be the primary area of improvement.

# Why Python for Data Science?

As the most popular language for data science, Python is also the fifth most important language for machine learning. Here are some of the machine learning features that poise it as data science's preferred choice of style:

## *An extensive set of packages*

Python possesses a robust and comprehensive collection of packages that different domains can get access to use. Some of the packages of Python include scipy, numpy, scikit-learn, pandas, and so on which are needed for data science and machine learning.

### Easy prototyping

Fast and easy prototyping is another essential feature of Python, which makes it the choice of language for data science. While on the developing stage of the new algorithm, this feature can be useful.

### Collaboration feature

Good collaboration is quite critical in the field of data science, and this situation is straightforward with several useful tools that Python provides.

### Many domains with one language

Some of the numerous fields of a typical data science project may have feature extraction, data manipulation, modeling, data extraction, updating the solution, deployment, and evaluation. Python provides the opportunity for data scientists to address all these domains from a common platform since it is a multi-purpose language.

# Machine Learning Techniques with Python

For us to build models to solve real-life problems with the use of data, we can use different machine learning algorithms, methods, and techniques. There are four techniques of Python machine learning, and they are:

## Machine learning regression

In a layman's term, sometimes one that is often less developed, to regress may mean getting back to a previous position. According to statistics, regression is the relationship between the corresponding values of other values, and it is a degree of how one variable's mean. A technique of machine learning that discovers its foundation in supervised learning is a regression. It is in the prediction of a numerical and continuous target that we use it and the work starts on the values of data set on which we have access already. While it labels the difference between the values of prediction and expectation as the residual/error, it also compares known and predicted values.

### Regression to the mean

Over generations, half-cousin to Charles Darwin, Francis Galton observed the sweet peas sizes. Galton concluded that it would get to a variety of sizes if we let nature do its job. However, larger ones may come up when we selectively breed sweet pears for size. With time, and with the steering wheel in the control of nature, there will perhaps be the production of bigger peas as smaller offspring are produced over time. For the variables in some peas, we have a particular size, yet it is to a specific curve or line that we can map these values.

Types of regression in machine learning

Regression is generally two types to observe, and they are:

- Linear regression – we use linear regression through the intent to denote the connection between a straight line target and a predictor;

$y = P_1 x + P_2 + e$

- Non-linear regression – it may not be possible for us to denote it as a straight line with a non-linear correlation observation between a predictor and a target.

## *Classification of machine learning*

With permission for us to predict group membership for data instances, a technique of data mining is the classification of machine learning. As this method falls under supervised learning, it makes use of labeled data beforehand. That is, by training the data, our expectation of it is for its future prediction. And we mean the classification of data into the modules they belong when we say 'prediction.' There are two types of available attributes for this, and they are:

- Output attribute which also means the dependent attribute
- Input attribute which also means the independent attribute

Classification methods

- Induction of decision tree – it is from the set identified tuples that we create a decision tree. This has internal nodes, leaf nodes, and branches. It is on an attribute test that the internal nodes denote, the outcome of the trial is what the branches indicate, and the label of the class is what the leaf nodes mean. Though they are fast, the two essential steps are testing and learning.

- Classification of rule-based – it is on the rules of IF-THEN that this classification is based. When there is a denote on a rule, it is –

THEN conclusion IF condition

- Backpropagation classification – mostly referred to as connectionist learning, neural network learning builds connections. And one of the mainly trendy neural-network learning algorithms is backpropagation. With the results to learn, it compares the target value and processes data.
- Lazy learner – the training tuple is what the machine stores and awaits a test tuple in a lazy learner approach. Sustenance of incremental learning is what this approach pertains. The strategy of early learner has a contrast to this.

For example, if you are to learn various codes and QR codes, Code 93 Barcodes, ITF Barcodes, Aztec, data matrices, and some others are presented to you. The next thing is the classification of the code when they show one them to you. As testing and training examples, this is supervised learning.

## Clustering

Unsupervised classification is clustering. With no availability of labeled data, this classification is an analysis of exploratory data. When we make use of clustering, we are doing the process of separating data that are unlabeled into discrete and finite collections of data composition that are hidden and natural. Here are two types of clustering for your observation:

- Hard clustering – a single cluster fits in with one object
- Soft clustering – multiple groups belong to one object

Designing the clustering algorithm after selecting the features and then validate the clusters are the first steps in clustering. As a result, interpreting the outcomes is what we do in conclusion.

## Anomaly detection

Something that has a deviation from its predictable pattern is an anomaly. Spotting an outlier is something we may sometimes wish with machine learning. For example, we may want to detect per hour bill of a dentist for 85 fillings. Per patient, the seconds are 42. Finding the bill of a specific dentist just for Tuesdays is another example. Suspicion may arise from these situations and to emphasize on these anomalies, and since it is not what we are looking for specifically for, we can use anomaly detection.

# Data Loading for Machine Learning Projects

What is the most essential and the first thing required of you when you are attempting to start a machine learning project? Well, to start any of the machine learning projects, loading the data is what we need to do. And the format of data that is most common for projects of machine learning is CSV, which stands for comma-separated-values, concerning data.

As a format in a simple file, they use CSV for tabular data storage, text, and number, including plain text spreadsheet. Before we load CSV data, we need to deal with some considerations even though we can load CSV data with different ways in Python.

## *Consideration while loading CSV data*

The format that is most common for machine learning data is CSV data format; however, while our machine learning projects are being packed with the same, we may need to take care of certain essential aspects.

### File header

Each file in CSV data files contains the information for each field in the header. For the data file and the header file, it is imperative to make use of similar delimiter since how we should interpret data fields is what the header file specifies. Here are some of the cases common to file header of CSV that need proper consideration:

- **Case 1**: where a file header is in data file – when a file header is as a result of the data file, each column of data will automatically get assigned the names.
- **Case 2**: where a file header has no data file – when there is no file header in the data file, it is with a manual approach that each column of data will be assigned names.

Whether our CSV file contains a header or not in the two scenarios, there is a need to have an explicit explanation on this.

## Comments

With comments in any data file, there is now a significant implication. At the beginning of the line in the data file of CSV, the indication of comments is through a hash (#). In the process of loading into machine learning projects the CSV data, there must be a consideration for comments since, depending upon the method we choose for loading, we may have to indicate whether to expect those comment or not if the file contains comments.

## Delimiter

The standard delimiter in the data files of CSV is comma (,) character. Separating the standards in the domains is the purpose of delimiter. As a result, while uploading the CSV file into a machine learning project, and because we can make use of a different delimiter like white space or tab, considering the delimiter's purpose is essential. However, we need to give it an explicit specification if we want to use another delimiter than the standard one.

## Quotes

The default quote character is double quotation (" ") mark in CSV data file. Again, as we attempt to upload the CSV file into a machine learning project, we must consider the purpose of quotes so we can use other quote characters than double quotation mark. However, there is a need to be clear when we are using a different quote style other than the standard quote.

## *Methods of loading CSV data file*

It is critical to load the data correctly when you are working with machine learning projects. CSV is the most common data format for machine learning projects, and CSV has varying difficulties in parsing and various flavors. There are three conventional approaches in Python to load CSV data file, and they are:

## *Load CSV with Python standard library*

When you attempt to load CSV data file, the first and most used approach is the use of the Python standard library, which provides us different built-in modules such as the `reader() function` and `csv module`.

### Load CSV with MumPy

Another way of loading CSV data file is through `numpy.loadtxt()` and *NumPy* function.

### Load CSV with Pandas

Through `pandas.read_csv() function` and *pandas*, you can load CSV data file. As a flexible function, it returns a pandas.DataFrame which you can use immediately for plotting.

# Applications of Machine Learning with Python

### Virtual personal assistants

The capacities of virtual assistants bring to our mind some names such as Alexa and Siri. You request Siri to play music for you or make a call. Also, to know the weather forecast, you can ask Alexa. Sending an SMS or even setting the alarm is possible. The only thing required of you is to speak to it simply, and it will listen to your command. For those differently abled, this comes in handy. Such assistants take note of your interactions with them, and for better future experience, they make use of that.

### Social media services

Facebook has so many features which you would have been aware of by now, and some of them are 'face recognition' and 'people you may know.' To monitor your activities, it makes use of machine learning. It observes which people send requests to you or vice versa, what profiles you visit or who visit your profile, others that you tag, requests you accept, and so on. So that people can use their platform regularly, Facebook uses this to provide more productive experience for their users on their platform.

## Online customer support

To help you with your questions, shopping and education platforms will most times use a live chat pop up. With a visitor that has several queries may leave instead of staying and likely make a purchase. As for other websites, they make use of chatbots to pull information to the site and attempt to deal with the questions of their customers.

## Online fraud detection

You will realize your trust with PayPal if you have any experience with it. With the use of machine learning, PayPal can defend against illegal acts such as money laundering. When it makes a comparison of millions of transactions, it can identify the one with illicit transactions.

## Product recommendations

Jabong and Amazon are some of the shopping platforms that suggest similar products to you when they notice what products you look at with your experience using their platforms. For them, it is a win-win situation since you are likely to make a purchase when they show you some favorite products to you. Also, they use a cart and wishlist content for this.

## *Refining search results*

When you search online using Google, the search engine will monitor your response. Do you stick around for some time when you visit a top listing? Or without clicking any link, you get to the second page and close the tab? Google is aware of all these activities, and it aims to enhance user experience.

## *Fighting web spam*

Several email clients use rule-based spam filtering. For spammers to get around this, they develop new tricks. Consequently, to keep their spam filter updated, clients such as Gmail use machine learning. Also, for Google and other search engines, spam is a big problem for them. Standard spam-filtering techniques are C 4.5 Decision Tree Induction and Multi-Layer Perceptron.

## *Automatic translation*

We have the luxury of translating text into another language through machine learning. How words fit together and thus uses this information to improve the quality of a translation is what the machine learning algorithm for these tackles. Also, people can translate the text on images with the use of neural networks to identify letters with automatic translation.

## Video surveillance

If it is possible to be aware of some crimes, people can avoid them. Through a video surveillance system, people will be mindful of the behaviors of others toward someone else, a situation, or a place.

# Chapter 9: K – Nearest Neighbor Algorithms – K – Means Clustering

An easy-to-implement, simple supervised machine learning algorithm that you can use to solve both regression and classification problems is K – nearest neighbor (KNN). But wait; let's try to take a deep dive.

As a process of learning a function that creates an appropriate output when given new labeled data, a supervised machine learning algorithm is one that bases its reliance on input data, as against the algorithm of an unsupervised machine learning. For finding a solution to regression and classification problems, you may want to turn to supervised machine learning algorithms.

As its output, a discrete value is as a result of the problem of classification. For example, these sentences are distinct: "likes pizza on Friday" and "does not like pizza on Friday." No middle ground appears to exist in this circumstance. In a classification data, we will have a label as well as a predictor, or a set of predictors.

As an integer number like 1, -1, or 0, characterization of the output (label) of the algorithm of classification is the accepted routine. These numbers are representational in this instance. It will be meaningless if you make an effort to perform a mathematical operation on them. You need to know that we cannot add "likes pizza" + "does not like pizza" together because their numeric representations should not be combined.

As a number with a decimal point as its output, a regression problem has a real number. When you use a data in a regression analysis, you will have dependent variables, which are the thing we are attempting to guess given our independent variables, and an independent variable, or set of independent variables. For example, we can take the weight to be the dependent variable and height to be the independent variable.

Also, for data used in a regression analysis, it is typical for each column, without the inclusion of dependent variable or label, to be called dimension, predictor, feature, and independent variable, while row can be observation, data point, or example. Without any tags, an unsupervised machine learning algorithm uses input data, which means, no label informs the computer to self-correct when it has made a mistake or when it is right. For getting more insight into the data, unsupervised learning attempts to learn the basic structure of the data, while supervised learning, given some new unlabeled data, tries to learn a function that will permit us to make a prediction.

# K – Nearest Neighbors

In close proximity, the existence of similar things as an assumption is the sum of the algorithm of KNN. Furthermore, close to each other, similar objects are in the same surrounding. For the algorithm to be functional, the concept of the KNN is that assumption is sufficiently accurate. Sometimes referred to as closeness, proximity, or distance, the idea of similarity captures KNN with some mathematics some of us might have learned in our childhood, which is to calculate the distance between points on a graph.

We have various ways of calculating distance, and depending on the problem we are trying to solve, one of them might be preferable. However, the standard and popular choice is the Euclidean distance, which is the straight-line distance.

## The KNN Algorithm

1. Load the data
2. To your preferred quantity of neighbors, initiate K
3. For each data example,
3.1 Calculate the current instance from the data and the case of the query.
3.2 As well as the distance to an efficient compilation, pop in the sample index
4. Sort the ordered collection of indices and ranges in ascending order, from smallest to largest by the gaps.
5. From the sorted collection, pick the first K entries.
6. Chosen K entries labels are the next things to get
7. Return the mean of the K entries if regression
8. Return the mode of the K labels of a classification

## Selecting the right value for K

You will need to run the algorithm of KNN several times for you to pick the K that is right for your data. While maintaining the ability of the algorithm to make accurate predictions when it's given data it hasn't seen before, you can choose the K that reduces the number of errors.

Keep some of these things in mind:

1. We have less stable predictions when we cut down on the value of K to 1. Let's imagine K = 1, and we have a query point around one green and several reds, however, the single nearest neighbor is the green. Since KNN that is K = 1, implies that the query point is green, which is an incorrect prediction, we would think the query point is most likely red.

2. Inversely, our predictions get more stable because of majority averaging and voting as we step up the value of K. As a result, up to some extent, making an accurate prediction is more likely. Ultimately, we will start seeing a rise in the number of errors. By now, we have stressed the K value too much when reality dawns on us.

3. Usually, to have a tiebreaker, we make K, an odd number in situations where we are taking a majority vote such as selecting the mode in a classification problem, among labels.

## Advantages

1. To implement and use the algorithm is easy and simple
2. You may not need of making added assumptions, tuning a variety of parameters, or creating a model.
3. Versatility is the nature of the algorithm. You can use it for search, regression, or classification.

## Disadvantages

1. With the increase in the number of independent variables, predictors, and examples, so the algorithm slows significantly.

## *KNN in practice*

In an impractical choice in settings where people need to make prediction more quickly, and with the increase in the volume of data, KNN can become significantly slower, and that is its main disadvantage. Besides, the results of regression and classification can be faster for some algorithms to produce more accurately.

However, for solutions that depend on identifying the same objects, KNN can still be quite useful in solving problems provided you have sufficient computing resources to handle the data you are using to make predictions speedily. For example, when we use an application of KNN search, the algorithm of KNN in recommender systems.

# How to Implement K – Nearest Neighbors in Python

We will follow the steps below with some of the main points of the process:

1. Handle data: from CSV, open the dataset and then split into train/test datasets
2. Similarity: between two data instances, analyze the distance
3. Neighbors: detect the data instances most similar to K
4. Response: from a set of data instance, generate a response
5. Accuracy: review the predictions' accuracy
6. Main: tie it all together

## *Handle data*

Loading our data file is the opening line of the process. In CSV format, the data can be without any quotes or a range of the header. With the open function, it will be possible to launch the file and in the CSV module, use the reader function to read the data lines.

After doing that, for KNN to make predictions when it uses it, it is into a training dataset that we need to split the data, and we can use a dataset test to evaluate the accuracy of the model. First, for the numbers that we can work with, we have to make the conversion of the measures of flower that were loaded as strings. Then, by splitting the data set randomly, we have to train the datasets. The standard ratio for us to use is the test/train of 67/33. loadDataset, a function that loads a CSV is what we can use for function definition with the given filename and with the use of given split ratio, split it randomly into the train and test datasets. Then, download to the local directory, the iris flowers dataset CSV file.

## Similarity

Between any two given data instances, we need to calculate their similarity so we can make predictions. For an assigned member of the test dataset and sequentially make a prediction, doing this is quite crucial for us to locate the K most related data instances in the training dataset.

The Euclidean distance measure is what we can use if the units of all four measurements of the flower are the same and are numeric. Between the two sets of numbers, this defines as the square root of the sum of the squared differences. At least for a few more times, you may want to let that sink in by rereading it. Also, the inclusion of which field in the calculation of distance calculation is another thing we want to control. Specifically, to contain the first 4 attributes is what we only want. While ignoring the final dimension, then to a fixed length with one approach, you need to limit the Euclidean distance. You can make the Euclidean Distance definition when you put all of this together.

## Neighbors

Now we can use a measure of similarity that for a given unseen instance, we have to collect the K most similar cases. For subset selection with the values of the smallest distance and calculating the range for all the circumstances, this process is a straightforward one.

## Response

Based on these neighbors, what we have to do next is to devise a predicted response after locating the neighbors that are most similar for an instance of test. This can be achieved when the prediction takes the majority vote after giving each neighbor the chance to vote for their class attribute.

## Accuracy

Now, all the KNN algorithm pieces are in place. The accuracy evaluation of the prediction is an essential remaining concern. And evaluating the model accuracy is an easy way, and it is called classification accuracy, which is, out of all predictions made, the ration calculation of the total correct predictions.

## Main

Then, it is time to tie them together with the primary function since we have all the elements of the algorithm.

# K – Means Clustering

As an unsupervised learning type, you can use K – means clustering in a circumstance where data are unlabeled, i.e., data that has no defined groups or categories. Identifying groups in data, with the variable K representing the groups' number, is the goal of this algorithm. Based on the features that are provided, assigning every data point to any member of the K groups is the iterative work of the algorithm. And also based on feature similarity, there is a cluster of data points. Here is the K – means algorithm clustering:

1. As they also use for new data labeling, the K clusters' centroids,
2. Training data labels (assign a particular cluster to each data point)

It becomes possible for you to analyze and find the organically formed groups instead of defining groups before looking at the data. As you read on, you will understand how you can determine the groups' number. Each cluster's centroid defines the resulting groups as the feature values' collection. You can interpret what kind of group each cluster represents while the centroid features weights examination.

## *Clustering*

The technique of data analysis that is most common exploratory that they use for intuition acquiring about the data structure is clustering. While data points in different clusters are quite varied such that data points in the same subgroup, cluster, are quite the same, clustering is the task of identifying subgroups in the data. In other words, according to a similarity measure like correlation-based distance and Euclidean-based distance, data points in each cluster are as similar as possible when we attempt to identify homogenous subgroups within the data. Application-specific is the verdict of the measure of similarity to use.

You can do clustering analysis based on the features where you attempt to identify samples subgroups derived from elements or based on models where we strive to identify features subgroups founded in samples. However, feature-based clustering is what we will discuss here. In market segmentation, clustering is what we use; in a situation where we attempt to identify the same customers whether in the conditions of image compression or segmentation, attributes or behaviors; document clustering based on topics, and so on, in a circumstance where we attempt to group the same region.

Because there is no comparison of ground truth to the actual label to the clustering algorithm output for evaluation of its performance, clustering is an unsupervised learning method, unlike supervised learning. It is through the process data points grouping into distinct subgroups that we have access to investigate the structure of the data.

# K – Means Algorithm

Where each data point belongs to only one group, as an interactive algorithm and also into *K*pre-defined distinct non-overlapping subgroups, clusters, Kmeans algorithm attempts to have segregation of the dataset. Although keeping the clusters as separate as possible, Kmeans attempts to make the data points of inter-cluster quite comparable. The total of the squared distance is at the minimum involving the centroid cluster and the data points when it assigns data points to a cluster. Within the same cluster, the more homogenous, similarity, the data points, the less variation that we have within clusters.

For a final result generation, the K-means clustering algorithm makes use of iterative refinement. The data set and also the clusters' number are the inputs of the algorithm. And for each data point, the data set is a features' collection. In the initial, it is with the K centroids' approximation that the algorithms start, which, from the data set, can either be selected or generated indiscriminately. For the process of iteration, here are the steps used by the algorithm:

## *Data assignment step:*

The definition of the individual clusters is through each centroid. With this process, based on the squared Euclidean distance, they dispense each data point to its nearest centroid.

On a more formal level, based on if $c_i$ is the collection of centroids in set $C$, each data point $x$ is designated to a cluster. Where dist( - ) is Euclidean's standard distance(L2). For each $i^{th}$ cluster centroid, let the data point set assignments be $S_i$.

## *Centroid update step:*

It is though this way that they compute the centroids; by assigning to the cluster of that centroid, they do this by taking the mean of all data points.

Between steps one and two, the iteration process of the algorithm takes place until stopping criteria are met, i.e., some maximum number of iteration is reached, there is a minimum in the sum of the distances, or no change clusters in data points. There is a conversion guarantee with this algorithm. Though it may not be the best possible result, a local optimum may be the result. What this means is that, with randomized starting centroids, when you assess more than one run of the algorithm, you may get a better outcome.

Kmeans algorithm works this way:

- Specifying the clusters K number
- Randomly, and without replacement, selecting data points of K for the centroids and shuffling the dataset while initiating centroids

- Till the centroids produce no change, let the iteration process continues, i.e., no transformation to the clusters when assigning data points to it
- As well as all centroids, the total data points, and the squared distance need computation
- Putting each data point to the closest cluster (centroid)
- You need to have the average of the same category of data points by computing the centroids for the clusters.

Expectation-Maximization is the K-means' approach results in solving the problem. The E step is when the closest cluster is designated to the data points. The M stage is when each cluster is computed to the centroid. There are a few things you need to take notice at this point, and they are:

- It is recommended to standardize the data to have a mean of zero and a standard deviation of one because clustering algorithms as well as shaping the comparison between data points, it is the distance-based measurements that K-means uses. This analysis is because, like income vs. age, there would have different units of measurements in nearly all the features in any dataset.
- At the onset of the algorithm, given the arbitrary initialization of centroids and K-means iterative natures, K-means algorithm may not converge to global optimum or at a local optimum, it may be stuck, and many boots may result in different clusters. As a result, using a

variety of centroids initialization and select the execution's results that yield the squared distance's lower sum is recommended to run the algorithm.

# Choosing K

Identifying the labels of data set tags and clusters for a specific pre-selected $K$ is the role of the algorithm described above. You may have to process the K-means clustering algorithm to identify the number of clusters in the data for $K$ values' collection and make a comparison for the outcomes. Generally, you can obtain a precise approximate by using the technique even though for determining accurate values of K, there is no method for that.

The mean distance connecting the data points and their centroid's cluster is one the measures people commonly use for results comparison across various values of $K$. When the similarity of the number of data point is K, there will always be a decrease in metric with the increase in K because increasing the clusters' number will always result in the distance to data points' reduction. We cannot use this metric, therefore, as the only target. Instead, to determine $K$, we can use the case where the rate of decrease sharply shifts, which is "elbow point" and as a function of $K$ is plotted, mean distance is to the centroid.

# Business Uses

For identification inside data, groups they are yet to label explicitly, they make use of the K-means clustering algorithm. Using it confirms the assumptions of business for unknown groups identification in complex data sets or about the existence of groups. It will be easy to assign any new data to the correct group when they have defined the groups and also run the algorithm. This algorithm is so versatile that they can use it for grouping of any type. Some of the use cases for this include:

## *Behavioral segmentation:*

- Purchase history segmentation
- Activities on website, platform, or application segmentation
- Interest-based personas definition
- Activity-based monitoring profile creation

## *Inventory categorization:*

- Sales activity in group inventory
- Manufacturing metrics in group inventory

## *Measurements of sorting sensor:*

- Motion types of sensor activity detection
- Images of the group
- Separate audio
- Identification of health supervision groups

## *Anomalies and bots detection:*

- Bots separation from groups' valid activity
- Cleaning up outlier detection against the legitimate exercise of the group

Also, they use it for meaningfully changed detection in data and monitors such situation if, over time, there is a switch between groups by a tracked data point.

# Chapter 10: Neural Networks – Linear Classifiers

Fashioned loosely after a human brain with a purpose for patterns recognition, neural networks combine a group of algorithms. With a machine perception, clustering, or labeling raw material, they interpret sensory data. Vectors that contain numeric are the models they identify and translate to entire data of real-world such as sound, images, time series, or text.

We can classify and cluster through the help of neural networks. With an advantage of the information you manage and store, they are classification and clustering layers. With their help, you can train on data as they classify it when their datasets have labels, or unlabeled data is what you can organize according to the model inputs' similarities. Also, the extraction of other algorithms' fed features for classification and clustering is the role of neural networks. Therefore, it is useful to have the imagination of more significant components applications of machine learning in deep neural networks which involve algorithms for regression, classification, and reinforcement learning.

Have you thought of the kind of solution deep learning can offer to some problems, and more fundamentally, your problems? Ask some of these questions to get to the root of things:

- What results do you want? Labels are the outcomes with which you apply to data. Here are some examples; in the filter of an email; `spam` or `not_spam`, in fraud detection; `bad_guy` or `good_guy`, in client relationship management; `happy_customer` or `angry_customer`.
- Along with data, is it possible for you to supplement those labels? In other words, for you to train your algorithm on the connection between inputs and labels, can you build a dataset that is labeled related to Mighty.ai, Figure Eight, or AWS Mechanical, or can you identify labeled data in which spam receives the label of spam?

The map of outputs and inputs is deep learning. Being an "approximator of universal," identifying correlation is its role. Assuming there is causation or correlation between any output $y$ and any input $x$, approximating, $f(x) = y$, an unknown function, is what it can learn. A neural network discovers the true f, in the process of learning, in the case that it is $f(x) = 9x - 0.1$ or $f(x) = 3x + 12$, transforming x into y in the correct manner.

## Neural Network Elements

With networks made up of various layers, stacked neural networks have its name in deep learning.

Nodes are the sum of the layers. The environment where the process of computation takes place is a node, somehow related to the human brain's neuron that triggers when plenty stimuli run into it. With a combination of weights or coefficients that either dampen or amplify that input, a node combines feedback from the data, in respect of the brief the algorithm tends to attempt to learn, thereby assigning significance to inputs that are devoid of any error, such as for data classification, which is most useful input? After being summed, these products of input-weight are passed through the activation function of the node, and to affect the ultimate result through the network like the classification act, it is to determine the extent or whether that signal should make further progress. There is an "activation" of neuron if the signal passes.

As the net feeds the input, those neuron-related controls strings that turn off or on is a node layer. And simultaneously, beginning from the first data-receiving layer, the output of each segment is the subsequent input of the layer. With regards to the process of clustering and classification of input by the neural network, those features have a significant dispensation in pairing the adjustable weights of the model with input features.

## Deep Neural Networks Key Concepts

By their depth, from the ordinary neural networks with a layer that is single-hidden, deep-learning networks are distinguishable, a multistep pattern recognition process which is the node layers' number that data have the requirement to pass through. The original form of perceptron were the neural networks' earlier versions and in between is a hidden layer, of one output composition and one input layer, and they were shallow. With the exclusion of output and input, what qualifies as "deep" in the learning are layers that are more than three. For the algorithms to pay attention to the ensemble, no one hasn't hard yet and read Sartre, so it is not common buzzword with the *deep* in the learning. With an extension more than a single hidden layer, the term, indeed, is a strict definition.

It is based on the output of the previous layer that each layer in the networks of deep-learning trains. Your nodes can categorize more complex features since they combine and aggregate previous layer's features as you further your advance into the neural net.

Feature hierarchy is the meaning of this, and as such, it is that of increasing abstraction and complexity. With the passage of nonlinear functions through parameters in their billions, handling high-dimensional and large data sets is what deep-learning networks can do.

Essentially, within unstructured, unlabeled data, discovering latent is possible through the neural nets. *Raw media* is a further term for data of unstructured, i.e., texts, images, audio recordings, and video. As a result, deep learning explains part of the troubles in clustering and processing the world's unlabeled, raw data, discerning anomalies and, in a comparative database or to which no one has ever mentioned, similarities in data which no one has organized.

For example, according to their similarities, it is possible for deep learning to take millions of images and then group them; a picture of your grandmother, in one side, is ice breakers, and cats in the other corner. It is in respect of the smart photo album that this analysis is all about.

At this point, for the other types of data, let's apply the same idea; for raw clustering text, including news articles or emails is the function of deep learning. In the vector area by one side, spambot messages or satisfied customers might cluster, while others might have the cluster of emails full of angry complaints. This dynamic is as a result of several messaging filters, and while voice messages have a similar situation, they use it in CRM, customer relationship management.

Clustering of data may happen around healthy or normal behavior and behaviors that are dangerous or anomalous with time series. When a Smartphone generates the time series data, it will impart knowledge into the habits and health of the users. Also, they can use it for catastrophic breakdowns prevention in a circumstance where an auto part generates it.

Without the intervention of a human, and unlike the algorithms of nearly all conventional machine learning, automatic extraction of feature is the functioning of deep-learning networks. Deep learning can be a means of circumventing the limited experts' chokepoint given that to accomplish the task of feature extraction can take years for squads of a data scientist. Which they do not scale by their nature, it gives a boost to the powers of the teams of data science.

Within a deep network, it is automatic for each node to learn features when preparing labeled data by attempting difference minimization connecting the probability distribution of the input data itself and guesses of the network and also from its samples' sources, trying to reconstruct the input. For example, in the manner, the creation of the supposed reconstructions is the machines of Restricted Boltzmann.

With this process, to draw connections between the representational of those features and feature signals, whether with data that are labeled or a reconstruction that is complete, relationships recognition is what these neural networks learn between specific optimal results and relevant features. It is practical to apply that on labeled data, and unstructured data, that a network of deep-learning directed more than the nets of machine-learning. This gives deep learning admittance to a lot more input. It is high-performance recipe since the more accurate a net is likely to be with the more data on which it can train. There can be outperformance when it is on a lot of data that bad algorithms trained against training on quite a little by good algorithms. Machine learning has a distinct advantage over previous algorithms because of its ability to learn and process from massive unlabeled data quantities. The output layer is the end of the networks of deep-learning: a softmax, logistic, classifier working with dispensing a probability to a specific label or result. Though in a huge implication, it is predictive, a term given to that. For example, when, in an image form, it has raw data, a network of deep-learning can choose that the representation of a person is the data of input of 90 percent.

## Feedforward Networks

As quickly as possible, reaching the least error is the purpose we have with using the neural net. In a loop, we pass a similar point continually because, on all sides of a track, we are running a race. In the situation where we initialize our weights is the starting line for the race and those parameters' condition. Once they can produce sufficiently accurate predictions and classifications is the finish line.

There are several steps involved in the race with those individual steps resembling the previous steps and the subsequent one. For us to arrive at the finish line, we will submit ourselves to the engagement in the act of repetition, like a runner. As it learns to take notice of the most critical features, there is an involvement of a guess with each step of a neural network, an adjustment to the coefficient, and its weights with a minor revision and an error measurement.

A model, whether in the state of end or beginning, is a collection of weights since it attempts to understand the structure of the data, as well as modeling relationship of data to labels of ground-truth, is the effort it attempts. Ordinarily, the conclusion may be a bit bad for models even though they have a bad beginning since its parameters get updates by the neural network; they change over time. The close reason is that it is in ignorance that the conception of a neural network happens. Concerning biases or weights, and guessing correctly, it has no knowledge that will best translate the input. And with more knowledge about its mistakes, making better sequential guesses is what it continues to do even though it starts with a hypothesis. Through a scientific method with a blindfold on, what you can imagine as an enactment miniature of the scientific technique is a neural network, making more attempts as they test hypotheses. Or more like a child; they have zero exposure in their birth and gradually learn to provide a solution to the world's tribulations through their life experience exposure. As such, data becomes the sole experience in support of neural networks.

As the simplest architecture to explain, in the course feedforward neural network learning, what happens is what can be described in plain details. The network experiences the presence of the input. The guesses the network make at the end is what the map, coefficient, or a set of guesses for weights input.

```
input * weight = guess
```

The characteristic of input is what a guess is to the result of the weighted information. Then, to the data's ground-truth, makes a comparison as the neural takes its guesses, inquiring from an authority effectively whether it has the right result.

```
ground truth - guess = error
```

Its *error* is the distinction between the ground truth and the guess of the network. Contributing to the error as they measure the error with an extensive weight adjustment, it is over its model that the network walks back the error.

```
error * contribution of weight to error = adjustment
```

For them to apply an update to the model, the neural networks' three essential functions' account is the above three pseudo-mathematical formulas, loss calculation, and scoring input. Then, they will start the step of three processes once more. A collective feedback loop is a neural network that is set to punish weights that result in an error and for weights that support its guesses, reward them.

## Multiple Linear Regression

Typical of any algorithm of other machine learning, simple code and math are all about artificial neural networks, in spite of their biologically inspired name. Indeed, in statistic, part of your learning techniques, in the beginning, is linear regression. And it will be easy for anyone who understands how neural network work to have a clear grasp of linear regression. Linear regression, in a form so simple, the following is the expression of linear regression;

```
Y_hat = bX + a
```

The input $x$ where output estimation is $Y\_hat$, on the vertical axis, a line interception of a graph with two-dimension is $a$, and $b$ is the slope. Let's concretize this: the risk of cancer risk could be $Y$, and the radiation exposure could be $x$; your benchpress' total weight could be *Y_hat*, and daily pushups could be *x*; the crop's size could be *Y_hat*, and the fertilizer quantity could be *x*. As you can see, on the *X*-axis, regardless of how far along you are, there is a proportional increase in the dependent variable *Y_hat* all the time there is an addition to a unit to *x*. Between two variables, a starting point is a simple relation that moves them together up or down.

For us to imagine linear regression in their multiplicity is the next step, where several input variables produce a single output variable. Typically, one can express it as follows:

$$Y\_hat = b\_1 * X\_1 + b\_2 * X\_2 + b\_3 * X\_3 + a$$

With all three affecting *Y_hat*, in the fertilizer variable to a planting season, you can attach the quantity of rainfall and sunlight to extend the example above.

At a neural network's node, happening now is multiple linear regression form. From the previous layer's node, there is a combination of input from every other node with input for each node of a single layer. This means, with the effect of their coefficients and leading to an individual node of the ensuing layer, there is a blend of inputs in different proportions.

And it has passed through a non-linear function when, to arrive at *Y_hat*, you total the inputs of your node. The reason is this: there will be linearly increased in *Y_hat*, and yet that doesn't serve our purpose with the increase of *X* without limit and if there is a mere execution of multiple linear regression by every node.

Regardless of whether or not the input signal should influence the crucial evaluations of the network when it has access to the input, a switch, similar to a neuron which turns off and on, is what we are trying to create. There's a problem of classification at hand once you possess a switch. Is there any indication from the signal of the input that the classification of the node must be sufficient, off or on, or not enough? Through 1 and 0, it is possible to express a binary decision and between 0 and 1, to translate it to space, squashing input is a logistic regression which is as a result of a non-linear function.

Similar to logistic regression, they are usually s-shaped functions as at each node, the nonlinear transforms. "S," sigmoid, in Greek term, is the name that they have and they are shaping each node's output. Between 0 and 1, with an s-shaped space being the output of squashed nodes, and in a feed-forward neural network, it will then pass as the subsequent layer's input to reach the decision-making space where it will go on pending the signal's arrival at the net's ultimate layer.

# Different Types of Classifiers

As an algorithm, a classifier maps the input data to a particular category. There are various types of classifiers, and some of them are:

1. Naive Bayes
2. Perceptron
3. Logistic Regression
4. Decision Tree
5. Support Vector Machine
6. K – Nearest Neighbor
7. Artificial Neural Networks/Deep Learning

Some of the ensemble methods are Bagging, AdaBoost, Random Forest, and so on. For a given data, we will get a similar output all over again as we discussed earlier. And whether regression or classification, machine learning gives us different outcomes. As such, when it comes to supervised learning, they work on random simulation, similar to the manner with which the artificial neural networks use random weights. Irrespective of the technique you use, a level of accuracy of prediction is imminent for these machines learning to reach with given data input. These are patterns of artificial intelligence. Therefore, we can distinguish them as generative algorithms and discriminative algorithms.

The perceptron classifiers are a concept that springs from artificial neural networks. So, classifying this into two classes of

# Conclusion

Thank you for making it through to the end of *Python Machine Learning: The Ultimate and Complete Guide for Beginners on Data Science and Machine Learning with Python (Learning Technology, Principles, and Applications)*. Let's hope it was informative and able to provide you with all of the tools you need to achieve your goals whatever they may be.

For you to get to this point, chances are you want to know so many things about Python, data science, machine learning, and so other related fields. You can be the next innovator. Building innovative technology begins with an idea, and your plan can become a reality when you make a move.

Right now, all you have to do is to imagine. Imagine how your world would be if you can take some steps to learn more about machine learning or perhaps neural networks. Imagine yourself a great data analyst who uses data science to make decisions and predictions with the use of machine learning.

Imagine having all the secrets about data science lifecycle where you can make several analyses. Imagine knowing everything about probability, statistics, fundamental, as well as data types you've read in this book. Imagine knowing all aspects of linear algebra and how you can proffer solution to many representational problems of linear algebra.

In this book, you have read about the fundamentals of machine learning. There are details about the prerequisites to start with machine learning and some details about machine learning roadmap. You have the knowledge you may need in the world of data science and Python with this book. The next step you need to take is to go out there and conquer the world.

Finally, if you found this book useful in any way, a review on Amazon is always appreciated!

www.ingramcontent.com/pod-product-compliance
Lightning Source LLC
Chambersburg PA
CBHW071057050326
40690CB00008B/1051